2/06

THE RISE OF ISLAM

Titles in the Series
Greenwood Guides to Historic Events of the Medieval World

The Black Death

The Crusades

Eleanor of Aquitaine, Courtly Love, and the Troubadours

Genghis Khan and Mongol Rule

Joan of Arc and the Hundred Years War

Magna Carta

Medieval Castles

Medieval Cathedrals

The Medieval City

Medieval Science and Technology

The Puebloan Society of Chaco Canyon

The Rise of Islam

THE RISE OF ISLAM

Matthew S. Gordon

Greenwood Guides to Historic Events of the Medieval World
Jane Chance, Series Editor

GREENWOOD PRESS
Westport, Connecticut • London

Library of Congress Cataloging-in-Publication Data

Gordon, Matthew.
    The rise of Islam / Matthew S. Gordon.
       p. cm.—(Greenwood guides to historic events of the medieval world)
    Includes bibliographical references and index.
    ISBN 0–313–32522–7 (alk. paper)
    1. Islam—History. I. Title. II. Series.
  BP55.G67   2005
  297'.09'021—dc22   2005003392

British Library Cataloguing in Publication Data is available.

Library of Congress Catalog Card Number: 2005003392
ISBN: 0–313–32522–7

First published in 2005

Greenwood Press, 88 Post Road West, Westport, CT 06881
An imprint of Greenwood Publishing Group, Inc.
www.greenwood.com

Printed in the United States of America

(∞)™

The paper used in this book complies with the
Permanent Paper Standard issued by the National
Information Standards Organization (Z39.48–1984).

10 9 8 7 6 5 4 3 2 1

To Susan with gratitude and love

CONTENTS

Photo essay follows Chapter 6

SERIES FOREWORD

The Middle Ages are no longer considered the "Dark Ages" (as Petrarch termed them), sandwiched between the two enlightened periods of classical antiquity and the Renaissance. Often defined as a historical period lasting, roughly, from 500 to 1500 C.E., the Middle Ages span an enormous amount of time (if we consider the way other time periods have been constructed by historians) as well as an astonishing range of countries and regions very different from one another. That is, we call the "Middle" Ages the period beginning with the fall of the Roman Empire as a result of raids by northern European tribes of "barbarians" in the late antiquity of the fifth and sixth centuries and continuing until the advent of the so-called Italian and English renaissances, or rebirths of classical learning, in the fifteenth and sixteenth centuries. How this age could be termed either "Middle" or "Dark" is a mystery to those who study it. Certainly it is no longer understood as embracing merely the classical inheritance in the west or excluding eastern Europe, the Middle East, Asia, or even, as I would argue, North and Central America.

Whatever the arbitrary, archaic, and hegemonic limitations of these temporal parameters—the old-fashioned approach to them was that they were mainly not classical antiquity, and therefore not important—the Middle Ages represent a time when certain events occurred that have continued to affect modern cultures and that also, inevitably, catalyzed other medieval events. Among other important events, the Middle Ages saw the birth of Muhammad (c. 570–632) and his foundation of Islam in the seventh century as a rejection of Christianity which led to the imperial conflict between East and West in the eleventh and twelfth centuries. In western Europe in the Middle Ages the foundations for modern

nationalism and modern law were laid and the concept of romantic love
arose in the Middle Ages, this latter event partly one of the indirect consequences of the Crusades. With the shaping of national identity came
the need to defend boundaries against invasion; so the castle emerged as
a military outpost—whether in northern Africa, during the Crusades, or
in Wales, in the eleventh century, to defend William of Normandy's
newly acquired provinces—to satisfy that need. From Asia the invasions
of Genghis Khan changed the literal and cultural shape of eastern and
southern Europe.

In addition to triggering the development of the concept of chivalry
and the knight, the Crusades influenced the European concepts of the
lyric, music, and musical instruments; introduced to Europe an appetite
for spices like cinnamon, coriander, and saffron and for dried fruits like
prunes and figs as well as a desire for fabrics such as silk; and brought
Aristotle to the European university through Arabic and then Latin
translations. As a result of study of the "new" Aristotle, science and philosophy dramatically changed direction—and their emphasis on this material world helped to undermine the power of the Catholic Church as
a monolithic institution in the thirteenth century.

By the twelfth century, with the centralization of the one (Catholic)
Church, came a new architecture for the cathedral—the Gothic—to replace the older Romanesque architecture and thereby to manifest the
Church's role in the community in a material way as well as in spiritual
and political ways. Also from the cathedral as an institution and its need
to dramatize the symbolic events of the liturgy came medieval drama—
the mystery and the morality play, from which modern drama derives in
large part. Out of the cathedral and its schools to train new priests (for-
merly handled by monasteries) emerged the medieval institution of the
university. Around the same time, the community known as a town rose
up in eastern and western Europe as a consequence of trade and the necessity for a new economic center to accompany the development of a
bourgeoisie, or middle class. Because of the town's existence, the need
for an itinerant mendicancy that could preach the teachings of the
Church and beg for alms in urban centers sprang up.

Elsewhere in the world, in North America the eleventh-century settlement of Chaco Canyon by the Pueblo peoples created a social model
like no other, one centered on ritual and ceremony in which the "priests"

were key, but one that lasted barely two hundred years before it collapsed and its central structures were abandoned.

In addition to their influence on the development of central features of modern culture, the Middle Ages have long fascinated the modern age because of parallels that exist between the two periods. In both, terrible wars devastated whole nations and peoples; in both, incurable diseases plagued cities and killed large percentages of the world's population. In both periods, dramatic social and cultural changes took place as a result of these events: marginalized and overtaxed groups in societies rebelled against imperious governments; trade and a burgeoning middle class came to the fore; outside the privacy of the family, women began to have a greater role in Western societies and their cultures.

How different cultures of that age grappled with such historical change is the subject of the Greenwood Guides to Historic Events of the Medieval World. This series features individual volumes that illuminate key events in medieval world history. In some cases, an "event" occurred during a relatively limited time period. The troubadour lyric as a phenomenon, for example, flowered and died in the courts of Aquitaine in the twelfth century, as did the courtly romance in northern Europe a few decades later. The Hundred Years War between France and England generally took place during a precise time period, from the fourteenth to mid-fifteenth centuries.

In other cases, the event may have lasted for centuries before it played itself out: the medieval Gothic cathedral, for example, may have been first built in the twelfth century at Saint-Denis in Paris (c. 1140), but cathedrals, often of a slightly different style of Gothic architecture, were still being built in the fifteenth century all over Europe and, again, as the symbolic representation of a bishop's seat, or chair, are still being built today. And the medieval city, whatever its incarnation in the early Middle Ages, basically blossomed between the eleventh and thirteenth centuries as a result of social, economic, and cultural changes. Events—beyond a single dramatic historically limited happening—took longer to affect societies in the Middle Ages because of the lack of political and social centralization, the primarily agricultural and rural nature of most countries, difficulties in communication, and the distances between important cultural centers.

Each volume includes necessary tools for understanding such key events in the Middle Ages. Because of the postmodern critique of authority that modern societies underwent at the end of the twentieth century, students and scholars as well as general readers have come to mistrust the commentary and expertise of any one individual scholar or commentator and to identify the text as an arbiter of "history." For this reason, each book in the series can be described as a "library in a book." The intent of the series is to provide a quick, in-depth examination and current perspectives on the event to stimulate critical thinking as well as ready-reference materials, including primary documents and biographies of key individuals, for additional research.

Specifically, in addition to a narrative historical overview that places the specific event within the larger context of a contemporary perspective, five to seven developmental chapters explore related focused aspects of the event. In addition, each volume begins with a brief chronology and ends with a conclusion that discusses the consequences and impact of the event. There are also brief biographies of twelve to twenty key individuals (or places or buildings, in the book on the cathedral); primary documents from the period (for example, letters, chronicles, memoirs, diaries, and other writings) that illustrate states of mind or the turn of events at the time, whether historical, literary, scientific, or philosophical; illustrations (maps, diagrams, manuscript illuminations, portraits); a glossary of terms; and an annotated bibliography of important books, articles, films, and CD-ROMs available for additional research. An index concludes each volume.

No particular theoretical approach or historical perspective characterizes the series; authors developed their topics as they chose, generally taking into account the latest thinking on any particular event. The editors selected final topics from a list provided by an advisory board of high school teachers and public and school librarians. On the basis of nominations of scholars made by distinguished writers, the series editor also tapped internationally known scholars, both those with lifelong expertise and others with fresh new perspectives on a topic, to author the twelve books in the series. Finally, the series editor selected distinguished medievalists, art historians, and archaeologists to complete an advisory board: Gwinn Vivian, retired professor of archaeology at the University of Arizona Museum; Sharon Kinoshita, associate professor of French literature, world literature, and cultural studies at the University of California–Santa Cruz; Nancy Wu, associate museum educator at the Metropolitan Museum of Art, The Cloisters, New York City; and Christopher A. Snyder, chair of the Department of History and Politics at Marymount University.

In addition to examining the event and its effects on the specific cultures involved through an array of documents and an overview, each volume provides a new approach to understanding these twelve events. Treated in the series are: the Black Death; the Crusades; Eleanor of Aquitaine, courtly love, and the troubadours; Genghis Khan and Mongol rule; Joan of Arc and the Hundred Years War; Magna Carta; the medieval castle, from the eleventh to the sixteenth centuries; the medieval cathedral; the medieval city, especially in the thirteenth century; medieval science and technology; Muhammad and the rise of Islam; and the Puebloan society of Chaco Canyon.

The Black Death, by Joseph Byrne, isolates the event of the epidemic of bubonic plague in 1347–52 as having had a signal impact on medieval Europe. It was, however, only the first of many related such episodes involving variations of pneumonic and septicemic plague that recurred over 350 years. Taking a twofold approach to the Black Death, Byrne investigates both the modern research on bubonic plague, its origins and spread, and also medieval documentation and illustration in diaries, artistic works, and scientific and religious accounts. The demographic, economic, and political effects of the Black Death are traced in one chapter, the social and psychological patterns of life in another, and cultural expressions in art and ritual in a third. Finally, Byrne investigates why bubonic plague disappeared and why we continue to be fascinated by it. Documents included provide a variety of medieval accounts—Byzantine, Arabic, French, German, English, and Italian—several of which are translated for the first time.

The Crusades, by Helen Nicholson, presents a balanced account of various crusades, or military campaigns, invented by Catholic or "Latin" Christians during the Middle Ages against those they perceived as threats to their faith. Such expeditions included the Crusades to the Holy Land between 1095 and 1291, expeditions to the Iberian Peninsula, the "crusade" to northeastern Europe, the Albigensian Crusades and the Hussite crusades—both against the heretics—and the crusades against the Ottoman Turks (in the Balkans). Although Muslim rulers included the concept of jihâd (a conflict fought for God against evil or his enemies) in their wars in the early centuries of Islam, it had become less important in the late tenth century. It was not until the middle decades of the twelfth century that jihâd was revived in the wars with the Latin Christian Crusaders. Most of the Crusades did not result in victory for the Latin Christians, although Nicholson concedes they slowed the advance of Islam. After Jerusalem was destroyed in 1291, Muslim rulers did permit Christian pilgrims to travel to holy sites. In the Iberian Peninsula, Christian rulers replaced Muslim rulers, but Muslims, Jews, and dissident Christians were compelled to convert to Catholicism. In northeastern Europe, the Teutonic Order's campaigns allowed German colonization that later encouraged twentieth-century German claims to land and led to two world wars. The Albigensian Crusade wiped out thirteenth-century aristocratic families in southern France who held to the Cathar heresy, but the Hussite crusades in the 1420s failed to eliminate the Hussite heresy. As a result of the wars, however, many positive changes occurred: Arab learning founded on Greek scholarship entered western Europe through the acquisition of an extensive library in Toledo, Spain, in 1085; works of western European literature were inspired by the holy wars; trade was encouraged and with it the demand for certain products; and a more favorable image of Muslim men and women was fostered by the crusaders' contact with the Middle East. Nicholson also notes that America may have been discovered because Christopher Columbus avoided a route that had been closed by Muslim conquests and that the Reformation may have been advanced because Martin Luther protested against the crusader indulgence in his Ninety-five Theses (1517).

Eleanor of Aquitaine, Courtly Love, and the Troubadours, by ffiona Swabey, singles out the twelfth century as the age of the individual, in which a queen like Eleanor of Aquitaine could influence the development of a new social and artistic culture. The wife of King Louis VII of France and later the wife of his enemy Henry of Anjou, who became king of England, she patronized some of the troubadours, whose vernacular lyrics celebrated the personal expression of emotion and a passionate declaration of service to women. Love, marriage, and the pursuit of women were also the subject of the new romance literature, which flourished in northern Europe and was the inspiration behind concepts of courtly love. However, as Swabey points out, historians in the past have misjudged Eleanor, whose independent spirit fueled their misogynist attitudes. Similarly, Eleanor's divorce and subsequent stormy marriage have colored ideas about medieval "love courts" and courtly love, interpretations of which have now been challenged by scholars. The twelfth century is set in context, with commentaries on feudalism, the tenets of Christianity, and the position of women, as well as summaries of the cultural and philosophical background, the cathedral schools and universities, the influence of Islam, the revival of classical learning, vernacular literature, and Gothic architecture. Swabey provides two biographical chapters on Eleanor and two on the emergence of the troubadours and the origin of courtly love through verse romances. Within this latter subject Swabey also details the story of Abelard and Heloise, the treatise of Andreas Capellanus (André the Chaplain) on courtly love, and Arthurian legend as a subject of courtly love.

Genghis Khan and Mongol Rule, by George Lane, identifies the rise to power of Genghis Khan and his unification of the Mongol tribes in the thirteenth century as a kind of globalization with political, cultural, economic, mercantile, and spiritual effects akin to those of modern globalization. Normally viewed as synonymous with barbarian destruction, the rise to power of Genghis Khan and the Mongol hordes is here understood as a more positive event that initiated two centuries of regeneration and creativity. Lane discusses the nature of the society of the Eurasian steppes in the twelfth and thirteenth centuries into which Genghis Khan was born; his success at reshaping the relationship between the northern pastoral and nomadic society with the southern urban, agriculturalist society; and his unification of all the Turco-Mongol tribes in 1206 before his move to conquer Tanquit Xixia, the Chin of northern China, and the lands of Islam. Conquered thereafter were the Caucasus, the Ukraine, the Crimea, Russia, Siberia, Central Asia, Afghanistan, Pakistan, and Kashmir. After his death his sons and grandsons continued, conquering Korea, Persia, Armenia, Mesopotamia, Azerbaijan, and eastern Europe—chiefly Kiev, Poland, Moravia, Silesia, and Hungary—until 1259, the end of the Mongol Empire as a unified whole. Mongol rule created a golden age in the succeeding split of the Empire into two, the Yuan dynasty of greater China and the Il-Khanate dynasty of greater Iran. Lane adds biographies of important political figures, famous names such as Marco Polo, and artists and scientists. Documents derive from universal histories, chronicles, local histories and travel accounts, official government documents, and poetry, in French, Armenian, Georgian, Chinese, Persian, Arabic, Chaghatai Turkish, Russian, and Latin.

Joan of Arc and the Hundred Years War, by Deborah Fraioli, presents the Hundred Years War between France and England in the fourteenth and fifteenth centuries within contexts whose importance has sometimes been blurred or ignored in past studies. An episode of apparently only moderate significance, a feudal lord's seizure of his vassal's land for harboring his mortal enemy, sparked the Hundred Years War, yet on the face of it the event should not have led inevitably to war. But the lord was the king of France and the vassal the king of England, who resented losing his claim to the French throne to his Valois cousin. The land in dispute, extending roughly from Bordeaux to the Pyrenees mountains, was crucial coastline for the economic interests of both kingdoms. The series of skirmishes, pitched battles, truces, stalemates, and diplomatic wrangling that resulted from the confiscation of English Aquitaine by the French form the narrative of this Anglo-French conflict, which was in fact not given the name Hundred Years War until the nineteenth century.

Fraioli emphasizes how dismissing women's inheritance and succession rights came at the high price of unleashing discontent in their male heirs, including Edward III, Robert of Artois, and Charles of Navarre. Fraioli also demonstrates the centrality of side issues, such as Flemish involvement in the war, the peasants' revolts that resulted from the costs of the war, and Joan of Arc's unusually clear understanding of French "sacred kingship." Among the primary sources provided are letters from key players such as Edward III, Etienne Marcel, and Joan of Arc; a supply list for towns about to be besieged; and a contemporary poem by the celebrated scholar and court poet Christine de Pizan in praise of Joan of Arc.

Magna Carta, by Katherine Drew, is a detailed study of the importance of the Magna Carta in comprehending England's legal and constitutional history. Providing a model for the rights of citizens found in the United States Declaration of Independence and Constitution's first ten amendments, the Magna Carta has had a role in the legal and parliamentary history of all modern states bearing some colonial or government connection with the British Empire. Constructed at a time when modern nations began to appear, in the early thirteenth century, the Magna Carta (signed in 1215) presented a formula for balancing the liberties of the people with the power of modern governmental institutions. This unique English document influenced the growth of a form of law (the English common law) and provided a vehicle for the evolution of representative (parliamentary) government. Drew demonstrates how the Magna Carta came to be—the roles of the Church, the English towns, barons, common law, and the parliament in its making—as well as how myths concerning its provisions were established. Also provided are biographies of Thomas Becket, Charlemagne, Frederick II, Henry II and his sons, Innocent III, and many other key figures, and primary documents—among them, the Magna Cartas of 1215 and 1225, and the Coronation Oath of Henry I.

Medieval Castles, by Marilyn Stokstad, traces the historical, political, and social function of the castle from the late eleventh century to the sixteenth by means of a typology of castles. This typology ranges from the early "motte and bailey"—military fortification, and government and economic center—to the palace as an expression of the castle owners' needs and purposes. An introduction defines the various contexts—military, political, economic, and social—in which the castle appeared in the Middle Ages. A concluding interpretive essay suggests the impact of the castle and its symbolic role as an idealized construct lasting until the modern day.

Medieval Cathedrals, by William Clark, examines one of the chief contributions of the Middle Ages, at least from an elitist perspective—that is, the religious architecture found in the cathedral ("chair" of the bishop) or great church, studied in terms of its architecture, sculpture, and stained glass. Clark begins with a brief contextual history of the concept of the bishop and his role within the church hierarchy, the growth of the church in the early Christian era and its affiliation with the bishop (deriving from that of the bishop of Rome), and the social history of cathedrals. Because of economic and political conflicts among the three authorities who held power in medieval towns—the king, the bishop, and the cathedral clergy—cathedral construction and maintenance always remained a vexed issue, even though the owners—the cathedral clergy—usually held the civic responsibility for the cathedral. In an interpretive essay, Clark then focuses on Reims Cathedral in France, because both it and the bishop's palace survive, as well as on contemporary information about surrounding buildings. Clark also supplies a historical overview on the social, political, and religious history of the cathedral in the Middle Ages: an essay on patrons, builders, and artists; aspects of cathedral construction (which was not always successful); and then a chapter on Romanesque and Gothic cathedrals and a "gazetteer" of twenty-five important examples.

The Medieval City, by Norman J. G. Pounds, documents the origin of the medieval city in the flight from the dangers or difficulties found in the country, whether economic, physically threatening, or cultural. Identifying the attraction of the city in its urbanitas, its "urbanity," or the way of living in a city, Pounds discusses first its origins in prehistoric and classical Greek urban revolutions. During the Middle Ages, the city grew primarily between the eleventh and thirteenth centuries, remaining essentially the same until the Industrial Revolution. Pounds provides chapters on the medieval city's planning, in terms of streets and structures; life in the medieval city; the roles of the Church and the city government in its operation; the development of crafts and trade in the city; and the issues of urban health, wealth, and welfare. Concluding with the role of the city in history, Pounds suggests that the value of the city depended upon its balance of social classes, its need for trade and profit to satisfy personal desires through the accumulation of wealth and its consequent economic power, its political power as a representative body within the kingdom, and its social role in the rise of literacy and education and in nationalism. Indeed, the concept of a middle class, a bourgeoisie, derives from the city—from the bourg, or "borough." According to Pounds, the rise of modern civilization would not have taken place without the growth of the city in the Middle Ages and its concomitant artistic and cultural contribution.

Medieval Science and Technology, by Elspeth Whitney, examines science and technology from the early Middle Ages to 1500 within the context of the classical learning that so influenced it. She looks at institutional history, both early and late, and what was taught in the medieval schools and, later, the universities (both of which were overseen by the Catholic Church). Her discussion of Aristotelian natural philosophy illustrates its impact on the medieval scientific worldview. She presents chapters on the exact sciences, meaning mathematics, astronomy, cosmology, astrology, statics, kinematics, dynamics, and optics; the biological and earth sciences, meaning chemistry and alchemy, medicine, zoology, botany, geology and meteorology, and geography; and technology. In an interpretive conclusion, Whitney demonstrates the impact of medieval science on the preconditions and structure that permitted the emergence of the modern world. Most especially, technology transformed an agricultural society into a more commercial and engine-driven society: waterpower and inventions like the blast furnace and horizontal loom turned iron working and cloth making into manufacturing operations. The invention of the mechanical clock helped to organize human activities through timetables rather than through experiential perception and thus facilitated the advent of modern life. Also influential in the establishment of a middle class were the inventions of the musket and pistol and the printing press. Technology, according to Whitney, helped advance the habits of mechanization and precise methodology. Her biographies introduce major medieval Latin and Arabic and classical natural philosophers and scientists. Extracts from various kinds of scientific treatises allow a window into the medieval concept of knowledge.

The Puebloan Society of Chaco Canyon, by Paul Reed, is unlike other volumes in this series, whose historic events boast a long-established historical record. Reed's study offers instead an original reconstruction of the Puebloan Indian society of Chaco, in what is now New Mexico, but originally extending into Colorado, Utah, and Arizona. He is primarily interested in its leaders, ritual and craft specialists, and commoners during the time of its chief flourishing, in the eleventh and twelfth centuries, as understood from archaeological data alone. To this new material he adds biographies of key Euro-American archaeologists and other individuals from the nineteenth and twentieth centuries who have made important discoveries about Chaco Canyon. Also provided are documents of archaeological description and narrative from early explorers' journals and archaeological reports, narratives, and monographs. In his overview chapters, Reed discusses the cultural and environmental setting of Chaco Canyon; its history (in terms of exploration and research); the Puebloan society and how it emerged chronologically; the Chaco society and how it appeared in 1100 C.E.; the "Outliers," or outlying communities of Chaco; Chaco as a ritual center of the eleventh-century Pueblo world; and, finally, what is and is not known about Chaco society. Reed concludes that ritual and ceremony played an important role in Chacoan society and that ritual specialists, or priests, conducted ceremonies, maintained ritual artifacts, and charted the ritual calendar. Its social organization matches no known social pattern or type: it was complicated, multiethnic, centered around ritual and ceremony, and without any overtly hierarchical political system. The Chacoans were ancestors to the later Pueblo people, part of a society that rose, fell, and evolved within a very short time period.

The Rise of Islam, by Matthew Gordon, introduces the early history of the Islamic world, beginning in the late sixth century with the career of the Prophet Muhammad (c. 570–c. 632) on the Arabian Peninsula. From Muhammad's birth in an environment of religious plurality—Christianity, Judaism, and Zoroastrianism, along with paganism, were joined by Islam—to the collapse of the Islamic empire in the early tenth century, Gordon traces the history of the Islamic community. The book covers topics that include the life of the Prophet and divine revelation (the Qur'an) to the formation of the Islamic state, urbanization in the Islamic Near East, and the extraordinary culture of Islamic letters and scholarship. In addition to a historical overview, Gordon examines the Caliphate and early Islamic Empire, urban society and economy, and the emergence, under the Abbasid Caliphs, of a "world religious tradition" up to the year 925 C.E.

As editor of this series I am grateful to have had the help of Benjamin Burford, an undergraduate Century Scholar at Rice University assigned to me in 2002–2004 for this project; Gina Weaver, a third-year graduate student in English; and Cynthia Duffy, a second-year graduate student in English, who assisted me in target-reading select chapters from some of these books in an attempt to define an audience. For this purpose I would also like to thank Gale Stokes, former dean of humanities at Rice University, for the 2003 summer research grant and portions of the 2003–2004 annual research grant from Rice University that served that end.

This series, in its mixture of traditional and new approaches to medieval history and cultures, will ensure opportunities for dialogue in the classroom in its offerings of twelve different "libraries in books." It should also propel discussion among graduate students and scholars by means of the gentle insistence throughout on the text as primal. Most especially, it invites response and further study. Given its mixture of East and West, North and South, the series symbolizes the necessity for global understanding, both of the Middle Ages and in the postmodern age.

Jane Chance, Series Editor
Houston, Texas
February 19, 2004

Advisory Board

PREFACE

Muslims are those who adhere to the Islamic religious tradition. They make up a growing proportion of the world's population. The frequently cited figure of 1 billion Muslims worldwide is an estimate, since accurate census figures are difficult to come by in many regions of the world. The number is probably much higher. But even an estimate clearly shows Islam's place as a world faith. The community of Muslims (*umma*) is represented today in nearly all regions of Asia and Africa, often as a majority faith. In Europe and the Americas, Muslims make up a substantial and growing minority population.

The present book is intended as an introduction to the early history of Islam. The origins of the Islamic religious tradition, and the formation of Islamic society, date to events that unfolded roughly 1400 years ago in the Arabian Peninsula. A set of chapters will trace the trajectory of that history from the lifetime of the Prophet Muhammad to the collapse of the Islamic Empire by the early tenth century. The chapters contain a mix of narrative history and analysis of particular topics. My interest lies, first and foremost, with social and political history: this bias runs through the book. The teachings and practice of Islam as a sophisticated religious system will not be ignored, but they also will not command the lion's share of attention. The Islamic religion—its doctrines, practices, and institutions—has been the subject of countless writings. A number of these are listed in the bibliography for readers seeking to understand these topics in greater depth.

The opening chapter provides an outline of the history of early Islamic society from the early seventh to the early tenth century. It concentrates on pre-Islamic Arabia and the life of the Prophet. Subsequent chapters treat the Arab-Islamic conquests; the early Islamic Empire; and society and religion, particularly in the early Abbasid period (750–925). Of particular interest is the spread of urbanization throughout the early Islamic world. Prior to the tenth century, as the first chapter makes clear, Islamic society was largely concentrated in al-Andalus (Islamic Spain), the Maghrib (North Africa) and the Near East. Inroads into Saharan Africa, Central Asia, and the Indian Ocean area still had far to go at this point.

The book is meant to respond, in part, to a growing interest in Islam in the United States and Europe (the West). Curiosity and, in many circles, concern about Islamic teachings have quickened in recent decades. The reasons are many, ranging from intellectual interest and an appreciation for the remarkable contributions of Islamic scholarship to anxiety sparked by the rise of militant Islamic movements. The events of September 11, 2001, were terrible on many fronts. Viewed from roughly three years later, one serious long-term effect of the attacks on New York and Washington was the rise of a particularly skewed and fearful image of Islam, especially in the United States. The image is of a culture and religious tradition in perpetual conflict with the West. It is, for the most part, an image built upon ignorance and/or deeply seated biases. Its unfortunate rise underscores the need for the dissemination of knowledge about Islamic history and society. The hope is that this volume will go some way toward satisfying that need.

ACKNOWLEDGMENTS

I wish to thank the following individuals for their suggestions and comments: Jonathan Berkey, William Chittick, Joseph Lowry, Chase Robinson, Omid Safi, and the anonymous reader for Greenwood Publishing Group. I also wish to thank Jane Chance, Michael Hermann, Marcia Goldstein, and the editorial staff at Greenwood, as well as Diane Cipollone at Westchester Book Group.

CHRONOLOGY

540–562	Wars between Byzantium (under Justinian I) and the Sasanid Empire (under Anushirvan the Great [Khusraw I]).
570	Traditional year of birth of Muhammad ibn Abdallah (the Prophet of Islam).
591–628	Reign of Khusraw II Parwiz in Iran. His campaigns in the Near East (611–627) spark the last round of conflict with Byzantium.
595	Traditional year of the marriage of Muhammad and Khadija.
610	Traditional year for the beginning of Muhammad's prophetic mission.
613–615	Emigration of early Muslims to Abyssinia. Muhammad remains in Mecca and continues his mission in the face of mounting Qurayshi hostility.
619	Deaths of Khadija, Muhammad's first wife, and Abu Talib, his uncle and protector against the Quraysh.
622	The *Hijra*, Muhammad's emigration to Medina, and the establishment of the early Islamic community; year 1 of the Islamic calendar.
630	The early Muslims, under Muhammad's leadership, take Mecca.

632	Death of the Prophet Muhammad.
632	Arab-Islamic forces take Jerusalem from the Byzantine Empire.
632–661	The reign of the *Rashidun* (Rightly guided) caliphs. Continuation of the Arab-Islamic conquests and the consolidation of the Medinan polity in the Arabian Peninsula.
634	Death of Abu Bakr (the first of Muhammad's successors).
636	Battle of Yarmuk in southern Syria (defeat of Byzantine forces).
636	Battle of al-Qadisiya in lower Iraq (defeat of Sasanid forces).
639	Invasion of Egypt by Arab-Islamic forces. Campaigns launched in the 640s against North Africa.
644	Murder of Umar ibn al-Khattab (second of the Prophet's successors).
656	Murder of Uthman ibn Affan (third of the Prophet's successors).
656–661	Reign of Ali ibn Abi Talib (first of the Twelver imams and the last of the Rashidun caliphs).
661–684	Establishment of the Umayyad caliphate under Mu'awiya with its capital in Damascus. Mu'awiya and his two successors are members of the Sufyanid branch of the Umayyad clan.
678	Death of A'isha, daughter of Abu Bakr and prominent wife of the Prophet.
680	Succession of Yazid I. Umayyad troops kill al-Husayn ibn Ali at Karbala.
680–692	The Second Civil War. Caliphate of Ibn al-Zubayr.

684	The Sufyanid Umayyads are replaced by the Marwanid branch of the Umayyad family. Marwan ibn al-Hakam assumes control in Damascus.
685–705	Reign of Abd al-Malik ibn Marwan. Known for significant advances in the conquests, notable administrative reforms, and construction of the Dome of the Rock in Jerusalem.
724–743	Reign of Hisham ibn Abd al-Malik, last significant ruler of the Umayyad dynasty. His reign witnesses important fiscal reforms and a complex and ultimately successful campaign along the Central Asian frontier.
728	Death of Hasan al-Basri, prominent religious scholar.
747–748	Following a long clandestine period, an anti-Umayyad movement in Khurasan turns to open revolt with the unfurling of black banners, henceforth the symbolic color of the Abbasid caliphate. Umayyad troops are forced out of Khurasan.
749–750	Overthrow of the Umayyad dynasty and foundation of the Abbasid caliphate. The Umayyad family is destroyed, but one male survivor, Abd al-Rahman ibn Mu'awiya, escapes to al-Andalus (Spain).
754–775	Reign of Abu Ja'far al-Mansur, founder of Baghdad.
756–788	Reign of Abd al-Rahman I in Spain; foundation of the Umayyad dynasty in Spain.
765	Death of Ja'far al-Sadiq, a key figure in the formation of Twelver Shi'ism. Considered one of the twelve imams, he was also a formidable scholar and teacher.
786–809	Reign of Harun al-Rashid, perhaps the best-known of the Abbasid caliphs. Civil war between his sons,

Muhammad al-Amin and Abdallah al-Ma'mun, nearly brings an end to the Abbasid caliphate.

789–985   The Idrisid dynasty, among the first autonomous dynasties of the early Islamic imperial period, reigns in Morocco.

795   Death of Malik ibn Anas, prominent religious scholar. His teachings form the basis for the foundation of the Maliki school of law.

820   Death of Abu Abdallah Muhammad al-Shafi'i, an early religious scholar. His writings become the foundation for the Shafi'i school of law.

836–892   The Abbasids rule from Samarra, a sprawling capital north of Baghdad.

838–923   Lifetime of Abu Ja'far Muhammad al-Tabari, historian and exegete. His principal works include a multivolume *History* and a renowned commentary on the Qur'an.

909–969   The Fatimid dynasty rules in the central Maghrib (modern-day Tunisia).

945–1055   The Buyid dynasty reigns in Iraq; Abbasid authority is sharply curtailed.

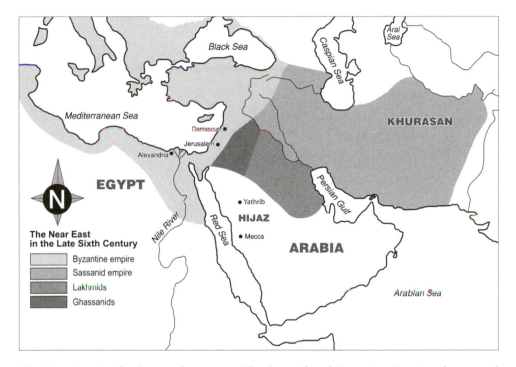

The Near East in the late sixth century. The Sasanid and Byzantine Empires dominated the Near East and eastern Mediterranean in the period known as Late Antiquity. War between the two powers erupted periodically, notably in the early seventh century (see Chapter 1). The Lakhmid and Ghassanid tribal polities, until the late sixth and early seventh century, were clients respectively of the Sasanids and Byzantines. *Miami University.*

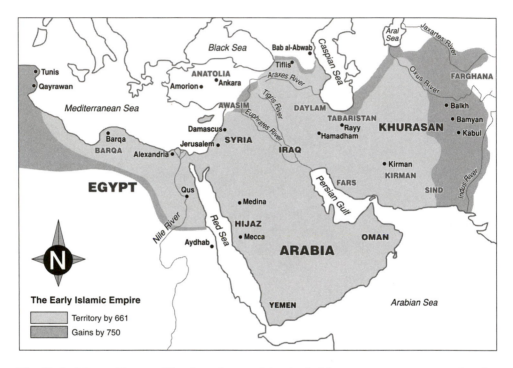

The Early Islamic Empire. The first phases of the Arab-Islamic conquests occurred under the Prophet Muhammad's four successors, the so-called Rashidun Caliphs, between roughly 632 and 661. The Umayyad caliphs made further gains from their center in Syria. The conquests resulted in the destruction of the Sasanid Empire and the ouster of the Byzantine Empire from most of the Near East. *Miami University.*

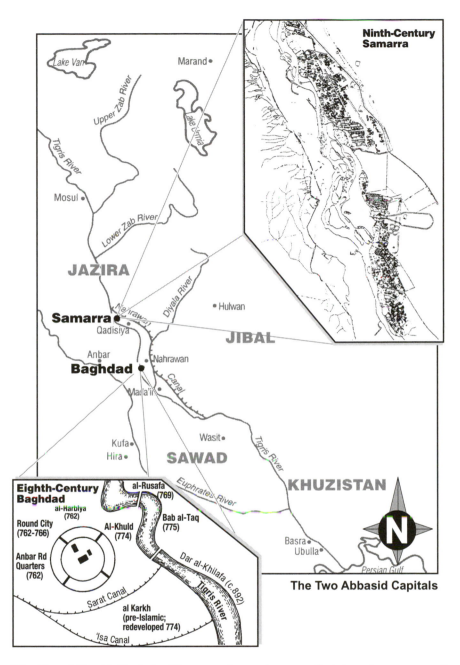

The Two Abbasid Capitals

The Two Abbasid Capitals. The map shows the two administrative centers of the Abbasid Caliphate. Samarra replaced Baghdad as the imperial hub from roughly 836 to 892 (see Chapter 4). The diagram of Baghdad highlights principal features of the original Abbasid settlement founded by al-Mansur. Samarra (top box) was vast, stretching many kilometers along the Tigris River. *Miami University.*

CHAPTER 1

HISTORICAL OVERVIEW

THE PRE-ISLAMIC NEAR EAST

The Islamic tradition traces its origins to the reception of divine revelation by a forty-year-old merchant, Muhammad ibn Abdallah. The body of revelation received by Muhammad is known as the Qur'an. Like his clansmen, the Banu Hashim, the Prophet belonged to the Quraysh, the principal tribe of Mecca, a small town in the Hijaz region of northwestern Arabia. Muhammad was an Arab by language, religion, and culture.

Sixth-century Arab culture was largely confined to the Arabian Peninsula and areas of southern Syria and Mesopotamia. A long-held view among historians that pre-Islamic Arabia was wholly isolated from the wider Near East has given way in recent decades to a more subtle and useful description. The peninsula was, both in geographic and cultural terms, at a considerable distance from the cosmopolitan societies of Egypt, Syria, and Iran. But the political, religious, and commercial influences emanating from those regions into Arabia are clear. Also clear is the influence of Arab culture, in turn, upon the history of the pre-Islamic Near East. These mutual influences were the inevitable result of centuries of cultural and commercial exchange between the Arabs (nomads and settled folk), including inhabitants of the Arabian Peninsula, and their non-Arab neighbors.

For over 500 years, the Near East had been the staging ground of a bitter conflict between the imperial states of Rome and Iran. By the sixth century, the heirs to the conflict were Byzantium (the Eastern Roman Empire), with its capital at Constantinople, and the Sasanid Empire, based in Ctesiphon, a prosperous city located on the Tigris River. Both empires relied upon deeply rooted imperial traditions of the Near East (Roman and Persian); the backing of well-entrenched religious and civilian elites; revenue from trade and a vast agrarian tax base; and the muscle of well-organized, experienced armies. There is good evidence that by the early sixth century, the effects of internal unrest and a period of renewed fighting between the two imperial foes had taken a toll upon the stability of both states. In Byzantium, a series of natural disasters had dire effects as well.

The internal difficulties for both empires had to do, in part, with their religious and cultural complexity. Elite families in the cities of Egypt and Syria—Alexandria, Damascus, and Antioch among them—usually identified with the Byzantine Empire through a shared Hellenistic culture. They participated in economic life through commerce and land tenure, so they had a stake in the stability of the empire. In much of the countryside, however, the Byzantine state and its official church were at odds with local society. These differences were in good part religious: the local churches of Syria and Egypt (as well as of Armenia and Ethiopia) were Monophysite, a form of Christian teaching rejected by the Byzantine Orthodox Church. The differences were exacerbated by the use—for example, by the majority Coptic Church in Egypt—of local languages and traditions in both liturgy and everyday life. Alienation from the empire was furthered by the heavy-handed conduct of Byzantine officials and their tax agents.

The Sasanid Empire (224–651) had as its official faith Zoroastrianism, an ancient Iranian faith headed by an ambitious religious establishment led by the magi, the chief priests. In addition to their veneration of Ahura Mazda (the God of Light), the Iranian shahs (kings) also claimed personal divinity, in contrast with their Byzantine counterparts. Due, in part, to notions of this kind, relations between the Iranian state and substantial minorities under their control, among them a large Jewish population and an even larger Nestorian Christian community, had soured badly by the onset of the seventh century. The Sasanid state also had to deal with ambitious local aristocratic families, some of whom claimed lineages as venerable as that of the Sasanids themselves.

Hostility between the two empires was driven by opposing strategic and geopolitical claims. These often had strong religious and ideological overtones. War erupted following the murder of the Byzantine emperor Maurice (r. 582–602) by mutinous troops. Seizing the moment, the young Sasanid ruler, Shah Khusraw II Parwiz (r. 591–628), sent his armies into Syria, Anatolia, and Egypt. The Sasanid occupation proved short-lived. In 622, the Byzantine emperor, Heraclius (r. 610–641), organized a brilliant campaign that drove the Sasanids back into Iraq by 626–627. Modern historians are divided over the extent to which this final round of warfare undermined the ability of the two empires to resist the campaigns of Arab-Islamic forces riding north from the Arabian Peninsula. It can be said, however, that neither empire fully anticipated an assault of this kind.

Byzantine and Sasanid observers had long been aware of the culturally distinct Arab population of southern Syria and Arabia. In prior centuries, small Arab principalities along the eastern and southern edges of the Arabian Peninsula had been clients of outside powers, including Iran and Ethiopia. The Nabataean kingdom (fourth century B.C.E.–106 C.E.), like the third-century city-state of Palmyra, flourished as a commercial power. In the fifth century, the Arabian kingdom of Kinda unified much of southern Arabia, then disappeared in the later sixth century. All three local states operated in the shadow of the two Near Eastern empires. Similarly, for much of the sixth century and into the early seventh century, Byzantine and Sasanid patronage supported, respectively, the Arab Ghassanids in southern Syria and, in southern Iraq, the Lakhmid princes. It is a measure of the religious and political complexity of the Near East in this period that the Ghassanids were Monophysite Christians despite their close association with the (Orthodox Christian) Byzantine Empire.

Of particular interest to the Near Eastern powers was the highly profitable trade that crossed the western Arabian Peninsula from the Indian Ocean into the Red Sea and, from there, into the Mediterranean region. No less lucrative was the trade in frankincense and myrrh, products grown in Yemen, in southwestern Arabia. Both forms of commerce dictated the long-term course of politics within Arabia because powerful nomadic tribes struggled for control over the flow of products and security privileges over the trade routes themselves. It appears that commerce also contributed to the establishment of small towns such as Mecca. These towns flourished as links in the panregional trade. It must be stressed, however, that by the sixth century, prior to the career of the Prophet Muhammad, the commerce in luxury goods from the Indian Ocean trade, along with the high-value perfumes of south Arabia, seems to have nearly disappeared. Recent scholarship, challenging the view that Mecca remained a center of the long-distance luxury trade, has pointed out that contemporary sources say nothing about the town in this period (in contrast to references in earlier periods). It may be that Mecca was a center of mostly local trade characterized by fairly mundane products (such as leather goods and dried foodstuffs) with a relatively limited value.

PRE-ISLAMIC ARABIA

Historians tread carefully when describing the society and culture of the peninsular Arabs in the pre-Islamic period. It was long the the practice among Western historians to rely on information concerning much later periods of Arabian history, even the nineteenth and twentieth centuries, to explain the early period up to and including the Prophet's lifetime. The question, of course, is whether such data are reliable. An approach of this sort clearly implies that "traditional" societies, such as that of pre-Islamic Arabia, undergo little change over many centuries. A related problem is that extensive archaeological work in the Arabian Peninsula (particularly in the Hijaz) has yet to be carried out. The problem has partly to do with official resistance to research of this kind, since many areas where archaeologists would want to carry out their work are historically and religiously sensitive. Important discoveries of early physical evidence have been made, and no doubt many more are to come, but to date the picture of pre-Islamic Arabian life remains incomplete. That said, historians of early Islam do agree on significant aspects of Arabian society at the time the Prophet was alive.

Unlike Egypt, Mesopotamia, and Iran, much of the Arabian Peninsula never experienced centralized state administration. Byzantine and Sasanid imperial control—even with the interest in Arabian trade, and campaigns waged along the edges of the peninsula—never extended into the interior of Arabia. For most peninsular Arabs, the tribe was the principal sociopolitical organization. Tribal affiliation provided a sense of identity, personal security, and livelihood. Scattered throughout fifth- and sixth-century Arabia were sedentary communities (towns), such as Mecca, Ta'if, and Yathrib. Many peninsular Arabs, however, lived as either semipastoralists or year-round nomads. Life and livelihood—particularly for the "pure nomads"—revolved around seasonal migration and the breeding, selling, and raiding of animals. This mode of socioeconomic life is known as pastoralism. For only a select group of tribes, the Quraysh of Mecca included, did pastoralism take second place to trade. The tribe, the central structure of Arabian society, was organized in terms of kinship. Claims of common lineage bound individuals, families, and clans to one another. Tribal organization appears to have cut across Arab society: pastoral nomads, small farmers and herders, and the inhabitants of towns all participated in this kinship-based system. Daily life centered on the immediate family and clan, the building blocks of the tribal groups. A wider tribal identity usually came into play when and where questions of security and the defense of property arose.

These were not incidental questions: raiding (*ghazw*) was a well-established pattern of pre-Islamic Arabian society. Given the scarcities of a semiarid environment and the absence of organized state institutions, this is hardly surprising. Raids were carried out regularly against opposing tribes and by nomadic groups against villages and towns. The evidence indicates that raids were conducted mostly to acquire property, such as animals, goods, and, when possible, prisoners rather than to inflict casualties. Prisoners often were used as slaves or hostages. To kill or wound one's (male) opponents, or to visit dishonor upon their women, was to invite acts of vengeance. The bond of kinship required that acts of violence be settled either through revenge or through compensation paid by the aggressor.

In both the pre-Islamic and the Islamic periods, poetry was the principal form of cultural expression. A surviving corpus of pre-Islamic verse provides crucial evidence on early Arab society.[1] The poems reflect an ethos of physical toughness, martial prowess, and a belief in the superiority of nomadic culture. No less prominent are themes of courage, generosity, and independence of spirit. Historians have argued that a society of this kind, in which raiding, feuding, the use of arms, and a high level of competition over resources were much in evidence, was "geared to warfare; among full members of the tribe (as opposed to slaves and others of low status) there were no 'civilians.' "[2] This is, in a sense, misleading. The martial ethos no doubt meant more to certain segments of Arabian society than to others. Of particular significance, here and to the course of early Islamic history, were the so-called camel nomads, Arab tribesmen whose livelihood centered on the breeding and use (in battle and commerce) of the camel. A creature ideally suited to desert conditions, the camel also was essential as a source of food (milk, meat) and hides and for long-distance travel. Poems and the accounts of the Arab-

Islamic conquests indicate that it was also customary for these tribes to keep horses. These were used mostly for warfare and were highly valued property.

Leadership in most Arab tribes was hereditary. In many tribal confederations, as a result, certain clans were predominant over several generations. New tribal chiefs were usually selected on the basis of ability rather than seniority, however, and all indications are that they wielded limited authority. The successful chief demonstrated generosity, physical courage, and a sense of justice. He was also required to have a keen sense of tribal politics, an ability to arbitrate conflicts between individuals and families, and a willingness to step aside when tribal elders deemed it time for him to do so. A trait greatly valued in Arab culture was *hilm*, a combination of wisdom, experience, and a keen sense of tribal politics.

A clear description of pre-Islamic Arab religion is difficult, largely because the formation of the Islamic tradition obliterated many of the traces left by previous religious practice in Arabia. It seems clear, however, that most Arab chiefs played little or no role in religious life. It also is clear that the major scriptural faiths had made inroads into local culture. In particular, Monophysite Christianity, the dominant form of the faith in Syria, Egypt, and Ethiopia, made its way into Arabia from southern Syria and across the Red Sea. Judaism also had deep roots in the region. Jewish tribes made up a sizable proportion of the population of Yathrib, a town north of Mecca, and a Jewish presence is known to have existed farther south, in Yemen.

Paganism existed alongside monotheism. The population of Mecca, like that of other locales in sixth-century Arabia, appears to have remained solidly animist. Inhabiting the natural world, it was thought, were spirits of both good and evil natures known as *jinns*, whose presence was invoked through ritual sacrifices and offerings. More significant was an apparent hierarchy of beings at whose head stood Allah (*the* God, the one Lord), surrounded by his three daughters. These beings inhabited sacred grounds, usually adorned with idols, in which specific rules held sway, including the promise of sanctuary and a ban on violence.

A sanctuary was known as a *haram*. The ban on violence in such areas had commercial and political value, since tribesmen could engage in commerce without fear of loss. They could also engage in negotiations and alliance-building, activities of great concern in any tribal environment. Of special standing in the fifth- and sixth-century Hijaz was the *haram* of Mecca, a significant center of animist practice. Its prominence had to do with two closely related features: the central location of its *haram* and the presence of the Ka'ba, an ancient, cube-shaped structure. Embedded in a corner of the Ka'ba was (and is) a black stone, perhaps a meteorite, that appears to have been the object of rituals of pilgrimage, such as circumambulation, carried out by the faithful. By the sixth century, the Prophet's tribe, the Quraysh, had emerged as guardians of the Ka'ba. As the heads of a local commercial network and leaders of the local cult, they had the most to lose if and when traditional values and practice were put in question.

THE PROPHET MUHAMMAD

Such was the environment into which the Prophet Muhammad was born. Even a simple reconstruction of the Prophet's life is fraught with difficulty, since none of his early Arabic-Islamic biographies are contemporary. The earliest surviving works date to the early ninth century, long after the Prophet's death, traditionally dated to 632. These works rely upon information transmitted from earlier periods, even the Prophet's lifetime, but also contain much material from later periods that reflects the natural tendency of any religious tradition to embellish the life of a venerated person, either as an expression of reverence or to impose views developed in the course of later religious debate. The challenge is to identify the earliest material, a task to which historians continue to devote their efforts.

Muhammad's career as prophet and as leader of the nascent Muslim community is described in a series of early Islamic texts. These include biographies (known as the *sira* literature), the most significant of which was written by the scholar Muhammad ibn Ishaq (d. 770). It survives in various versions, perhaps the best-known of which is the edition by Abd al-Malik ibn Hisham (d. 834), an Iraqi author.[3] The Prophet's life is also laid out in historical works such as the great *History of Prophets and Kings* by the Baghdadi historian Muhammad ibn Jarir al-Tabari (d. 923).[4] No less valuable a source is the Hadith, the copious record of the Prophet's words and deeds that stands as a scriptural complement to the Qur'an.[5] It is an essential guide to Muslim thought and worship. The Qur'an itself is also used as a source for the Prophet's life. On the basis of these early sources, later authors developed more popular accounts that include songs and poetry commemorating the Prophet's life.

According to traditional accounts, Muhammad was born in 570. Orphaned at a young age, he was reared by other members of the Banu Hashim, notably his uncle Abu Talib. He acquired a reputation for honesty and intelligence and, at some point, was nicknamed *al-Amin* (the Trustworthy). Like others of the Quraysh, Muhammad became a merchant and, in that capacity, journeyed outside the Hijaz. The sources tell us that early predictions revealed the mission for which he was soon to be chosen. A pair of angels, for example, is reported to have cleansed his heart of a black clot, and on a number of occasions, Jewish and Christian figures are said to have recognized the young Muhammad as a future prophet.

Muhammad's first marriage occurred prior to his prophetic mission. Impressed with his moral probity, Khadija bint Khuwaylid (d. 619), an older woman and a merchant in her own right, proposed the union. According to various accounts, the couple had as many as six children. One or perhaps two sons died at a young age. Four daughters would convert to Islam and accompany their father on the *Hijra* (see below). Among them was Fatima (about whom more will be said later). Modern social historians are impressed with Khadija's independence and high social standing (as a woman in pre-Islamic Mecca). Khadija would provide vital support to Muhammad following his first, and overwhelming, vision of the archangel Gabriel. Ibn Ishaq says of her: "She strengthened him, lightened his burden, proclaimed his truth, and belittled men's opposition."[6] He goes on to describe her as the first convert to Muhammad's new teaching. Upon her death, Muhammad's situation became precarious, deprived as he was of her unwavering support and wealth.

According to Islamic tradition, Muhammad's mission began in his fortieth year (610). On Mount Hira, located above Mecca, a figure, usually identified as the archangel Gabriel, announced to him: "You are the Messenger of God." Gabriel later summoned him to recite the first words of revelation, the body of teaching that was to become the Qur'an. The moment is commemorated as "the Night of Destiny [or Power]" (*Laylat al-Qadr*), to which the Qur'an makes reference: "And what will explain to you what the Night of Destiny is? The Night of Destiny is better than a thousand months" (*Surat al-Qadr*, 97:2–3).

Muhammad would receive revelation in serial form until his death. An official version of the Qur'an was sanctioned and distributed only later, during the caliphate of Muhammad's third successor, Uthman ibn Affan. The Qur'an, composed of 114 *suras* (chapters), each of which is made up of a number of verses (*aya*; pl., *ayat*), is held by the Islamic tradition to be the divine, unalterable word of God. It conveys, in often intense and unambiguous language, the central idea of divine unity and power, and the requirement that the believer (the Muslim) choose between submission to the will (or law) of God, the promise of which is salvation, and an unrighteous life whose outcome is eternal damnation. "For those whom God has left astray, there will be no protector thereafter" (*Surat al-Shura*, 42:44). *Islam* means "submission," and thus the *Muslim* is one who submits or surrenders.

Muhammad initially preached his new message in private, then more publicly. He attracted converts from within his clan and among other, usually more humble, groups in Mecca. (That many of the early converts included members of disenfranchised groups has led some modern historians to argue that the rise of Islam should be understood in sociopolitical rather than religious terms.) The Qurayshi leadership, however, wanted no part of his teachings. Their hostility turned particularly bitter as Muhammad's denunciation of their pagan beliefs grew more pointed. Among Muhammad's first converts was a young cousin, Ali ibn Abi Talib. He was the son (*ibn* is Arabic for "son") of Abu Talib, the Prophet's patron and protector in the early years. Ali would later marry Fatima, the Prophet's daughter, which strengthened his ties to the Prophet.

It was also in this period that Muhammad is said to have undergone a miraculous nighttime journey (*Isra'*) to Jerusalem, followed by an ascent into heaven (*Mi'raj*). Upon reaching Jerusalem, according to his biographers, the Prophet prayed with Abraham and others of the line of monotheistic prophets. He then, with Gabriel's help, arose to heaven, where he encountered Jesus, Moses, and Abraham and, finally, entered into the presence of God. Commenting on the Night Journey, one of Ibn Ishaq's informants says: "It was certainly an act of God by which He took him by night in what way He pleased to show him. . . . His mighty sovereignty and power by which He does what He wills to do."[7] The huge rock that stands at the center of the Dome of the Rock, an early Islamic structure in Jerusalem, is held to be the spot from which the Prophet arose into the Divine Presence.

THE *HIJRA*

Faced with Qurayshi resistance, the Prophet sought support outside Mecca. In an event known as the *Hijra* (622), Muhammad departed Mecca for the northern town of Yathrib, known henceforth as Medina. The *Hijra* (emigration, flight) marked a new phase for the Prophet and his following. Adopted later as the beginning of year 1 of the Islamic calendar, the *Hijra* became the founding moment of the Islamic *umma* (community) and thus the dawn of a new age. The Muslims—literally, "those who submit" (i.e., to God's will)—as they would come to be known, could now worship openly. As their leader, Muhammad assumed often daunting responsibilities. He had now to balance religious guidance and political leadership. The believers also looked to him to establish social regulations, that is, rules to govern their daily affairs. The content of the Qur'an and the Prophet's own instruction provided a foundation for the gradual formation of early Islamic law. The Arabic sources portray Muhammad as a leader of wisdom, grace, and magnanimity.

The Medinan phase of the Prophet's career will be considered in more detail in the next chapter. The conflict with Mecca was a crucial aspect of the period. Several years of warfare culminated in the surrender of the Quraysh and the capitulation of Mecca (630) to Muhammad and his forces. Near the end of the conflict the Jewish tribes of Medina were exiled and, in one case, destroyed. Reentering the town of his birth, the Prophet immediately "purified" the Ka'ba by ridding it of its pagan idols. In this way, he incorporated the Ka'ba and its ritual patterns into the nascent faith of Islam. In a sympathetic gesture typical of his leadership style, he forgave most of the Qurayshi leadership for its opposition. Controversy would later surround the rise of his former Qurayshi opponents to positions of influence in early Islamic society and politics.

In the last years of his life, Muhammad devoted no less attention to the creation of alliances with influential tribes throughout Arabia. Most pacts were settled through diplomacy, but when this failed, the Muslim leadership relied on force. Following Muhammad's death, a number of these tribes, only some of which had accepted the new religious teachings, broke ties with the leadership in Medina. This obliged Muhammad's successors to wage campaigns to reestablish control over the Arabian Peninsula. An open question is whether the Prophet intended the unification of Arabia as preparation for a more ambitious campaign against Byzantine territory. In any case, he appears to have initiated attacks on Byzantine outposts in southern Syria.

The Prophet's death (632) sparked a fierce debate over his succession that threatened to tear apart the young Islamic community. Abu Bakr, close friend and adviser to the Prophet, finally was chosen to fill his shoes. He adopted the title "caliph," from the Arabic *khalifa* (representative or deputy); his office was the caliphate. Abu Bakr, and his immediate successors, would not only reunify the Arabian Peninsula but also, and more important, launch the early Arab-Islamic conquests. These campaigns proceeded with great rapidity. An abiding question is whether the Byzantine and Sasanid empires were poorly prepared to face the Arab-Islamic forces because of the losses each had incurred during the warfare of the late sixth century. Though these losses were certainly a reason for the success of the Arab campaigns, they by no means stand alone. An equally significant factor must have been the unifying power of the message contained in the Qur'an and the Prophet's own teachings. History has shown repeatedly that ideas can provide powerful motivation for extraordinary deeds.

THE ARAB-ISLAMIC EMPIRE

The campaigns of expansion lasted for nearly a century. An initial series of victories faltered as internal conflict and civil war erupted within the Islamic Empire. Uthman, the fourth of the Prophet's successors to the caliphate, fell to an assassin (656). His murder sparked upheaval, during which Ali ibn Abi Talib was chosen as his successor. Ali's assassination (661) brought a close to the Medinan caliphate as well as a pause in the conquests. Ali's chief opponent, Mu'awiya ibn Abi Sufyan, was given the oath of allegiance (*bay'a*) as the new caliph. Mu'awiya, at the time governor of Syria, was a member of the Umayyad clan, a powerful branch of the Quraysh. He quickly transferred the capital of the empire to Damascus and, in doing so, founded the Umayyad caliphate (661–750).

The Umayyads initiated two distinct though closely related policies, the combination of which was to transform Near Eastern society: Arabization and Islamization. Arabization involved the spread of Arab culture and language. Within several centuries of the early conquests, the Arabic language became the lingua franca of a region stretching from al-Andalus (Spain) across the Maghrib (North Africa) into the Near East. Though other regions, such as Iran, Central Asia, and India did not adopt Arabic as a principal language, Arabic became a major world language. No less a result of Umayyad rule was the spread of the Islamic faith. Conversion occurred among substantial numbers of Coptic-speaking Egyptians, Aramaic-speaking populations in Syria and Palestine, and other subject peoples over several centuries. It appears that majority Muslim populations emerged in areas of the Near East, Iran, and North Africa by the late tenth century. The Umayyads were not solely responsible for the transformation of the religious landscape, but they certainly did much to make it possible.

The Umayyad period ended with the Abbasid revolution (750), the details of which will be discussed later. It fell to the Abbasids to recognize and exploit deep-seated resentment of Umayyad rule throughout the empire. It is unclear when the Abbasids actually gained control of the anti-Umayyad movement. What is clear is that they won sufficient backing to claim the caliphate by the late 740s. Once the destruction of the Umayyad house was complete, the new dynasty moved quickly to consolidate its authority. The true founder of the Abbasid state, Abu Ja'far al-Mansur (r. 754–775), is credited with a number of achievements, including the foundation of a new imperial capital in Iraq. For at least 300 years, that city—Baghdad—remained the nexus of remarkable cultural and religious development. It was replaced as the imperial capital in the mid-ninth century by Samarra (for roughly sixty years). Even then, Baghdad remained the undisputed urban center of the eastern Mediterranean.

At its height, at the end of the eighth century, the Abbasid Empire stretched from central North Africa across the Near East and southern Anatolia into eastern Iran. From that point forward, however, the unity and stability of the empire would suffer. In the early ninth century, civil war and the transfer of the capital from Baghdad to Samarra contributed to a weaker Abbasid state. Internal difficulties were joined by political fragmentation. By the end of the ninth century, Abbasid authority gradually gave way to autonomous regimes in two important provinces, Egypt and Khurasan (eastern Iran). In Khurasan, the Samanids controlled economic and political life through the tenth century despite relatively cordial relations with the Abbasids. Egypt fell under the control of the

Tulunids, a Turkish military family. Finally, northern Iraq and much of Syria would fall to the control of the Hamdanids, centered in the cities of Mosul and Aleppo. The Hamdanids faced large campaigns conducted by the Byzantine Empire over the tenth century. In turn, military and political crises badly eroded trade and agricultural production. The result was a prolonged period of economic instability at the heart of the Abbasid Empire.

Finally, the Abbasids surrendered control over Iraq to the Buwayhids (or Buyids). The head of the family, Ali ibn Buya (d. 949), was a warlord from the northern province of Daylam, along the south Caspian coast. He and his family established a base of support in Fars, along the Persian Gulf. Soon thereafter, Ahmad ibn Buya (d. 967), Ali's brother, pushed into Iraq and occupied Baghdad (945). He was recognized by the Abbasid caliphate with the newly coined title *Amir al-umara* (literally "Commander of the Commanders"). In this way, the Abbasids abandoned most of what remained of their decision-making powers. The Abbasid dynasty was to survive until 1258 (and, in Egypt, to 1517). From the Buwayhid period on, however, its role was usually symbolic: the later caliphs often reigned over little more than their palaces. The Abbasids had certainly left their mark upon the history of the Islamic world, but no less upon the history of the premodern world.

NOTES

1. A good introduction to this poetry is Michael Sells, trans., *Desert Tracings: Six Classic Arabian Odes*.

2. Hugh Kennedy, *The Prophet and the Age of the Caliphates*, p. 18.

3. See Alfred Guillaume, trans., *The Life of Muhammad: A Translation of Ibn Ishaq's Sirat Rasul Allah*.

4. Now available in a multivolume translation, *The History of al-Tabari*.

5. For more on Hadith, see Chapter 5.

6. Ibn Ishaq, *Life of Muhammad*, p. 155.

7. Ibid., pp. 181–182.

CHAPTER 2

THE ARAB-ISLAMIC CONQUESTS AND THE MEDINAN STATE

The Arabic *written* accounts of the earliest period of Islamic history first appeared around the early ninth century, many decades after Muhammad's death. To make sense of events up to that period, the authors of these works had to rely on information transmitted *verbally* by one generation of Arabic-speakers to the next. Such information is known as *oral tradition.* Across human history, societies have relied heavily upon oral tradition, which preserves history and customs and provides a powerful source of identity and social unity. Orally transmitted information is subject to change, however—sometimes radical change. (Written sources are subject to alteration as well, so the distinction between the kinds of information should not be exaggerated.) Change may be accidental—memories, after all, are often faulty—but also may come about deliberately. Individuals or groups rework, even invent, information that they present as an authentic record of the past. The way in which early Islamic society remembered the Medinan period is a case in point. Little wonder, then, that historians devote great energy to making sense of these sources. Debate over the reliability of such evidence often grows heated. Similar debates have long surrounded, for example, the life of Jesus and the history of the early Christian movement. Even in the face of such persistent questions, an account of the first period of Islamic history can (and ought to) be made.

MUHAMMAD AND THE EARLY COMMUNITY

The *Hijra* (622), which divided the Prophet's career into the Meccan and Medinan periods, occurred because of the violent response of the

Quraysh to Muhammad's teachings. No sooner did Muhammad arrive in Medina than he set about organizing his followers into a formal group. The term *umma* is used in the Qur'an to refer to human communities in a religious sense, that is, it denotes a human collective—a society— founded principally upon prophetic teachings. The followers of Abraham constituted such a society, as did, according to this Qur'anic meaning, Jews and Christians. When *umma* refers specifically to Muhammad's following in Medina, it indicates that the first Muslims constituted the fullest expression of human religious life. The stress falls upon the religious as opposed to the social, economic, or political. These elements are not absent from society and, indeed, are necessary to its survival. But they are of secondary importance: a society of this sort is defined by its devotion to the One God and the determination to do His will.

The Prophet's early biographers indicate that Muhammad set his sights on unifying his followers, providing them with sources of livelihood, and building the sorts of political arrangements that would assure their survival. Historians use the biographies, alongside other sorts of evidence, to argue that Muhammad's genius lay in bringing together traditional patterns of Arabian religion, society, and politics with the new socio-religious message of the Qur'an. Muhammad appealed to his followers with a mix of the familiar and the new.

Muhammad's domestic arrangements are interpreted in this light. Among his first steps was the construction of a simple but good-sized building in central Medina. Though intended in part as a dwelling for himself and his growing family, it had other, more significant functions as well: as a site for prayer, meals, and other communal needs; a staging ground for military campaigns; and a sanctuary during conflict. It consisted of a vast, open-air courtyard along one wall of which was a covered area; built into a second wall was a set of private rooms used by the Prophet's wives and children. The covered space marked the direction (*qibla*) in which believers were to pray. In Islamic tradition the building, known as "the Prophet's house," is seen as the first mosque in Islam, and thus the model for mosque construction from then on, though this is a point much disputed by modern art historians. It served "as the nerve center of the burgeoning Muslim community":[1] it was a symbol of the new community and its headquarters.

Muhammad's marriages are often viewed in political terms. The early biographers state that Muhammad consummated marriage with at least eleven women in Medina, most of whom survived him. The majority of his wives fell into two categories. One group was the daughters of close supporters from the Quraysh—including A'isha, the daughter of Abu Bakr, and Hafsa, daughter, of Umar ibu al-Khattab (the second of the Prophet's successors)—and other prominent Hijazi tribes. The second group consisted of widows of slain Muslims (Hafsa was in this category as well). Marriage served, in these cases, as a means to secure or create political bonds. There is nothing to indicate that such conduct was unusual for a man in Muhammad's position. The evidence shows that polygyny (having more than one wife) was among several marriage patterns in pre-Islamic Arabia. Muhammad's wives, and A'isha in particular, assumed a prominent role in early Islamic society. A'isha, said to have been the favorite of Muhammad's wives after Khadija, became a authority on the Prophet's teachings following his death.

Once his domestic affairs were settled, Muhammad turned to overcoming divisions among his followers. A remarkable document, known misleadingly as the "Constitution of Medina," provides important evidence of the Prophet's approach. The Constitution was a set of agreements between the different elements of Muhammad's following. Ibn Ishaq's *Sira* (his biography of Muhammad) contains the earliest surviving version of the agreement. Historians argue over whether it was a single document and differ widely over its significance. They agree, however, that it is authentic. The details of these debates can be set aside.[2] The concern here is Muhammad's effort to create a sense of common purpose among his followers. Prior to the *Hijra*, the Prophet had won a loyal following in Medina by arbitrating between two feuding tribal blocs, the Aws and the Khazraj. Both were confederations consisting of numerous clans. Though Muhammad won the confidence of clans on both sides, decades would pass before their long-standing differences disappeared. The Prophet's Medinan followers, the *Ansar*, included members of most of these clans. Divisions also existed between the *Ansar* and the other principal group of believers, the *Muhajirun*, the Meccans who had accompanied the Prophet to Medina.

To bridge these divisions, the Prophet appealed to the believers to think of themselves in new terms. The Constitution refers explicitly to the Prophet's followers as "one community" (*umma wahida*) and recognizes that forming a new-style community of this kind would be difficult, requiring great initiative and, in all likelihood, armed conflict against its opponents. A portion of the text follows:

> A believer shall not take as an ally the freedman of another Muslim against him. The God-fearing believers shall be against the rebellious or him who seeks to spread injustice, or sin, or enmity, or corruption between believers; the hand of every man shall be against him even if he be a son of one of them. A believer shall not slay a believer for the sake of an unbeliever, nor shall he aid an unbeliever against a believer. God's protection is one, the least of them may give protection to a stranger on their behalf. Believers are friends one to the other to the exclusion of outsiders. To the Jew who follows us belong help and equality. He shall not be wronged nor shall his enemies be aided. The peace of the believers is indivisible. No separate peace shall be made when believers are fighting in the way of God.[3]

The believers (those soon to be known as Muslims) were to embrace, in sum, a new form of identity, one that turned on acceptance of the unfolding revelation and Muhammad's leadership.

Modern historians suggest that the new *umma* resembled the tribe as western Arabian society knew it. It was led, like any other tribe, by a strong, respected leader—the Prophet. It provided its members with identity, security, and a significant source of livelihood—namely, raiding—that had been an integral aspect of Arabian society well before Muhammad's day. Raids—or, as some historians describe them, "localized warfare" between opposing tribes—was the means by which tribes increased their wealth (by capturing flocks, slaves, and goods) and widened their sphere of authority. These organized campaigns, in one sense, reflected an age-old pattern and, as practiced by the Muslims under Muhammad's guidance, served much the same function. But they were now defined in quite different terms, the terms provided by the dynamic ideas of the Qur'an. Muhammad, in other words, had introduced something new: the early believers were to belong to a "tribe" that was like no other. Rather than the mundane affairs of everyday tribal life, the Prophet's following was to devote itself to a higher purpose: the creation of a new, divinely inspired social order.

Muhammad's second and more difficult task was to organize a response to the formidable opposition posed by the Jews of Medina and the

Quraysh-led forces of Mecca. The Constitution, as seen above, deals explicitly with the Jews of Medina, hinting clearly at growing strains between them and the early Muslims. The Jewish presence in the Hijaz was long-standing, and good evidence exists that the Jewish leadership had held sway over Medina in the pre-Islamic period. Muhammad posed an obvious challenge that would explain, in part, the rise in tensions. If the Constitution is a bit ambiguous on this point, other early Arabic sources provide clearer evidence. They indicate that Muhammad initially cultivated ties with the Medinan Jews. He is reported to have adopted such Jewish practices as formal prayer in the direction of Jerusalem. As the relationship soured, however, he ordered his followers to pray toward Mecca, that is, the Ka'ba. The believers duly carried out a reorientation of the *qibla*, the direction of prayer, in the "Prophet's house."

Poor relations with the Jewish tribes gave way to outright conflict precisely at the point when the struggle against Mecca was reaching its peak. Reports have Muhammad ordering the expulsion of two of the Jewish tribes and, shortly thereafter, the massacre of the males of a third tribe, the Banu Qurayza. The Banu Qurayza were accused of betraying the Muslims by backing the Quraysh-led forces sent from Mecca. But Muhammad's attempts to instill a sense of purpose among his followers no doubt played a part as well. As seen earlier, Arabia, like the wider Near East, was suffused with Jewish and Christian ideas and lore. The Qur'an, and Muhammad's own teachings, reflect the influence of the older traditions upon the emerging new faith. It is hardly surprising that, at some point, Muhammad sought to distinguish his teachings from those of Judaism and Christianity. The two steps—opposing the Jewish tribes in Medina and providing his own teachings with sharper definition—can only have contributed to his goal of unifying the early Muslims and providing them with a sense of direction.

The conflict against the Quraysh of Mecca was more difficult. To gain the upper hand, Muhammad turned to a subtle mix of armed force and diplomacy. Small-scale raiding, mostly against Meccan trade caravans, turned gradually to outright warfare. The first raids are often understood as having a dual purpose: to attack the Meccans and to provide income to the believers. In the major fighting that followed, however, the stakes were primarily military and ideological. A victory at the Battle of Badr (624), a defeat at Uhud (625), and a final victory at the Battle of the Ditch (627) provided Muhammad's forces with a sense of both momentum and triumph. The tide now turned against the Quraysh; as influential members of the tribe rushed to convert to Islam, the Quraysh leadership sued for peace. Muhammad, acting to counter lasting effects of the conflict, quickly incorporated the Qurayshi elite into positions of authority, much to the chagrin of his other followers. Symbolic of Muhammad's victory was the "cleansing" of the Ka'ba (630), in which the idols representing the pagan faith of the Quraysh were destroyed. Muhammad then required the Quraysh to pay homage.

MUHAMMAD AND THE QUR'AN

To organize and inspire his followers, Muhammad relied chiefly upon the body of revelation that he had begun to receive in Mecca (in 610, according to traditional dating). The revelation—the Qur'an—continued from the Meccan into the Medinan period until the end of the Prophet's life (632). It served the Prophet's goals in several ways.

The Qur'an identifies Muhammad's followers, in one verse after another, as a distinct community. This is not to say that it ignores the respective tribal or clan identities of the early believers. On the contrary, it encourages pride in family and clan, and urges believers to see to the health, protection, and honor of those closest to them. A well-known Qur'anic verse refers to God having created "nations and tribes" precisely so that believers would recognize the significance of God's project (*Surat al-Hujurat*, 49:13). The idea, it seems, is that differences (of background, language, and region) are the outward characteristics of every group. That which unites them as believers is their essential humanity before God and the shared responsibility to heed His will. One belonged to family, clan, and tribe but, more significant still, one belonged to a universal body charged with the duty to serve God in dynamic fashion.

The Qur'an urges believers to dedicate themselves to God through ritual devotion. These expressions of faith include prayer, fasting, pilgrimage, and the distribution of alms. These practices are discussed later in conjunction with Document 10, which contains a very well-known text, the Hadith of Gabriel. Islamic law came to define these acts as religious duties that Muslims were to perform regularly. They were seen, as they are today, as the means by which to bind and strengthen Islamic society. Ritual devotion also was a reminder to believers of their common history. For example, Ramadan, the Islamic month during

which a daylong fast (*sawm*) occurs, commemorates the appearance of
Gabriel to Muhammad and, therefore, the onset of revelation. Ramadan was also the month during which the early Muslims defeated
their Meccan opponents at Badr, their first collective experience in
armed conflict.

The Qur'an is no less clear on the obligation to attend to social needs,
defined in both general and specific terms. It places high value upon the
virtues of humility, generosity, mercifulness, patience, and restraint, and
urges believers to observe a caring attitude or "mindfulness" in every
realm of activity. The Qur'an also makes a great deal of the moral and
spiritual equality of Muslims: all humans, notwithstanding distinctions of
origin and wealth, stand equally before God. These principles are to in-
form Muslim conduct in both the private and the public arenas. More
specific rules include a ban on fornication, adultery, lying, stealing, and
murder. Other Qur'anic rules deal with family and home: marriage, divorce, and inheritance. These elements provide a framework upon which
later generations of Muslim scholars would construct a system of law.

Muslim and non-Muslim scholars alike are deeply interested in the
egalitarian message that, in the view of many readers, lies at the heart of
the Qur'an. This goes in part to the complex subject of women and gender in Islam. A well-known verse reflects the message:

> For all men and women who have submitted to God, for believing
> men and women, for devout men and women, for all men and
> women who are true [to their word], for all men and women who
> are patient and constant, for all men and women who humble them-
> selves [before God], for all men and women who give in charity, for
> all men and women who fast [or deny themselves], for all men and
> women who are mindful of their chastity, for all men and women
> who waver not in evoking God's name, God has made ready for-
> giveness and great reward.
>
> (*Surat al-Ahzab*, 33:35)

The verse addresses men and women as standing on equal terms before
God. Other verses of the Qur'an, however, hold that sharp distinctions
were to be made between men and women. They clearly indicate, for example, that men are to wield authority over women, particularly in marriage, in which husbands are empowered to discipline, even strike, the
disobedient wife. In addition, according to an often-cited verse (*Surat al-*

Nisa, 4:3), men are permitted to take up to four wives at once under specific conditions (the same verse insists that each woman be treated equitably). A similar verse reads thus:

> And it will not be in your power to act with equal fairness towards the women [or wives], however much you may desire to do so, and so do not allow yourselves to incline [to one woman] so as to leave [another] as if in a state of suspense [i.e., as if without a husband].
>   (Surat al-Nisa, 4:129)

Commentators, particularly in the modern period, have understood such verses as a clear warning against polygyny. Similar interest is shown in the matter of veiling, which is not explicitly mandated by the Qur'an; the verse usually cited (Surat al-Nur, 24:31) requires women to dress and comport themselves modestly—and directs the same instruction to men. The central point, for present purposes, is that the Qur'an directs believers to attend closely to relations between men and women, as well as those between family members. Modern commentators, like their medieval counterparts, have shown a strong interest in the ways in which Qur'anic prescriptions on gender and family are to be applied in contemporary society.

The Qur'an also displays strong interest in the nature and dynamics of warfare—hardly surprising, given the context in which it was revealed. It makes general references to warfare and its effects. It also refers, according to Muslim commentators, to the specific conflicts of the Medinan period: the war with Mecca and the simultaneous clashes with Medina's Jews. The cited references are not always explicit: the Quraysh, for example, are seldom named directly in this context, so it is uncertain whether the war with Mecca is what the Qur'an has in mind. Finally, the Qur'an addresses specific facets of warfare, such as the use of weapons, treatment of prisoners and noncombatants, and the collection of revenue and spoils of war from conquered peoples. Many of these verses concern relations with non-Muslims.

Few would argue, however, that the Qur'an contains a clear doctrine of warfare, and scholars often point out that the references to warfare are ambiguous and, at times, contradictory. Scholars generally see the shifting terms by which the Book treats warfare as a reflection of changing conditions in Muhammad's conflict with Mecca, the Jews of Medina, and other opponents. One well-known verse (*Surat al-Tawba*, 9:5), for example, urges believers to fight idolaters until they convert to Islam, but a number of other verses urge either patience or tolerance toward those who reject or ignore God's teachings.

Two terms occur most often in the Qur'an in reference to armed struggle: *qital*, often translated as "fight," or "armed struggle," and, far less frequently, *jihad*, which is best translated as "struggle," or "striving" (to meet a particular goal). Since it is "struggle" with specific religious goals, however, many readers translate the term as "holy war."[4] A critical step is the connection made between warfare and service to God: a prominent theme of the Qur'an is that of struggling "on the path of God" (*fi sabil Allah*) as a principal duty of Muslims. "Struggle," as suggested earlier, is understood in different ways: piety, faith, and service to the community all involve strength of will and commitment. The Qur'an is clear, however, that service to God is also accomplished through participation in warfare when it is required. The relevant passages indicate that warfare was a principal activity around which the early Muslim community was organized. At least one modern historian has argued, in fact, that these elements of the "struggle on the path of God" were the very basis on which Muhammad organized his following in Medina.[5]

THE MEDINAN POLITY AND THE ARAB-ISLAMIC CONQUESTS

The triumph of Medina over its opponents owed everything to the force of Muhammad's leadership and the power of the Qur'an. One debate among historians is whether to begin speaking of a "Medinan state." Those who are uncomfortable with such a formal definition point out that under Muhammad and his four successors, Medina was a "state" in only a primitive sense. It had no standing army, no formal institutional life, no formal mechanisms for collecting taxes. It did, however, have a dynamic leadership, with the Prophet at its head, able to organize the resources and population under its control. It also had a sense of purpose provided by the Qur'an and the Prophet's own instruction. Whether this constitutes a "state" remains open to question. Some historians prefer the term "polity," the term that is used here.

In treating Muhammad's immediate legacy, historians debate a further question: Did the Prophet seek to expand Medina's sphere of influence beyond the Hijaz? One view is that the Prophet died before making his intentions clear. A counterargument, that Muhammad intended to push his advantage, makes reference to Qur'anic verses that press believers to wage offensive warfare against nonbelievers. Also, precisely at the point that Meccan resistance was crumbling, Muhammad began to receive delegations bearing messages of submission from throughout Arabia. In addition, the early Arabic sources refer to Muslim raids against the Byzantines in southern Syria late in the Prophet's lifetime. Much evidence makes clear, in any case, that Muhammad had put in place the elements required for campaigns of expansion.

Following Muhammad's death (632), a crisis of succession nearly destroyed the early Islamic community. The crisis pitted the *Muhajirun* against the Medinan Muslims (*Ansar*), who feared an alliance between the *Muhajirun* and the Qurayshi elite. It was settled when leading Muslims, chief among them Umar ibn al-Khattab (d. 644), threw their support behind Abu Bakr (r. 632–634), the Prophet's father-in-law and close companion, and thus a highly respected member of the Muslim leadership. Abu Bakr and his three successors—Umar ibn al-Khattab (r. 634–644), Uthman ibn Affan (r. 644–656), and Ali ibn Abi Talib (r. 656–661)—later came to be known as the *Rashidun* (rightly guided) caliphs. The four men reigned less as rulers than as "first among equals," another indication that the Medinan state was still in its infancy. They held office because they enjoyed broad acceptance among their fellow Muslims. This was particularly true of Abu Bakr and Umar; Uthman and Ali faced far greater opposition and fell victim to assassination, a measure of the fissures that were to divide early Islamic society.

The reigns of the Rashidun caliphs were crowned by two related achievements. First, they prevented the collapse of the Medinan polity following Muhammad's death. Shortly after the Prophet's demise, a number of the Arab tribes, particularly those far from Medina, severed ties to the Muslim leadership, feeling, it appears, that they owed allegiance to the Prophet but not his successors. A few tribes, in particular, took steps to reassert influence over their respective regions. The campaigns launched by Abu Bakr against these Arab tribes are known as the *Ridda* wars. The Islamic sources use the term *ridda* in the sense of "rejection," or "repudiation." For many of the tribes, the act may have been simply political: to end their alliance with the polity in Medina. A few others appear to have reacted against the Prophet's teachings as well. The Arab-Islamic sources treat their activity in religious terms, as "apostasy." They are described as having adopted prophetic leaders to replace Muhammad. A prominent example was Maslama ibn Habib, better known as Musaylima (d. 632), in the Yamama region.

The *Ridda* campaigns involved a mix of diplomacy and force. Abu Bakr's approach was to treat the outlying tribes as subject to Medinan authority. Thus, for example, he forbade them from participating in the campaigns of expansion, and, to ensure their submission, he held hostage members of each tribe. His successor, Umar ibn al-Khattab, took a different tack, reversing the overall policy soon after assuming office (634). He is reported to have freed the prisoners and to have invited their tribes to participate alongside those allied to Medina. In military terms, the step was momentous: Medina was now assured of greater numbers of fighters. This helps explain the conquest of the Near East, the second and more significant achievement of the Rashidun caliphs.

Often described as a demanding, even harsh, leader, Umar is also known in the sources as *al-Faruq* (one who distinguishes truth). As a young man, he vigorously opposed the Prophet before deciding to embrace his cause. After his conversion, when he was in his twenties, he quickly joined the Prophet's inner circle and provided Muhammad with sage, if often hard-edged, advice. He went on to lend critical support to the caliphate of Abu Bakr, remaining a significant ally of the older man even when they disagreed on specific policies. His devotion to Islam is described as unyielding. The great historian al-Tabari reports that Abu Bakr, in a sermon delivered in 634, spoke of *jihad* (the struggle in the path of God) as that through which God "bestowed nobility in this world and the next."[6] The words no doubt met with Umar's strong approval.

The Arabic sources credit Umar with initiating the Arab-Islamic conquests. The campaigns sent Arab-Islamic tribal forces against the Byzantine and Sasanid empires. Leading these forces were, among others, Amr ibn al-As (d. 663) and Khalid ibn al-Walid (d. 642). Like Umar, both men, as members of the Quraysh, had opposed Muhammad until, sensing that the tide had turned in the Prophet's favor, they converted to Islam. Amr is best known for his efforts in Egypt (as seen below). Khalid, nicknamed *Sayf al-Islam* (the sword of Islam) for his devotion to *jihad*, played a key part in the *Ridda* wars. Following the early conquests, he became governor of Syria.

The two commanders led Arab fighters against Byzantine armies throughout southern and central Syria in pitched battles including those at Ajnadayn, Fahl, Marj al-Suffar, and along the Yarmuk River (634–636). In his *Futuh al-Buldan*, a history of the conquests, al-Baladhuri (d. 892) describes the fall of Damascus (635) and Jerusalem (638).[7] A clash on the Yarmuk River that took the life of Theodorus (brother of the Byzantine emperor Heraclius) is viewed as the crowning event of the Arab-Islamic capture of Syria. The Byzantines retreated north into Anatolia.

The other regional power, the Sasanid Empire, fared much worse. Khalid led the initial Arab attack on Iraq and southern Iran. When Khalid returned to Syria, Sa'd ibn Abi Waqqas (d. c. 675) took over, leading new forces into Iraq. (Sa'd, an early Qurayshi convert to Islam, had been one of Muhammad's closest followers.) His efforts followed a rout of Arab forces at the Battle of the Bridge, a brief setback from which the Arabs quickly recovered. Sa'd's forces inflicted defeat (637) upon substantially larger Sasanid units at al-Qadisiya (near the modern city of Najaf). The victory, and subsequent smaller operations, left southern and central Iraq—and their considerable agricultural wealth—to the Arabs. The Sasanid administration abandoned its capital at Ctesiphon (known as also as al-Mada'in), a complex of urban settlements located along the Tigris just south of the site where Baghdad would later be built. The remarkable wealth discovered in al-Mada'in—money, livestock, slaves, and other forms of movable property—was subsequently distributed to Arab tribal units as conquest spoils. Pressing north, the Arabs crushed Sasanid resistance, particularly in the Zagros Mountains. Arab cavalry chased Shah Yazdigird III (r. 632–651), the final member of the dynasty, into the province of Khurasan, where he was killed.

To the west, following the victories in Syria and Palestine, Amr ibn al-As had moved into Byzantine-held Egypt. Bolstered by reinforcements from Medina, he overran Byzantine defenses at Heliopolis, the key Byzantine stronghold at Babylon. He then took Alexandria (641). Egypt—like Iraq a province of great agricultural and commercial wealth—was now under Arab-Islamic control. Its population was overwhelmingly Coptic, a form of Christianity sharply at odds with that practiced by the Byzan-

tine church. Tension between the Byzantine authorities and the Egyptian populace was palpable when the Arab-Muslim forces arrived. Op-
pressive Byzantine taxes, on the peasantry in particular, had made matters
worse. While the Coptic population did not welcome the Arab-Islamic
armies, it is likely that many native Egyptians simply refused to defend
the local Byzantine administration.

The campaigns in Egypt were followed by the establishment of an
Arab naval presence in the eastern Mediterranean. Utilizing the skills of
Syrian and Egyptian locals, Arab forces seized the island of Cyprus (647)
and destroyed (655) a large Byzantine fleet at the battle of *Dhat al-Sawari*
(Battle of the Masts) shortly thereafter. The rise of Arab-Islamic naval
strength was a blow to the Byzantines since the defense of Constantinople relied heavily on control of the seas. Arab-Islamic naval supremacy
would last only a short while, however, before the Byzantines were able
to reassert themselves. This was to be one of several fronts in the
Byzantine-Islamic conflict for centuries to come.

EMPIRE AND AUTHORITY

By roughly the mid-seventh century, Arab-Islamic forces controlled
regions stretching from Egypt across Syria and Iraq into central Iran. The
result was not simply a radical redrawing of the political map but a cultural and religious transformation of the Near East. The processes of Arabization and Islamization (considered later) would require centuries of
gradual change. The Arab-Islamic polity faced more immediate challenges in the meantime.

The seizure of territory—and, thus, control over well-established trade
networks and vast agricultural estates—yielded tremendous political and
fiscal rewards, but questions remained to be resolved. How were the newly
conquered regions to be administered? How were the spoils of war to be
distributed, and by whom? What policies were to govern the treatment
of subject peoples in towns and villages? And, finally, what role were the
Qur'an, the teachings of Muhammad, and the emerging principles of
Islam to play in the newly created empire?

The Arab-Muslim leadership lacked experience of the sort required to
rule an empire. The Byzantines had derived considerable administrative
knowledge from centuries of Roman imperial rule, and the Sasanids relied upon centuries of Iranian imperial history. The Medinan leadership

could draw upon no such history: they would have to learn most of the lessons of centralized government from scratch. A fundamental challenge for the caliphs, their governors, and the Arab military elite was to understand how large-scale agrarian economies functioned. Agriculture had long been practiced in the oasis towns of Arabia, but nowhere in central and northern Arabia did there exist anything resembling the large agrarian socioeconomic systems that had operated for centuries throughout the Near East.

No less a challenge was to establish control over a majority non-Arab, non-Muslim population. The development of regulations governing the affairs of non-Muslims was a gradual process, in good part, because of the sheer dimensions of the task of ruling such a variety of provinces. The status assigned to the non-Muslims (first the Jews and Christians, and, at a later date, Zoroastrians and other groups) was known as *dhimma* (protection). The Arab-Islamic administration offered protection and security in exchange for recognition of Islamic rule. The non-Muslims came to be known as *ahl al-dhimma* (those accorded protection) or, simply, *dhimmis*. Acceptance came largely in the form of a controversial poll tax known as the *jizya*, a key marker of non-Muslim status. The Qur'an's use of the term is evidence that a practice of this kind was used by the Prophet, perhaps in relations with the Jewish tribes of the Hijaz.

A third challenge was to define the authority of the caliphate. The Rashidun caliphs appear to have adopted two titles at this early stage. The first was *Amir al-mu'minin* (Commander of the Faithful), which suggests a combination of moral and military duties. Umar is said to have been the first to adopt the title, which was used in ceremonies and official correspondence. The second title—*khalifat Allah*—points more clearly to a claim of religious authority. (As noted earlier, "caliph" derives from the Arabic *khalifa*.) The sources indicate that nearly every caliph, from Uthman to the early Abbasids, adopted the title.[8] It translates as "deputy (or representative) of God." The claim was that the caliph's authority, like that of the Prophet, was of divine origin, giving him the right to interpret and enforce the law derived from the Qur'an and the Prophet's teachings.

Finally, there was the challenge of managing the military. The indications are that Umar took several steps to organize the Arab-Islamic tribal forces and increase the authority of the Medinan polity. But relations between Medina and the conquest forces were delicate. Rather than simply impose their will, the caliphs relied on persuasion, negotiation, and the cooperation of tribal chiefs. The armies remained tribal in nature: they were organized into tribal units, with clansmen fighting and living with clansmen. It is no surprise, then, that tribal leaders, in their capacity as commanders, exerted considerable authority at the local level, enhanced by the great distances between Medina and the newly conquered territories.

In an effort to exert control, Umar is reported to have insisted that the Arab-Muslim forces not settle among, nor interfere in the affairs of, local populations. The Arab fighters were not to lay claim to the lands they had conquered nor adopt the lifestyle of the majority peasant populace of Egypt, Syria, and Iran. The conquered territories instead were to be treated as the collective property of the Muslims. The fighters were to settle in garrison centers, each known as a *misr* (pl., *amsar*), located in strategically sensitive areas. Among the first of these garrisons were Basra and Kufa in Iraq, al-Fustat in Egypt, and Qayrawan in central North Africa. Other garrisons followed. These included settlements constructed alongside preexisting urban centers, such as Marw in Iran and other, perhaps smaller, centers of which there are few traces today.

To ensure that the Arab troops remained in the *amsar*, Umar arranged for the regular payment of salaries, funded out of tax revenue collected by the Medinan polity from local population centers throughout the Near East. To organize its fiscal affairs, the early Medinan administration relied on carefully managed payroll lists, known as *diwans*, organized by tribe and clan. While the origins of the term *diwan* are obscure, it is likely that the system of the military payroll was inspired by Byzantine and/or Sasanid models. Salaries for the Arab fighters were based on length of service to the Medinan state and, by extension, the Prophet's community. At this very early stage, only Arab Muslims were entitled to military salaries.

The use of Byzantine and Sasanid practice is significant. In the absence of Arab administrative traditions, the Arab-Muslim leadership was obliged to turn to pre-Islamic patterns. The caliphs and their governors, for example, used Byzantine and Sasanid coinage.[9] They also employed local officials who had served the previous empires. At first, these officials continued to use local practice and languages (Coptic, Greek, Aramaic, and Persian). The shift to Arabic as the official language of empire would occur in the Umayyad period. In addition, the Arab-Islamic administration relied on Byzantine and Sasanid systems of revenue collection. In the former Sasanid provinces, two kinds of taxes had been assessed: a land tax (Arabic, *kharaj*) and a poll tax levied directly on the population (calculated according to the size of each community). As seen above, a poll tax (*jizya*) was probably in use in Medina early on, so the Sasanid practice may have been simply fused with that tradition. Elsewhere—Egypt and Syria, for example—Byzantine practices were adopted although, due to the disruptions caused by the conquests, they underwent rapid change. The result was that local administration differed widely from one province to the next. Though clearly the situation was untenable if the empire was to function efficiently, the problem of bringing greater uniformity to imperial administration would fall to the Umayyad dynasty some decades later. Umar's assassination (644), at the hands of a Persian slave, led to internal upheaval that distracted the attention of Arab-Islamic society from the conquests and state reform.

DISSENSION AND CIVIL WAR

To appoint Umar's successor, the Muslim leadership turned to a process known as *shura* (consultative council), whereby a small, elite group worked together to find a worthy candidate. Following long debate, they settled on Uthman ibn Affan. Some historians believe that Uthman was a consensus candidate, chosen because of his relatively mild manner (quite in contrast with that of Umar). Uthman, a wealthy merchant and an early convert to Islam, later became the Prophet's son-in-law, marrying the latter's daughter Rukayya. Though a member of the Banu Umayya clan of the Quraysh, Uthman had not participated in the opposition to the Prophet led by his uncle, Abu Sufyan (d. 653).

The Arabic sources generally cast a positive light on Uthman's first years in office. Problems arose midway through his caliphate, however, when Uthman began to overstep the limits of his authority in an attempt to strengthen the caliphate. Controversy arose, for example, over his decision to create a uniform edition of the Qur'an. Later Arab-Islamic writers generally praise Uthman for this decision, seeing it as an important step toward the creation of a unified Islamic *umma*. But earlier sources suggest that, at the time, the decision was perceived by some as an arbitrary effort to impose one version of the text.

Uthman's decision to distribute key positions to his Umayyad clansmen sparked controversy over control and distribution of revenue produced in each of the newly conquered territories. Like Umar before him, Uthman faced resistance from local commanders to the idea of sending surplus revenue to Medina. Uthman's appointment of his clansmen was seen as a further attempt to wrest control over local resources. But a larger question loomed: Should one's status in Islamic society be based on family and tribal ties or on commitment to the Prophet's teachings and the needs of the *umma*? The debate hinged, in part, on when individual Muslims had converted to Muhammad's teachings and, in part, on how they had conducted themselves following conversion. The Banu Umayya, led by Abu Sufyan, had converted at a late date, so their detractors argued that they had no serious claim to influence over their fellow Muslims.

At first, Uthman was accused of nepotism, but as he dug in his heels, it grew to that of tyranny. Resentment led to violence: Arab tribesmen from Egypt laid siege to Uthman's residence, then broke in on the caliph. According to prominent accounts, he was assassinated as he sat, alone and unarmed, reading the Qur'an. The killing (656) sparked civil war.[10]

NOTES

1. Robert Hillenbrand, *Islamic Architecture*, p. 42.

2. For a discussion of the debate, see R. Stephen Humphreys, *Islamic History*, pp. 92–98.

3. Ibn Ishaq, *Life of Muhammad*, p. 232.

4. The term is a controversial one, particularly in recent decades with the emergence of extremist Islamic movements that define *jihad*, in many cases, as armed struggle against Western states and their allies in the Islamic world. Unfortunately, the term is often poorly understood; one particularly troubling tendency has been to equate the Islamic tradition, and Muslims as a group, with the teachings and activity of these movements.

5. K. Y. Blankinship, *The End of the Jihad State*, pp. 11–19. Also see Jonathan Berkey, *The Formation of Islam*, pp. 72–73.

6. Al-Tabari, *The History of al-Tabari*, vol. 11, *The Challenge of the Empires*, p. 80.

7. Document 3 contains extracts from a translation of his book.

8. Patricia Crone and Martin Hinds, *God's Caliph*, pp. 4–23.

9. See illustration 10 on the change from pre-Islamic to Islamic imagery on coins.

10. For one account of the civil war, see Hugh Kennedy, *The Prophet and the Age of the Caliphates*, pp. 69–90.

CHAPTER 3

THE UMAYYAD CALIPHATE (661–750) AND THE CRISIS OF AUTHORITY

The Arab-Islamic polity assumed greater complexity following the establishment of the Umayyad dynasty in Damascus. It became a "state" following the organization of new armies, new administrative offices, and a more unified system of tax collection. At the head of the emerging political system sat the caliph. Like Muhammad's four successors—the Rashidun caliphs—before them, the Umayyads would struggle to attract lasting support. Ultimately they would fail, but not before taking significant steps toward the creation of a new-style state. Their successors, the Abbasids, enjoyed greater success, but by the mid-ninth century they, too, were overwhelmed by two fundamental problems: the inability to create durable armies and a failure to find a widely accepted definition of leadership. This second problem centered on two thorny questions: Who was to govern the Islamic community? How was that person's authority to be defined? The present chapter will consider the Umayyad phase in the history of the caliphate.

THE GREAT *FITNA* (656–661)

The first period of civil war to beset the Islamic community is known as the Great *Fitna* (trial, temptation). Brought on mainly by the debate over Uthman's leadership, it was largely a conflict over caliphal authority and legitimacy. Uthman's supporters, who enjoyed the lion's share of influence in the early years, argued that he had ruled in proper fashion and that vengeance against his killers was required. His successor, they insisted, would have to see justice done. The new caliph, Ali ibn Abi Talib, assumed the caliphate on the strength of his relationship with the Prophet (his first cousin and father-in-law) and long service to Islamic society. However, in taking office, he relied upon the support of Uthman's opponents, including those involved in the assassination. This cast an immediate pall over Ali's caliphate.

Opposition to Ali was organized first by A'isha, the Prophet's widow and, by now, a prominent figure. She was joined by two influential Medinans, Talha ibn Ubayd Allah and al-Zubayr ibn al-Awwam, a former companion of the Prophet and well-regarded member of the *umma*. The three leaders rallied forces in Medina with two goals in mind: to avenge Uthman's murder and to protest the manner in which Ali had become caliph. In their view, Uthman's successor should have been chosen through the established practice of consultation and debate (*shura*). Ali, facing strong opposition, left Medina for Kufa, seeking military backing. Kufa and, to a lesser extent Basra, both in southern Iraq, were bastions of support for Ali and his descendants. Backed by Iraqi forces, Ali marched on his opponents. The Battle of the Camel (656) led to the deaths of Talha and al-Zubayr and the exile of A'isha to Medina. Ali's moment of triumph was short-lived; he now had to deal with the challenge posed by the Umayyad governor of Syria, Mu'awiya ibn Abi Sufyan.

As Uthman's kinsman, Mu'awiya had made it clear that he would not recognize Ali's caliphate until Uthman's murder was avenged. He decided to make a bid for power on the basis of the political and military support of Syrian tribal forces and a good number of Uthman's supporters. This support was enhanced by Mu'awiya's commitment to campaigns against the Byzantines along the northern Syrian frontier. Mu'awiya's opposition left Ali with little choice. Following several months of intermittent warfare, the two leaders agreed to open negotiations. The talks, held at the southern Iraqi town of Siffin (657), ended without resolution. They led, however, to a sharp erosion of Ali's support. He not only had recognized Mu'awiya as his equal simply by agreeing to talk but then had neglected to respond when Mu'awiya, sensing an opportunity, refused to address Ali by his caliphal title *Amir al-Mu'minin* (Commander of the Faithful). A small but vocal group of Ali's backers abandoned his army and established their own camp outside Nahrawan, to the north. They are known as the Kharijis (literally, "those who go out"), the name probably inspired by a Qur'anic verse ("He who departs his home on the path of God will find ready and welcome refuge in the world," *Surat al-Nisa*, 4:100).[1] Ali marched successfully against Nahrawan. His triumph, however, was short-term: the Kharijis would remain a potent movement under the Umayyad and Abbasid caliphs.

Against Mu'awiya, however, Ali's options were limited. Mu'awiya's position improved when he gained the backing of Amr ibn al-As, who was now governor of Egypt. At this point, Syrian supporters proclaimed Mu'awiya their caliph. The result was the presence of rival claimants to the office: Ali in Iraq, Mu'awiya in Syria (and Egypt). A confused situation ended when Ali fell to a Khariji assassin (661). Mu'awiya was left with only one pressing challenge: Ali's followers in southern Iraq had turned to his eldest son, al-Hasan, with a plea to take up his father's cause. Pressured by Mu'awiya to withdraw, al-Hasan declined.

Mu'awiya's triumph meant more than a change of rulers. Arab-Islamic history now entered a vital new phase. The location of Damascus, in the midst of a region noted for commerce and agriculture, meant that the resources needed to maintain an effective military and state were on hand. The location of Syria, in turn, meant greater access to, and greater opportunity for control over, surrounding regions. The caliphs now sat atop an emerging empire, and the resources at their disposal far exceeded those possessed earlier by Muhammad and his four successors. They had become emperors and, as a result, the questions surrounding their political authority now loomed larger than ever.

THE UMAYYAD PERIOD: CALIPHS AND CIVIL WARS

Mu'awiya I (r. 661–680)

Historians of early Islam point out that many Arabic sources date from the period of the Abbasid caliphate. The Abbasids, having overthrown the Umayyads (750), made every attempt to distinguish themselves from their opponents. They sought out scholars willing to characterize the Umayyads as unworthy of authority over Islamic society. These works often referred to the Umayyad rulers as "kings" (*malik*; pl., *muluk*) rather than caliphs (*khalifa*; pl., *khulafa*). "King" connotes, in this sense, that the Umayyads were little different from monarchs of the pre-Islamic period, and therefore could claim no legitimacy as proper Muslim rulers. The full historical record shows that Abbasid propaganda sought to distort the Umayyad record of achievement. Although the Umayyads reigned for less than a century, they contributed considerably more to the formation of Islamic society than the Abbasids wished anyone to know.

Hostility to the Umayyads notwithstanding, the early Arabic sources generally treat Mu'awiya with respect. They associate him with the Rashidun caliphs as a model of political rule. His reign relied on a combination of elements. He used to good effect a mix of patience, wisdom, and subtle manipulation, often through the use of material rewards (i.e., the spoils of war), a traditional Arabian approach to rulership known as *hilm*. Mu'awiya earned kudos from many observers for this preference of subtle persuasion over brute force. His traditionalist style can also be seen in his frequent meetings with Arab tribal delegations. It is useful to recall that the Prophet had been approached by similar delegations (*wufud*) as his authority spread. Meetings of this sort gave the caliph an opportunity to demonstrate his personal qualities and develop a network of loyalty throughout the empire.

Mu'awiya also relied upon tribal leaders (*ashraf*) and provincial governors, particularly in Syria and Iraq. Significant changes in the structure of Arab tribes had occurred as a result of the conquests. These changes were related, in particular, to the movement and resettlement of Arab tribesmen in the newly conquered territories of the Near East. The *ashraf* functioned as intermediaries: they worked to solve problems related to military service and pay, and to calm tensions produced by shifting patterns of settlement and social integration. But they were no less responsible for encouraging loyalty to the Umayyads and maintaining order in their respective provinces on behalf of the empire.

To be effective, the tribal chiefs had to work closely with Mu'awiya's provincial governors (*amirs*), who were responsible for collecting taxes, keeping the peace, and other tasks essential to imperial success. Most of the governors were members of the Umayyad clan or had close personal ties to Mu'awiya and his inner circle. It is significant that Mu'awiya seldom interfered in the local affairs of his governors. For example, he received only a small amount of the provincial tax revenue (most of the money remained with the governors to dispense as they saw fit). This high degree of local autonomy reflects the rudimentary nature of Mu'awiya's administration. There were few government offices, only a small number of officials (scribes, clerks, tax collectors, and so on), and relatively little ceremonial life of the elaborate kind developed later by the Abbasids.

The Syrian tribal armies constituted the other main support of Mu'awiya's state. Many of these forces came from the powerful Quda'a tribal confederation of central and northern Syria. They had previously served as auxiliary forces in the Byzantine Empire and, to Mu'awiya's credit, he knew to coax them into service of the Arab-Islamic state. This was not yet a professional (or standing) army, but it is clear that the Syrian forces were quickly becoming the mainstay of the Umayyad military and the guarantor of the Umayyad realm. Mu'awiya guaranteed the Syrian tribes, as reward for their service, a generous share of the conquest spoils. The conquests had resumed following the Great *Fitna*, with notable successes in North Africa and eastern Iran, and Mu'awiya devoted particular energy to the conflict with Byzantium. Rewards for the Syrian troops only multiplied.

To a great extent, then, Mu'awiya practiced a traditional, tribal-based form of governance. But new ideas of religiopolitical leadership were in the air as well. First, Mu'awiya probably used the title *khalifat Allah* (deputy of God), implying that the caliph had the duty and right to interpret God's Word (i.e., the Qur'an) and establish religious law. It does not seem, however, that Mu'awiya was very aggressive in promoting the idea. Second, Mu'awiya developed certain state offices. These would take clearer form later, but their appearance now suggests that a new form of imperial government was on the horizon. These offices, known by the term *diwan*, may have included a *diwan al-barid* (the office responsible for official mail and intelligence) and the *shurta* (an urban security office or police).

The third and final development was also the most controversial. Prior to his death (680), Mu'awiya appointed his son, Yazid ibn Mu'awiya, as his successor. The Arabic sources roundly condemn the decision. It is hard to know to what extent the sources are reflecting opinion as it was expressed at the time, but it was clearly an unpopular decision with many in Arab-Islamic society. One complaint was that Mu'awiya had ignored the process of *shura*, whereby candidates to the office were chosen through open debate. No less objectionable was that Mu'awiya was resorting to the practice of hereditary rule. In doing so, the sources write, Mu'awiya and the Umayyads who succeeded him were following the lead of the non-Muslim monarchs (i.e., the Byzantines and Sasanids) who had reigned in the dark days before Islam. It is in part for this reason that the later sources refer to the Umayyads with the perjorative "kings." Mu'awiya's decision appears to have been the principal spark of a second round of civil war.

The Debate over Leadership and Authority

A brief pause is in order at this point. The various conflicts that befell early Islamic society carried the seeds of long-term divisions. It would be useful to identify the different sides in these debates, but it needs to be emphasized that the movements born of these early divisions emerged slowly over subsequent centuries; they did not take shape overnight. It also should be pointed out that despite appearances, the debates of early Arab-Islamic society were not wholly about politics or political leadership. The question of who should rule the *umma* and on what terms was a significant religious matter as well. This is clear, for example, in the caliphs's use of the title *khalifat Allah* (deputy of God). It is also clear in the early debates over the meaning and direction of Islamic society: To what extent was it to adhere to Qur'anic principles and to the examples set by Muhammad and the first generations of Muslims?

The debates of the early Arab-Islamic world are not easy to grasp. Historians generally agree that three broad movements began to make their appearance during the Umayyad period: the Kharijis, Shi'a, and proto-Sunnis.[2] These movements would develop over time, with differences of doctrine and practice growing more pronounced. At this early stage, debate focused largely on the question of leadership and authority. (These are introductory comments, and all three movements will be considered again at a later point.)

One set of ideas on the caliphate was proposed by the Kharijis. Describing their ideas is difficult because the Kharij movement was generally amorphous, with a number of splinter groups. Also, except in small states in southern Arabia and North Africa, the Kharijis never became a dominant element of early Arab-Islamic society. The early Kharij model of political authority was based on merit: any free, male, adult Muslim, regardless of background, could become leader (*imam*) of the community. What mattered was the candidate's piety, integrity, and knowledge. Unlike the Umayyads and the followers of Ali, in other words, the Kharijis did not stress family or tribal origins. Occasionally Kharijis argued that even former slaves could hold office if they demonstrated the proper qualities. They also insisted on consistent leadership: if a chosen leader proved unworthy, he was to be removed from office. This was an idealistic vision of political leadership that failed to gain broad acceptance. But it was an attractive alternative, particularly in periods of political crisis.

The *Shi'at Ali*, the "followers" or "partisans" of Ali (and his family), or, simply, the Shi'a (or Shi'is) took another position on the problem of leadership. Out of the pro-Alid movement, concentrated in Kufa and Basra, the garrison centers of Iraq, would emerge a complex set of ideas with the central claim that only members of the Prophet's family, and specifically descendants of Ali ibn Abi Talib, could claim legitimate rule over Islamic society. They, too, would use the term *imam* to refer to their candidates. The use of the single term (Shi'i) is deceptive because the early Shi'is often were sharply divided over which member of Ali's clan deserved to don the mantle of leadership. Though Ali's death (661) led many Shi'is to transfer their allegiance to al-Hasan, other candidates from the family were sought out as well, especially Ali's second son, al-Husayn.

The third and final movement was hardly a "movement" at all until well into the mid-eleventh century. By then, the majority of Muslims would be known as Sunni Muslims. (Sunnis make up over 90 percent of Muslims in the modern Islamic world.) Sunni Islam (or Sunnism) would derive its name from the phrase *Ahl al-sunna wal-jama'a* (the people of the Prophet's way and community). The ideas embedded in the phrase will be considered later. Despite its later significance, the Sunni movement was the last of the three to take discernible shape. It emerged largely as a reaction against the Khariji and Shi'i movements. For this reason, the term "proto-Sunni" will be used from this point forward. Characteristic of early proto-Sunni Islam was a commitment to the teachings of Muhammad and the Qur'an, and an ambiguous stance regarding the caliphate. Many early Muslims came to dislike, often intensely, the wealth and arbitrary authority of the Umayyad house. Yet, when faced with the option of supporting armed struggle against the caliphs, these same voices would grow cautious or even fall silent. Over time, proto-

Sunni scholars would define this relationship to the caliphs in clearer terms.

The Second Civil War (680–692)

These introductory comments in place, the discussion of the Umayyad caliphate resumes. The new round of conflict began with significant opposition by several movements to the caliphate of Yazid ibn Mu'awiya (r. 680–683). It continued well after Yazid's death and led, in part, to the transfer of rule from the Sufyanids (Mu'awiya's line) to the Marwanids, a second branch of the Umayyad house.

The Kharijis in southern Iraq and northern Arabia were one source of opposition. More substantial was the opposition mounted by Abdallah ibn al-Zubayr (d. 692), whose father had fallen at the Battle of the Camel. Ibn al-Zubayr, after refusing to recognize Yazid's caliphate, escaped to Mecca, where, following Yazid's death, he declared himself caliph. His candidacy clearly struck a chord, proving how unpopular the Umayyads had become. Ibn al-Zubayr won supporters throughout all the provinces, including Syria, where Umayyad support was strongest. Further evidence of his success is the appointment of his brother, Mus'ab, as governor of Iraq and the minting of coins, even in outlying provinces of the empire, that bear his name and title.[3] In a new study, Chase Robinson makes the case for taking Ibn al-Zubayr as the rightful caliph and the Umayyads as his challengers.[4] The upshot is that for the second time in early Islamic history, rival caliphs laid claim to the office. It was a crisis of authority that would grow.

The Umayyads also were opposed by Ali ibn Abi Talib's charismatic son, al-Husayn ibn Ali, the younger brother of al-Hasan. Al-Husayn had fled to Mecca early in the conflict. When his family's followers in Kufa called on him to assert his family's claim to leadership, al-Husayn (unlike his brother) decided to act. He led a small force, which included his wives and children, from Medina into southern Iraq. Outside the town of Karbala, the group was attacked by Umayyad troops and decimated (680). The heads of al-Husayn and his male followers are reported to have been sent in baskets to Yazid in Damascus. This stunning but temporary defeat for the followers of Ali's family, the Shi'a, was to have a profound effect on the debate over the caliphate. The later Shi'i movement was to remember al-Husayn's death in highly charged religious terms. It was, in this view, an act of martyrdom, and in time, the Shi'a would develop elaborate annual rituals to commemorate the deed.

Anger over al-Husayn's death galvanized the Shi'a in Kufa. A new movement emerged, led by a certain al-Mukhtar (d. 687), a local military commander and activist. Though it was quickly crushed by forces sent by Ibn al-Zubayr (acting as caliph), the movement was noteworthy for at least two reasons. First, al-Mukhtar launched the revolt in the name of Muhammad ibn al-Hanafiya, a third son of Ali ibn Abi Talib. Ibn al-Hanafiya seems to have done relatively little to support al-Mukhtar. The popularity of the revolt in southern Iraq, however, indicates that support for Ali's family—among the early Shi'a—was on the rise. Second, many of al-Mukhtar's followers were non-Arab Muslims. Known as *mawali* (sing., *mawla*), these were primarily former prisoners of war and their descendents; most were Persian speakers. Enslaved in large numbers during the Arab-Islamic campaigns, they were settled (or had chosen to settle) in the Arab garrison cities. There they attached themselves to Arab tribes through clientage and, in most cases, converted to Islam. Their participation in al-Mukhtar's revolt probably reflected their frustration at being denied equal treatment with Arab Muslims.

The Second Civil War ended with the caliphate in the hands of the Marwanids, another branch of the Umayyad clan, named after Marwan ibn al-Hakam (r. 684–685), who was proclaimed caliph in Damascus (684). This followed several campaigns in which Marwan consolidated central rule over Syria, Palestine, and Egypt. To govern the all-important province of Egypt, he appointed his son Abd al-Aziz (d. 754). Following Marwan's sudden death, possibly from the plague, a second son, Abd al-Malik, assumed the office of caliph. Abd al-Malik carried out the final destruction of Abdallah ibn al-Zubayr and his brother. Ibn al-Zubayr was cornered in Mecca and killed (692) in fighting around the Ka'ba.

The debate over the authority of the caliphate had taken on tremendous weight by the time that Abd al-Malik took office. Significant forces throughout the empire violently opposed the Umayyads on the grounds that they were illegitimate rulers. The Umayyads were divided among themselves, with various factions struggling for control. For a majority of Muslims, it seems, Abd al-Malik and his family simply did not have a rightful claim to the caliphate. Ibn al-Zubayr, whose claim to the office had been widely embraced, was finished. For Abd al-Malik, newly sworn in, the question of authority remained very much unresolved.

Abd al-Malik ibn Marwan (r. 685–705)

It is difficult to exaggerate the importance of Abd al-Malik to early Islamic history and, in particular, the history of the caliphate. Over a twenty-year reign, he took significant steps toward establishing a centralized imperial state. A very important role was played by the longtime governor of Iraq, al-Hajjaj ibn Yusuf (d. 714), who through his entire career was a fierce ally of the Umayyad house. He helped defeat the Zubayrids in the Hijaz and brought order to the garrison cities of Iraq at the end of the Second Civil War. He served Abd al-Malik and his son and successor, al-Walid ibn Abd al-Malik (r. 705–715), with unwavering loyalty.

The creation of the imperial state involved, in part, a series of reforms. Abd al-Malik, with al-Hajjaj's support, shifted slowly from a reliance on tribal leaders and delegations to a more bureaucratic system in which state officials cooperated closely with governors and the caliph's court. More notably, Abd al-Malik and his governors moved decisively toward establishing a standing army, composed almost entirely of Syrian and northern Mesopotamian forces. The military reforms included the creation of new ranks of command and the inclusion of formal units of non-Arab fighters (i.e., mawali). The Syrian armies, as a result, clearly assumed a dual function. They were to carry on with the conquests as before. They were now, to a degree not seen previously, also responsible for defending the caliphate against its internal opponents.

More significant were the policies asserting the Arab-Islamic identity of the empire. It was pointed out earlier that the long-term significance of the Umayyad period lies in the twin processes of Arabization and Islamization. It would be an exaggeration to say that these were due solely to Abd al-Malik; it is likely that the use of Arabic was on the rise throughout the Near East while, at a slower rate, Jews, Christians, and other non-Muslims were converting to Islam. But there is also little question that Abd al-Malik's policies played an important part in these transformations of Near Eastern society.

Arabization was clearly related to the centralization of government under the new caliph. Up to that point, provincial government was largely conducted by officials using local languages, primarily Greek (Syria), Coptic (Egypt), and Persian (Iran). Abd al-Malik is said to have mandated that all government documents be written in Arabic. Though Arabic became the empire's official language only gradually, the process was largely complete by the early Abbasid period. The second process, Islamization, was tied even more directly to Abd al-Malik's effort to assert Umayyad imperial authority over his opponents both within the Islamic community and in the non-Islamic communities living under Umayyad control.

Abd al-Malik and his supporters worked to sharpen the definition of the caliph as the "deputy" of God through letters and other official documents, coinage, speeches, and sermons. In response to the caliph's patronage, poets dutifully recited verses praising the caliph in appropriate terms. The message conveyed was twofold. Abd al-Malik was the symbol of the Islamic faith; were he to vanish, the Islamic *umma* would lose its identity as a religious community. He was also the source of both religious and political guidance: in his absence, Muslims would be cut adrift in the world. Jarir ibn Atiyya (d. 729), one of the greatest of the early Arab poets, called Abd al-Malik "the blessed one [through whom] God guides his adherents."[5]

Abd al-Malik also created a specifically Islamic coinage. Up to this point, the Arab-Islamic state had relied upon either Byzantine or Sasanid currency. Gradual changes reflecting the new Arab-Islamic rule had been introduced earlier, but many pre-Islamic elements remained. In addition, different coinage systems were used from province to province, making trade and tax collection awkward. The new coins, after a short period of experimentation, featured only Arabic characters and, significantly, banned all figural representation. (See illustration 10.) By the late 690s, two coin types were in use: gold *dinars* and silver *dirhams*. Though the older coinage remained in local use for decades, particularly along the frontiers, the new monetary system was a firm step forward in the centralization of the imperial economy, specifically, the revenue collection system.

The most striking symbol of Abd al-Malik's reforms, however, was the Dome of the Rock, the first great Muslim building, located in Jerusalem. The Umayyads already had learned from the Sasanids and Byzantines about the symbolic power of architecture. A public building, properly built and situated, functioned as a powerful sign of authority and wealth.

The Dome of the Rock was erected in the early 690s, precisely when Abd al-Malik was developing his program of Islamization. Built atop the Temple Mount (the symbol of the historic Jewish presence in Jerusalem) and looking down upon the site of the Church of the Holy Sepulcher (one of Christianity's most revered sites), it conveyed the message that Islam had triumphed over the earlier monotheistic faiths. The interior of the monument is decorated with broad bands of Qur'anic text written in Arabic, refuting the Christian idea of the trinity. Historians understand the use of these Qur'anic verses to be an assertion of Islamic identity and distinctiveness. Most of all, the Dome was meant to make a political point: Abd al-Malik, as God's agent, stood at the head of a victorious Arab-Islamic state.

The Currents of Opposition

Abd al-Malik's policies represented a shift to a centralized and increasingly authoritarian state. How were such efforts viewed by Islamic society? The later part of Abd al-Malik's reign, and the reigns of his successors, his sons Walid I (r. 705–715) and Sulayman (r. 715–717), were relatively stable and prosperous. Syrian forces carried out a new wave of successful conquests to the east and west. Such achievements as the construction of the great Umayyad mosque in Damascus, under Walid I, point to a confident and well-managed state. Al-Hajjaj's ability to achieve a measure of calm in Iraq was also a contributing factor.

The calm was short-lived, and soon currents of dissatisfaction with Umayyad rule reemerged. Khariji activity remained at a high level, as did increasingly organized Shi'i opposition in Iraq. Two other sources of opposition also appeared: non-Arab Muslims, resentful at ongoing discrimination, and religious-scholarly circles, increasingly upset over the nature of Umayyad rule. The ideas expressed by different networks of scholars and their supporters were soon to take shape in the Khariji, Shi'i, and proto-Sunni religiopolitical traditions. Though they disagreed on many fronts, they shared a common distaste for the Umayyads' preoccupation with power, stability, and wealth over the needs of Islamic society. (The views expressed by the urban scholars will be treated in a subsequent chapter.)

The demands of the non-Arab Muslim minorities deserve a bit more consideration. It is difficult to judge the size of the non-Arab Muslim population at this point in Islamic history. Its numbers included slaves (or freedmen) who, as *mawali* of Arab tribes, were serving in many cases as auxiliary troops, and converts from non-Muslim (*dhimmi*) populations, mostly peasants, who had migrated into Arab-Islamic centers. It appears, given these trends, that conversion to Islam was just taking hold in the middle and upper tiers of Near Eastern urban society. Non-Arab converts faced ongoing patterns of discrimination. Many local Umayyad officials insisted that they continue to pay the *jizya* although, as converts to Islam, they should not have had to do so. Umar II ibn Abd al-Aziz (r. 717–720) reversed the practice and is credited with promoting the rights of non-Arab Muslims.[6] Due in part to these measures, Umar II is treated in later Arabic sources as the most praiseworthy member of the Umayyad dynasty. There is little to indicate, however, that his policies ever took hold. The best such indication is the broad appeal of the Abbasid movement among non-Arab Muslims (see below).

Hisham (r. 724–743), the fourth of Abd al-Malik's sons to inherit the caliphate, was the last major Umayyad ruler. During and after his reign, civil war sapped the strength of the dynasty and central administration. Factionalism undermined the Syrian armies' ability to defend the caliphate. The Arab-Islamic sources show that corruption was rampant among Umayyad governors in various provinces. As if internal difficulties were not enough, Umayyad armies suffered debilitating defeats in the Caucasus, Central Asia, and North Africa. The exhaustion of the Syrian regiments may have been the deciding factor: no agrarian-based empire could hope to survive without a stable and motivated military. No sooner had the strength of the Syrian regiments faltered than anti-Umayyad resistance surged as never before.

THE ABBASID REVOLUTION (746–750)

The revolutionary movement that brought the Abbasids to power originated in Iraq. It began, as such movements do, in clandestine fashion, probably in the early eighth century, with two descendants of al-Abbas ibn Abd al-Muttalib (d. 653), the Prophet's paternal uncle: his great-grandson, Muhammad ibn Ali (d. 743), and Muhammad's son, Ibrahim ibn Muhammad (d. 749). They gained a following first in southern Jordan, then in Kufa. A key moment was the death of a popular Shi'i figure, Abu Hashim, the son and successor of Muhammad ibn al-Hanafiyya (mentioned earlier). Muhammad ibn Ali claimed that Abu Hashim had designated him as his successor. The upshot was that the Abbasid family (named after the Prophet's uncle) gained a proto-Shi'i following in Iraq, particularly in Kufa, the center of Abu Hashim's following. Events then led the pro-Abbasid movement to construct a network of support in Khurasan, particularly among the mixed Arab and Iranian units based in Marw, an ancient commercial center located on the historic Silk Road. The Arab units, garrisoned in the eighth century during the conquests, had settled among the local Persian-speaking population.

It appears that the revolutionary movement first called for placing the caliphate in the hands of the most deserving member of the Prophet's family: authority over the *umma* belonged to "the chosen one from the family [or clan] of the Prophet," the Banu Hashim. Some historians see the reference to the Banu Hashim as a clever but deceptive attempt to win over two sizable constituencies in Iraq and Khurasan: the followers of Ali's family (the proto-Shi'is) and non-Arab Muslims. As seen earlier, many Shi'is had supported al-Husayn ibn Ali and, later, Muhammad ibn al-Hanafiyya, both direct descendants, through Ali ibn Abi Talib, of the Prophet. The latter movement, led by al-Mukhtar, had also tapped into the sentiments of the non-Arab Muslims of Iraq and elsewhere. The pro-Abbasid movement, in short, recognized the potency of this combination of claims and sought to turn it to the advantage of the Abbasid house. To appeal to as great a number of groups as possible, it kept its propaganda vague.

More likely, the movement simply reflected the deep but still undefined attachment of many early Muslims to the Prophet's family. The appeal of placing authority in the hands of a member of the Banu Hashim was deeply attractive, particularly as anti-Umayyad feelings grew, but it mattered less who that person was, and what line of the Banu Hashim he belonged to, than that he demonstrated the proper qualities of leadership. The argument is that Shi'ism had not yet come to mean support for the direct line of Ali ibn Abi Talib but was still a broad and indistinct movement that viewed the Banu Hashim as the only legitimate source of authority and guidance. If many Muslims (Arabs and non-Arabs alike) preferred Ali's direct line, others were less strict in this regard. In this case, the argument goes, leaders of the movement saw the Abbasids as the best available choice among the Banu Hashim.

The role of Abu Muslim al-Khurasani (d. 754) was crucial. Little is known of his background, though the evidence suggests that he was an Iranian *mawla* raised in Iraq. The Arabic sources provide better information concerning his role as head of the pro-Abbasid movement. They credit him with recruiting forces, in and around Marw, whose considerable experience in campaigns against Turkish nomadic forces on the Central Asian frontier recommended them highly. In 749, Abu Muslim launched the final, open stage of the revolution by unfurling black banners, the symbol of the revolt and soon the official color of the Abbasid caliphate. The Khurasani regiments quickly swept west into Iraq. Having routed the Umayyad armies, the rebel forces moved into Syria and Egypt. The destruction of the Umayyads soon followed, and with it, the end of the dynasty.

Abu Muslim is also said to have imposed the preference for the Abbasids upon the revolutionary movement following its seizure of Kufa. Umayyad agents had earlier arrested and executed Ibrahim ibn Muhammad, the designated head of the Abbasid family. Undeterred, Abu Muslim turned to a second member of the family, Abu al-Abbas Abdallah ibn Muhammad, who was in hiding in Kufa. Rushed to the city's principal mosque, Abu al-Abbas was proclaimed caliph (749). He assumed the title of al-Saffah ("the Generous," or perhaps "the Spiller of Blood"). (All subsequent Abbasid caliphs would be known by regnal titles of this kind.) Al-Saffah's reign was brief, and upon his death (754), he was succeeded by his brother Abu Ja'far al-Mansur (r. 754–775).

Al-Saffah, though a transitional figure, carried out the final destruction of the Umayyad clan (750) and the suppression of its Syrian-based supporters. His uncle, Abdallah ibn Ali (d. 764), made a bid for the caliphate shortly after al-Saffah's death, but was defeated by Abu Muslim on behalf of al-Mansur. Al-Mansur, recognizing Abu Muslim's popularity, betrayed his popular commander a short time later by arranging his assassination (755). It is fair to view al-Mansur as the proper founder of the new dynasty. Not only was he responsible, over his long reign, for the consolidation of Abbasid authority, but he also oversaw the transfer of power from Syria to a newly established capital, Baghdad, which he ordered built in the 760s. It quickly emerged as a premier commercial and cultural center of the Near East and Mediterranean worlds. It was a fitting site for the dawn of a new imperial era.

The succession of al-Mansur was a critical moment in early Islamic history. The Abbasid movement had been a Shi'i movement as it was understood at the time: a pro-Banu Hashim movement seeking to replace the hated Umayyads. When it became clear that the Abbasids intended to control the caliphate, those who supported the house of Ali ibn Abi Talib—in other words, the pro-Alid groups—protested loudly. In their view, the Alid house had a far better claim to power than any other branch of the Banu Hashim, including the Abbasids. Unlike the Abbasids, who were descended from the Prophet through his uncle, the Alid family could rightly claim *direct* descent. The most serious pro-Alid/Shi'i challenge to Abbasid rule occurred with the revolt of two descendants from al-Hasan ibn Ali, Muhammad al-Nafs al-Zakiyya (the Pure Soul) and his brother, Ibrahim. They enjoyed strong support: Muhammad in Medina, Ibrahim in Basra. Al-Mansur managed to suppress the revolt only after two years (762–763) of intensive effort. This was the last full-scale Shi'i uprising for some fifty years. It signaled, however, a deep division in Islamic political and religious affairs, that between Shi'is and non-Shi'is.

NOTES

1. See Patricia Crone, *Medieval Islamic Political Thought*, p. 54.
2. See the useful discussion by Jonathan Berkey, *The Formation of Islam*, pp. 83–90.
3. G. R. Hawting, *The First Dynasty of Islam*, p. 48.
4. Chase F. Robinson, *Abd al-Malik*.
5. Patricia Crone and Martin Hinds, *God's Caliph*, p. 36.
6. Hawting, *First Dynasty*, pp. 76–81.

CHAPTER 4

CITIES IN THE EARLY ABBASID PERIOD: SOLDIERS, MERCHANTS, AND SCHOLARS

The Abbasids faced serious political challenges from the outset of their reign. The defeat of Muhammad al-Nafs al-Zakiya (r. 762–763) had put an end, for the time being, to large-scale Shiʻi revolts. Shiʻi opposition, however, would persist in various regions, including southern Iraq. The Abbasids also had to contend with pro-Umayyad uprisings in Syria and northern Mesopotamia. These various sources of opposition undercut the stability of the empire and challenged the legitimacy of the Abbasid house. A related problem was the Abbasids' unremarkable history prior to the revolution of 750. To raise their standing, the Abbasids turned, in part, to propaganda.

The message of pro-Abbasid poets, writers, and preachers was that the revolution had been far more than a simple change of dynasties. Rather, it was, they argued, a seismic event of profound political and religious meaning. The Umayyads, as impious and tyrannical rulers, had led Muslims astray from the teachings of the Qur'an and the guidance of the Prophet. Realizing the depth of the crisis, the argument went, the Abbasids came forward to guide the *umma* back onto the proper path. They did so by placing power in the hands of those who most embodied the Prophet's model of leadership. They were referring, of course, to the members of their own house. The Abbasids later added a second argument: that the Prophet had bestowed his leadership upon his uncle, al-Abbas, rather than Ali ibn Abi Talib. In this way, according to their supporters, the Abbasids had reconnected Islamic society to its cherished origins.

These arguments may have served their purpose at least in the initial decades of Abbasid rule. The historian must recognize them as propaganda. Despite the shift from Umayyad to Abbasid rule, power remained in the hands of the Arab elite, so, in that sense, little had changed in Arab-Islamic politics. It is also doubtful whether the Abbasid revolution represented as radical a change as the pro-Abbasid campaign would have one believe. Modern historians have debated this point. It concerns, in part, the problem of periodization.

Until quite recently, it was customary to divide early Islamic history by dynastic rule. This meant that early Islamic history was best understood when carved neatly into the "Umayyad" and "Abbasid" periods. In more recent decades, however, historians have preferred a more nuanced description. Fred Donner, in a useful survey of early Islamic history, reflects this newer approach:

> The period of 700 to 950, then, represented the apogee of the caliphal empire—an age of political and communal expansion, great institutional and cultural development, and economic growth. The Umayyad dynasty was overthrown in 750 . . . [but] several key aspects of the evolution of the caliphate and the empire continued under both the late Umayyad and the early Abbasid caliphs, and for this reason, despite the change of ruling dynasty, it is fair to view the period of 700 to 950 as a single phase in the history of the caliphate and of the Islamic community.[1]

It is true that the Abbasid period bore prominent features that were largely absent under the Umayyads. But many characteristic features of the Abbasid era were the product not of a single, sudden event but of gradual, long-term processes that bridged the Umayyad and Abbasid periods. The Abbasids, in other words, were indebted to their Umayyad predecessors in a number of ways: the use of professional armies; a reliance on hereditary succession; and the representation of the caliph as "God's agent." The Abbasids also had inherited a large and unified empire. The early conquests had been permanent: the Abbasids were never required to retake the core regions of Egypt, Syria, Iraq, and Iran. Furthermore, to administer the empire, the Umayyads had helped set in motion the broad patterns of Arabization and Islamization. By the time of the Abbasid uprising, the Arabic language and Arab cultural patterns had taken root in most of these regions. Conversion to Islam was a slower process, but it, too, was gaining momentum among the diverse religious groups of the Near East.[2]

The early Abbasid period will be discussed over two chapters. The subject of the present chapter is early Abbasid urban life, with a particular emphasis on Baghdad and Samarra. Chapter 5 considers the formation of Islam as a complex religious system.

THE URBAN SETTING

Why the focus on cities in the early Abbasid period? To put it simply, Islamic civilization, as a complex religious, sociopolitical, and economic entity, sprang from its urban centers. As one historian puts it: "The history of the [Islamic] Middle East is the history of its cities, where commerce and learning, industry and art, government and faith flourished."[3] Albert Hourani remarks on the cities themselves:

> The creation of an Islamic empire, and then the development of an Islamic society linking the world of the Indian Ocean with that of the Mediterranean, provided the necessary conditions for the emergence of a chain of great cities running from one end of the world of Islam to the other: Cordoba, Seville and Granada in Andalus, Fez and Marrakish [or Marrakech] in Morocco, Qayrawan and later Tunis in Tunisia, Fustat and then Cairo in Egypt, Damascus and Aleppo in Syria, Mecca and Madina in western Arabia, Baghdad, Mosul and Basra in Iraq, and beyond them the cities of Iran, Transoxiana and northern India. Some of these cities had already existed in the time before the coming of Islam, others were creations of the Islamic conquest or the power of later dynasties.[4]

The urban centers of the early Islamic period emerged at different points in time and for different reasons; three broad categories can be identified. Cities such as Alexandria, Jerusalem, Damascus, Aleppo, and the eastern cities of Balkh, Marw, and Samarkand were among those that had existed long before the Arab-Islamic conquests. The Arab armies avoided these cities at first but, over time, the integration of Arab populations, and the adoption of Islam and Arab culture by long-established

populations, transformed the older cities. This was by far the largest category of the three. The postconquest transformation of Near Eastern
urban life was thus a central feature of early Islamic history.

But Arab-Islamic rule also brought about an unprecedented period of
new city-building under the Umayyads and Abbasids alike. Critically important sources of evidence on urbanization in the early Islamic period is
the works of geography that begin to appear in Arabic from the mid-ninth
century on. Among the foremost examples is the *Ahsan al-Taqasim fi
Ma'rifat al-Aqalim* (The Best Divisions for Knowledge of the Regions) by
al-Muqaddasi, a late tenth-century writer.[5] These works provide detailed
information on a second category of Arab-Islamic towns—Qayrawan, al-
Fustat, Basra, Kufa, and others—that originated in the garrison settlements, the *amsar*, built to house the conquest armies of the seventh and
eighth centuries. The settlement of large civilian populations, the construction of markets and other permanent structures (mosques, bathhouses, caravansaries, and prisons), and the creation of roads and water
systems transformed the *amsar* into thriving urban centers.

In a third category were the cities established as seats of government
(sometimes referred to as "palatine" cities).[6] The three major examples
are Baghdad, Samarra, and Cairo. A further example is the Moroccan
city of Fez, founded in the late eighth century by a newly arrived Arab
prince. More is said below about Baghdad and Samarra.

The history of each of these cities deserves to be studied in its own
right. When these differences are set aside, however, common patterns
and features emerge. First, as Hourani suggests, the creation of the Islamic
Empire brought significant change to the physical and economic landscape of the regions bordering the Mediterranean Sea and Indian Ocean.
The collapse of the Sasanid Empire, and the retreat of the Byzantines into
Anatolia, ended the political divisions that separated Syria and Iraq from
Iran and Central Asia. Travel and transportation from one region to the
next were eased considerably. Greater access to skills, goods, and finished
products and a boom in commerce and manufacturing occurred as well.
The growth of regional and transregional trade, and of urban manufacturing, produced new levels of prosperity across the city landscape. The
wealth generated by trade and other sources of income contributed directly to the rise of Arab-Islamic culture and learning as the urban elite
extended patronage to artisans, scholars, and artists of all sorts.

Cities were also the site of considerable cultural interaction. Of particular interest is the contact of Arab-Islamic armies with the non-Arabic-speaking populations of Egypt, Syria, and Iran. Interaction between Arabic speakers—nomads and townsmen of Arabia and southern Syria—with the highly urbanized cultures of the Near East long predated the Islamic period. The Arab conquests resulted, however, in cultural exchange of a more intense and complex sort. It operated at all levels, including the religious: in a variety of ways, only some of which are wholly clear to modern historians, early Islamic thought and practice were deeply influenced by patterns of Judaism and Christianity. No less clear are the significant changes that resulted in Judaism and Christianity in turn. Historians of Judaism, for example, have studied the effects of exchanges with Muslim scholarship and ritual upon contemporary Jewish life.[7]

The urban centers shared common physical features as well. This is not to argue that they adhered to a single model—Paul Wheatley remarks that the many towns of North Africa and the Near East each "had their own distinctive sights, sounds, colors, and smells"[8]—but that features of this kind appeared across the urban landscape. One prominent feature was (and is) the mosque, the building type used by Muslims for public prayer, education, housing (for travelers and pilgrims), and social interaction. Small-to-medium-sized mosques (*masjid*; pl., *masajid*), located throughout the urban landscape, were (and are) used on a daily basis. Larger urban centers, including Baghdad, Samarra, and Cairo, contained one or more congregational mosques (*jami*; pl., *jawami*). Built to accommodate the throng of worshipers who assemble each Friday noon, the *jawami* were (and are) imposing, impressive structures.

Figurative representation generally does not appear in religious contexts in Islamic art (though important exceptions exist). Thus mosques generally contain far fewer overt decorative features than, say, Catholic cathedrals or Buddhist temples. The most striking feature is the bands of inscription that adorn mosque walls, most of which contain Qur'anic and other religiously oriented texts. Calligraphy emerged early on as the preeminent form of art in the Islamic Near East and was used, as well, in illustrated manuscripts, miniature painting, and elsewhere. Other consistent features include the *mihrab*, a niche that marks the direction of prayer (*qibla*), often richly decorated with marble, ceramic tiling, columns, and small arches. Many of the major mosques also contain a *minbar* (platform)—a raised pulpit from which the Friday sermon (*khutba*) is delivered—often finely constructed of precious wood and stone. Art historians identify classical, Byzantine, and Sasanid influences in both *mihrab* and *minbar*, as in many other features of mosque construction, in the early Islamic period. The recessed niche, for example, was long a feature of Roman temples (containing sacred statues) or, on a larger scale, of churches (containing the altar).

The use of fine inscriptions bearing the names of patrons, rulers, and leading families associated with a given building remind one that the congregational mosques functioned as symbols not only of faith but also of the wealth and authority of the persons who constructed them. The *maqsura*—an enclosure, usually located near the *mihrab*, set aside for the ruler and other prominent persons—was a third common feature of the large mosques. Though probably meant, in part, to protect the ruler from assassins, its intent was mostly to separate, and thus highlight, the royal presence within the mosque. Significant examples of congregational mosques are those built by the Umayyad caliph al-Walid I in Damascus, Medina, and Jerusalem; two mosques constructed in Samarra by al-Mutawakkil (r. 847–861), of which only the ruins remain; and the mosque built in Egypt by Ahmad ibn Tulun, a military governor during the Abbasid period (see below), which stands today.

BAGHDAD: A BRIEF HISTORY TO 925

Urban historians lament the fact that few physical traces are left of eighth-century Baghdad, the most important urban complex of the early Islamic period. The city was founded around 762 by the Abbasid caliph al-Mansur. Using huge numbers of imported workers—from highly skilled artisans to common laborers—the caliph oversaw the construction of a formidable new capital. Designated officially as *Madinat al-Salam* (the City of Peace), it was built in the round; hence its nickname, al-*Mudawwara* (The Round City). The original settlement, completed around 777, was enclosed by fortified walls within which were the houses of the Abbasid family, government officials, officers, and court servants, along with small markets and guardhouses. The caliph's palace/residence and a congregational mosque stood at the center of this massive circular structure. The military—the forces of Khurasan that had brought the dynasty to power—was quartered to the northwest of the Round City, in an area known as al-Harbiya.

It is clear that al-Mansur intended the site to be a new administrative center. In this sense, Baghdad became the prototype for many later palatine centers in Islamic history. In each case, construction was carried out in underpopulated areas that were easier to defend than existing and very crowded urban centers. Like Baghdad, each new settlement contained several component parts: palaces for the ruling class and administration; markets and bathhouses; numerous barracks; and, of course, mosques. Imposing walls and guard towers generally functioned to defend the city and mark its physical boundaries. Each new center, more generally, was intended to serve the practical needs of administration and security, but also to symbolize the authority of the respective dynasty.[9] Baghdad was constructed for very specific and complex purposes.

Quickly, however, the growth of the city's population and other factors overwhelmed al-Mansur's careful plans.[10] A huge new neighborhood, known as al-Karkh, was built to accommodate a growing population of craftsmen, workers, and rural migrants. The presence of this growing and varied population attracted merchants and artisans of all sorts. An expanding population meant the appearance of new commercial and residential quarters. By the mid-tenth century, according to al-Muqaddasi, the markets of Baghdad were vast, both in number and in variety. Security demands also brought changes to the city's layout and use. Al-Mansur, according to the Arabic sources, became convinced that the Round City would be nearly impossible to defend. As Document 9 indicates, the caliph and his administration faced potential threats not simply from opponents operating in the provinces—such as the Shiʿa and Kharijis—but from restive elements of Baghdad's populace as well. Al-Mansur finally moved (775) to a newly constructed palace, Qasr al-Khuld, located along the Tigris River. Yet another palace complex, al-Rusafa, was constructed across the river shortly thereafter.

Into the tenth century and beyond, the expansion of Baghdad reflected its status as the premier commercial and cultural center of the Islamic world. Its political history, however, grew troubled; an initial period of stability under al-Mansur and his immediate successors collapsed with the onset of civil war in the early ninth century. The conflict (809–819) began as a clash over succession following the death of Harun al-Rashid (r. 786–809). Al-Rashid, following a pattern introduced by the Umayyads, had chosen his sons, Muhammad al-Amin (d. 813) and Abdallah al-Ma'mun (d. 833), to succeed him in that order.[11] When al-

Ma'mun (then governor of Khurasan) challenged his brother, the ensuing conflict led to years of war in and around Baghdad and, in many provinces, a collapse of central authority. It also led to the demise of the Khurasani army as the mainstay of the caliphate. The descendants of the original Khurasani fighters, living in al-Harbiya and adjoining areas of Baghdad, were known as the *abna al-dawla* (sons of the regime). A handful of *Abna* families participated at the highest levels of Abbasid politics and society, and retained their standing within Baghdad despite the civil war. The Khurasani military, however, experienced a rapid fall in status and effectiveness following defeat by the combined Iranian and Central Asian armies employed by al-Ma'mun.

Following his victory over al-Amin, and a campaign of reunification in Syria and Egypt, al-Ma'mun assumed the caliphate and slowly reinstated the authority of his office. (He returned to Baghdad from Khurasan in 819.) The civil war had been a turning point in the history of Baghdad and, therefore, of the caliphate. It led to a series of significant developments, including the transfer of the imperial capital out of Baghdad. Al-Ma'mun was succeeded by his younger brother, Abu Ishaq al-Mu'tasim (r. 833–842), a power broker in Baghdad in the later part of al-Ma'mun's reign. His reputation rested mostly to the strength and reputation of his personal guard, a new-style military force made up of Turkish-speaking slave troops. The Turkish fighters had been acquired from elite families in Baghdad in some cases, through a thriving Central Asian slave trade in most other cases. Al-Ma'mun had approved the creation of the Turkish guard, but al-Mu'tasim is to be credited with its formation and training. The Turkish guard slowly evolved into a field army following al-Mu'tasim's reign.

It was, in good part, to accommodate the military that al-Mu'tasim created a new administrative center at Samarra, located to the north along the Tigris River. Over ensuing decades, events in Samarra exacted a grim toll upon the public image and authority of the caliphate. Periods of rioting and general chaos erupted late in the Samarra period as poorly paid troops, Turks and non-Turks alike, took to the streets. Factionalism within Turkish ranks turned violent as rival units fought over revenue and other matters. Equally serious was a brief but costly war that led Samarran forces, mostly Turks, to lay siege to Baghdad in 865–866. The interference of the Samarran Turkish command in affairs of state proved no less detrimental to the fortunes of the caliphate. Following their as-

sassination of al-Mutawakkil (r. 847–861), Turkish high officers, with the
support of civilian allies, struggled to place pliable candidates on the
caliphal throne. The result was the quick turnover of six caliphs—four
of whom were assassinated—over less than ten years (861–870). Relative
order was eventually restored to the political process, and, some two
decades later, the Abbasids returned to Baghdad. The reputation of the
caliphate barely recovered from the violence at Samarra.

New setbacks to the stability and status of Baghdad occurred in the
tenth century, all closely related to a decline in caliphal authority. Egypt
and Khurasan, among other provinces, became independent, and as a result the flow of tax revenue to Baghdad slowed to a trickle. Declining
levels of income contributed in part to episodes of unrest within the city
that grew in number and intensity. Alongside the rise in ordinary crime,
Sunni-Shi'i clashes occurred in the mid-tenth century, as did incidents
of violence between civilian and military factions. The city remained a
large and vibrant place, a hub of commerce, culture, and politics; but
with the rise in lawlessness and the decline of entire neighborhoods, a
difficult period of its history began.

THE CALIPH AND COURTLY SOCIETY

Ninth-century Baghdad was home to a large political elite, the city's
"palace society." At its center was the caliph, the axis around which
palace society turned. To glorify the caliph and his office, an elaborate
system of state ritual was put in place. In designing this ornate (and very
expensive) system, the image makers of the Abbasid caliphate drew upon
various political traditions. The caliph was head of the Islamic *umma*, and
references to the Abbasid caliph as "God's agent" (the source of religious
law and guidance) remained very much in use. But the Abbasid court
also relied on pre-Islamic conceptions of imperial leadership: the caliphs
were portrayed as heirs to the monarchs of the ancient Near East. As one
modern historian puts it, the caliph was now "raised to a magnificent figure, remote in a world of awesome luxury, walled off by an elaborate
courtly etiquette, whose casual word was obeyed like divine law."[12]

In fashioning the image of the caliph as universal monarch, the Abbasids picked up where the Umayyads had left off. The later Umayyad
caliphs, based in former Byzantine Syria, had experimented with Roman
and Byzantine patterns of court ritual. The Abbasid transfer of capitals

from Syria to Iraq meant exposure to a greater range of Near Eastern influences. Two currents of political tradition, in particular, remained from the pre-Islamic period. In urban centers from northern Mesopotamia into eastern Iran, the heritage of ancient Greek literature, science, and political thought had survived as Hellenism. Christian scholars and laypersons, working in Syriac and Greek, preserved these ancient works into the early Islamic period, and transmitted their ideas as they participated in Abbasid political and intellectual life.

The literature and political traditions of Sasanid Iran formed the second source of influence. For centuries Iraq had been an important center of Iranian imperial culture and, during the Sasanid period, it was the location of Ctesiphon, the imperial capital. Persian language, literature, and sociopolitical patterns were therefore as prevalent in Iraq as they were in Iran. Of particular importance was the survival of a wealthy and influential Persian-speaking aristocracy from the Sasanid period. These men, educated in Persian language, culture, and tradition, carried these patterns with them following their recruitment into the Abbasid court, provincial administration, and officer corps.

Baghdad's palace society included large numbers of officials, administrators, and hangers-on of other ethnic and regional backgrounds. As participants in an increasingly complex bureaucracy, these individuals carried out many functions. Scribes, secretaries, and finance officials kept the books; drew up official correspondence; arranged the visits of ambassadors, envoys, and merchants; and enforced the decisions of the court. To coordinate their activities, the caliphs relied upon the vizier (Arabic, *wazir*), whose role as head of the imperial administration increased over the course of the eighth and ninth centuries. Elite servants, including palace guardsmen and the eunuchs of the imperial harem—the private household of the monarch, and thus of his wives, concubines, and children—oversaw other crucial functions. Poets, singers, musicians, and actors provided entertainment, often of a very high quality, but also carefully maintained the public image of the caliph and his court.

Since little remains in modern Baghdad of Abbasid-era palaces and elite homes, historians and archaeologists rely on written descriptions—often highly detailed and therefore very useful—as well as on surviving structures at other sites, such as the palace at Ukhaydir (southern Iraq) and the ruins at Samarra, some of which have been restored. They are usually immense structures consisting of "huge walled compounds with endless successions of apartments, courts, rooms, halls, and passageways, whose functions are not known,"[13] which indicates that large sums of money, and the skills of countless artisans, went into these buildings. Decorative elements included ornate, often painted stucco in many styles and large mural paintings depicting secular themes (hunting, dancing, music-playing, and drinking), animals, and other subjects. Hellenistic and Sasanid influences have been identified in many of these elements.

MERCHANTS AND THE COMMERCE OF BAGHDAD

Baghdad became a significant link in a complex trade network connecting the Indian Ocean with the Mediterranean world and was, as a result, home to a large and energetic merchant community. Evidence regarding the dynamics of this trade before roughly 900 is not as plentiful as one would like. Trade was conducted by merchants of all backgrounds, Jews and Muslims as well as Christians, including many from the Byzantine Empire and the Italian city-states (e.g., Genoa and Venice). Diverse merchant groups exchanged not only goods but cultural and religious ideas as well. Muslim merchants in subsequent periods played a central role in the dissemination of Islam; Muslim trade colonies were the seed from which Islamic society would spring in many regions outside the Near East. There is every reason to think the process began in the early Abbasid period.

The activity of Baghdadi merchants was driven, in good part, by the needs of the court. After all, the Abbasid caliphs, presenting themselves as heirs to the great monarchs of the past, required appropriate displays of luxury. This need extended not simply to the person of the ruler but also to his palaces; retinues of officials, guardsmen, and slaves; and public appearances as well: all had to reflect the dynasty's glory. Early Abbasid wealth can be measured by the levels of material consumption in the palaces and fine homes of Baghdad. The *Book of Gifts and Rarities*, an anonymous work from the late eleventh century, deals largely with gifts and treasures of early Islamic society. While it often exaggerates amounts and costs, its lists offer good evidence for the range of luxury goods that were available to elite urban households in the early Abbasid period. Included in these lists are fabrics (silks, brocades, linens); jewelry of gold, silver, and gems; carpets; intricate metalwork; weaponry; fine musical instruments; and an array of exotic foodstuffs.[14] The anecdotes that make up much of the book also refer to the wide availability of slaves for those who could afford to own them.

The wealth of the Iraqi merchant class was tied as well to trade in manufactured goods such as textiles and paper. Papermaking had spread into the Islamic world, from China through Central Asia, in the eighth century and rapidly became an important industry. The availability of paper had an immediate impact on record keeping (tax receipts, military payrolls, and so on) and contributed directly to the growth of the Abbasid bureaucracy. In Baghdad, the Suq al-Warraqin (the Stationers' Market) is said to have included over 100 shops. Even more significant was the important role played by paper production in the development of Arab-Islamic scholarship. Books, pamphlets, and other written material could now be more easily copied and distributed. Knowledge of all sorts was made more accessible than ever before.

Trade in more ordinary goods flourished as well. To feed an increasingly large population, Baghdad drew on the agricultural production of the Sawad, the highly fertile lands located between the Tigris and Euphrates rivers. Reliance on a surrounding hinterland was characteristic of most Near Eastern cities (one thinks of Cairo's dependence on the crops of the Nile Valley). Other agricultural products, such as rice and sugar, were imported from regions farther away. Many new types of fruits and vegetables came to be produced in the Near East, and therefore were available in the markets of Baghdad as a result of an "agricultural revolution" that occurred, according to Andrew Watson, during the early Islamic period.[15] It follows, of course, that the relationship between the large urban centers and the countryside was crucial to the Abbasid economy. The Abbasids, like the Umayyads before them, were fortunate in having inherited from the Sasanids a long-established and well-functioning irrigation system. High levels of agricultural production were maintained in the early Abbasid period. As Abbasid authority waned by the late ninth century, however, maintenance of the agricultural infrastructure suffered as well. This led to a decline in agricultural production and in tax revenue, to the detriment of the imperial state.

SLAVES

Slavery was a conspicuous feature of Near Eastern society prior to Islam and remained so well into the Islamic period (and, in some regions, into the modern age). Frequent references to slaves and slavery occur in the Qur'an and Hadith (the reports of the Prophet's words and deeds), and in most genres of early Arab-Islamic writing, including history, belles-lettres, and poetry. An important, if difficult, source of evidence on early Abbasid slavery is the works of Islamic law that appeared beginning in the late eighth century. Slaves, according to early Islamic law, fell into two categories: captives and those born into slavery. Muslims, legally speaking, could not be enslaved. The formal status of slaves was both object and person. The slave was a commodity and, therefore, could be bought, sold, inherited, or given away. The presenting of female slaves as gifts was, it appears, a common practice of elite Baghdadi society. The slave was also a person, though not fully so; the slave's legal rights were far less than those of an adult Muslim. Slaves did, however, have the right to marry (and divorce) and to bring grievances before legal authorities. It should be noted that considerable merit was attached to manumission as an act of piety (Qur'anic verses urge believers to free their slaves).

Slavery was thus an important component of transregional trade in the Abbasid period. The Arab-Islamic sources refer (often in passing) to the slave markets of Baghdad, Samarra, and other cities. Abbasid merchants acquired slaves from a variety of regions, notably East Africa, regions of North Africa, Eastern Europe, and the Central Asian steppe. It is, however, difficult to judge the scale of the slave trade in this early period. Slaves were employed in a number of ways, but in what numbers? Al-Ya'qubi (d. c. 900), an important Arab-Muslim historian and geographer, refers to an area of Baghdad known as Dar al-Raqiq (house of the slaves), and states that it held "the slaves of Abu Ja'far [al-Mansur] that he had purchased from distant lands." He acknowledges the purchase and use of slaves by the caliph, but otherwise the statement is vague. It is unfortunate that the Arabic sources do not provide better evidence regarding the level and costs of the eighth- and ninth-century slave trade.

To their credit, they do offer plenty of evidence on the roles assigned to slaves in Baghdad (and elsewhere). Elite households routinely employed slaves as maids and nursemaids, cooks and handymen, guards and messengers. Slave soldiers were employed in the Abbasid military, whether as field troops or as elite guardsmen assigned to defend the caliph and his court (see below). Many entertainers were of slave origin as well. Elite Iraqi households employed singers, dancers, poets, and musicians:

the slave trade met a significant demand. There is evidence, in fact, that one category of slave merchants specialized in the training of singing girls. Among the best-known musicians of the period was Arib al-Ma'muniya (d. 890), reported to have been trained as a singer and instrumentalist by her owner in Basra prior to her purchase in Baghdad.[16] Judging by evidence provided in a marvelous Arabic work, the *Kitab al-Aghani* (Book of Songs) by Abu al-Faraj al-Isfahani (d. 967), Arib was one of a large number of slave singers. It is worth adding that late in her career Arib owned and trained her own slave singers.

Her example is important in another regard. As the anecdote in Document 13 suggests, Arib enjoyed wealth and wide connections throughout elite Abbasid society in the final period of her life. The evidence, though spotty, suggests that most slave girls ended up as either domestic servants or ordinary prostitutes. A smaller number became concubines of wealthy merchants, officers, or state officials; it was common for elite males to keep concubines in their households. The occasional woman, Arib among them, found the means to climb the social ladder, however, and thus participate in contemporary society on rather different terms. Social mobility by those of slave origin was not uncommon in early Islamic society: one was legally a slave (Arib is said to have been manumitted), but this did not preclude access to wealth and position for those with wits and good fortune.

THE MILITARY: OFFICERS AND SOLDIERS

Agrarian empires, such as that ruled by the Abbasids, require force alongside wealth in order to prosper: no imperial center is complete without its men-at-arms. Among the first population groups to settle in Baghdad were the Khurasani troops who had ushered the dynasty into power. Though many of the Khurasani units had returned home upon conclusion of the Abbasid revolution, as many had opted to remain in Iraq. Providing decent housing for these troops was an important reason for the foundation of Baghdad.

The appearance of the Khurasani forces marked a significant development in Islamic history. By virtue of their victory over the Umayyads, the Khurasanis stepped into the shoes of the Syrian and Mesopotamian troops of the pre-Abbasid period. These had been primarily Arab tribal forces (though non-Arab *mawali* served as well). The Syrian forces were marginalized through the early Abbasid period; many units simply blended into the civilian populace. The Khurasani forces, by contrast, a mixed force of Arab and Iranian troops, were primarily Persian-speaking, and it appears that their loyalties remained as much with Khurasan as with Baghdad and the Abbasid state. They were subsequently replaced, as the mainstay of the empire, following al-Ma'mun's triumph over his brother (see above). Many of the new Iranian and Central Asian forces probably remained in Iraq through the death of al-Ma'mun and the accession of al-Mu'tasim.

The demands of the Iranian, Central Asian, and Turkish regiments were of paramount concern to al-Mu'tasim. The historian/geographer al-Ya'qubi, in a description of the caliph's settlement at Samarrra, indicates that the caliph distributed generous land grants to a number of civilian officials and military officers; the largest of these were assigned to prominent Turkish and Central Asian commanders.[17] Many of the regiments were settled alongside one another in neighborhoods scattered throughout the new capital but, as al-Ya'qubi indicates, the Turks and Faraghina (units from the Central Asian province of Farghana), probably the largest forces, were settled in segregated quarters designed to keep them at a distance from other regiments and from the population at large. (They were provided with their own mosques, markets, and bathhouses.) Al-Ya'qubi adds that al-Mu'tasim ordered slave women to be distributed to the Turkish troops, with whom they were to create families.

Initially the Turkish and Central Asian forces served the caliphate well, suppressing internal rebellions and participating in attacks on Byzantine soil. Two developments, it seems, turned their attention to domestic matters: an effort by the caliph al-Mutawakkil (r. 847–861) to bolster the authority of his office and a fiscal crisis that nearly bankrupted the treasury and, as a result, left the salaries of the rank and file unpaid. The first development led to political meddling by the Turkish command (with support from high-ranking civilians); the second, to riots by Turkish and non-Turkish soldiery. Upheaval ensued (as noted earlier).

The violence in Samarra, in the view of contemporary observers, was symptomatic of a deeper ill: the presence of rough and unwelcome "barbarian" outsiders. Modern historians offer a more nuanced explanation. Due to a mix of deliberate policy (the distribution of land grants and other arrangements in Samarra) and accident (a mid-ninth-century economic downturn), Abbasid military matters were left in the control of population groups with few ties to local Near Eastern society and only a partial commitment to the interests of the empire. The suggestion is that, in sociocultural terms, the Turks and other Samarran forces were indeed outsiders and, in political terms, the new military leadership in Samarra chose to support the caliphate only to the extent that its interests were well represented. In sum, for a combination of reasons, a divide arose that separated Near Eastern/Islamic urban society and the Abbasid military and political establishment.

The biography of a second-generation Samarran soldier lends further support to this view. Ahmad ibn Tulun (d. 884)—unlike his father, Tulun (d. 854), enslaved in Central Asia during al-Ma'mun's reign and brought to Iraq—was raised a Muslim (and was, therefore, of free status). Upon entering the military, according to his biographers, Ahmad gained the notice of his peers and, in due course, of the Turkish high command. Thus, though raised in Iraq, he was a product of Samarran/Turkish military society. His appointment as governor of Egypt followed, as did a close relationship with the caliph al-Mu'tamid (r. 870–892). Using his new post and the support of his father's network, he carefully exploited political divisions in Iraq to assert autonomy from the Abbasid center. As head of a newly created state, Ibn Tulun proceeded to create a new administrative center.[18] The Tulunid dynasty would rule Egypt for only a brief time (868–905) before being ousted by an Abbasid force. Ibn Tulun's career says much about the willingness of a new, largely Turkish military class to exploit opportunities, regardless of the cost to the Abbasid caliphate.

THE SCHOLARS: ESSAYISTS, PHILOSOPHERS, ASTRONOMERS, AND PHYSICIANS

Alongside slaves, soldiers, and scribes, the population of early Baghdad included a good number of scholars. The initial period of Islamic history had witnessed the rise of largely religious scholarship (see Chapter 5). The early Abbasid period produced a second and dynamic current of scholarship. Its emergence had everything to do with the expansion of Arab-Islamic urban society and, in particular, the growth in demand by urban dwellers and the caliphate for medical, scientific, and technological knowledge. To support the production of such knowledge, wealthy Iraqis, including members of the Abbasid house, offered financial and material support to scholars, their students, and their families. Patrons of scholarship and culture were in no short supply.

The result was rapid progress in a number of disciplines. As Arab-Islamic scholarship flourished, interest in the ideas of other, pre-Islamic cultures grew apace. It led to a wide-ranging translation program that began probably in the late Umayyad period and accelerated quickly, particularly in Baghdad, under the early Abbasids. Several of the Abbasid caliphs played a key role in this regard: al-Mansur, Harun al-Rashid, and al-Ma'mun provided direct support to the translation effort. Many of the translated works were housed in Baghdad in the *Bayt al-Hikma*, a fine library founded by al-Rashid and expanded by al-Ma'mun. The fruit of decades of work was the translation into Arabic of a large number of Greek, Persian, and Indian writings. It was due to these translations that the influences of Hellenistic and Iranian thought on Arab-Islamic scholarship and society occurred. Among those involved in the translation movement were the Banu Musa brothers, members of a wealthy Baghdadi family and leading patrons of scientific scholarship; Abu Zakariya ibn Masawayh (d. 857), court physician and patron of medical research; and, perhaps the best-known translator of the ninth century (when the greatest number of translations appeared), Hunayn ibn Ishaq (d. 873), a Nestorian Christian Arab. Working with a team of students, Hunayn produced translations of works in medicine, philosophy, and scientific fields including astronomy.

As this brief description suggests, scholars working in Arabic contributed original works in a number of fields. Philosophy was among the most important. It also quickly became controversial through its trust in human reason, logic, and natural laws. Religious scholars responded angrily to this reliance upon human reason, particularly when it came to discussions of God and the Qur'an. Were these not, after all, solely matters of faith? Despite such questions, Arab-Islamic philosophy flourished. Abu Yusuf al-Kindi (d. c. 866), usually seen as the first significant Muslim philosopher, was active in Baghdad and Samarra, and is reported to have been close to both al-Ma'mun and al-Mu'tasim. A later figure, Abu Bakr al-Razi (d. 925/932), an Iranian scholar, contributed some 200 works on philosophy, medicine, alchemy, and other fields.

More extensive work was carried out in astronomy, mathematics, and medicine. The influence of Greek thought was particularly strong in as-

tronomy. Muhammad ibn Musa al-Khwarizmi was among the most prolific writers of the period. As a young man, he was active in Baghdad and
studied in the *Bayt al-Hikma*. He is credited with influential works in geography, mathematics, and astronomy. His *Zij al-Sindhind*, a set of tables
of solar and planetary movements, remained a standard work of astronomy for centuries, and his *Kitab al-Jabr wa al-Muqabala*, probably the first
formal work of algebra (the term derives from the title of his book), was
a milestone in the history of mathematics. The significance of his work—
like the work of many Arab-Muslim scholars of the Abbasid period—lies
not simply in the role it played in Near Eastern scholarship. Rather, it
also lies in the impact it had particularly in early Western scholarship:
the *Kitab al-Jabr* was among a large number of Arabic works to be translated into Latin and Hebrew in early medieval Europe.

NOTES

1. Fred Donner, "Muhammad and the Caliphate," in John Esposito, ed., *The Oxford History of Islam*, pp. 19–20.

2. For a discussion of conversion in early Islamic history, see Richard Bulliet, *Conversion to Islam in the Medieval Period*.

3. Basim Musallam, "The Ordering of Muslim Societies," in Francis Robinson, ed., *Cambridge Illustrated History of the Islamic World*, p. 165.

4. Albert Hourani, *History of the Arab Peoples*, p. 110. For a challenging dis-
cussion of urbanization in the early Islamic period, see Paul Wheatley, *The Places Where Men Pray Together*.

5. Many of the documents in this book deal with urban life in the early Islamic period. Document 7 contains an excerpt from al-Muqaddasi.

6. See Wheatley, *Places Where Men Pray*, pp. 269–287.

7. See Jonathan Berkey, *Formation of Islam*, pp. 91–101.

8. Wheatley, *Places Where Men Pray*, p. 337.

9. Document 14 contains a partial description of al-Qata'i', the palace complex built by Ahmad ibn Tulun, the founder of the short-lived Tulunid dynasty
in Egypt. His career is described briefly below.

10. See Wheatley, *Places Where Men Pray*, pp. 54–55, 269–278.

11. See Document 5 for a description of the succession documents.

12. Marshall Hodgson, *The Venture of Islam*, vol. 1, p. 283.

13. Richard Ettinghausen et al., *Islamic Art and Architecture*, p. 55 (with fine
illustrations, pp. 51–59).

14. See *Book of Gifts and Rarities*, translated by Ghada al-Qaddumi, pp. 34–41. Document 8 contains extracts from the book.

15. See Andrew M. Watson, *Agricultural Innovation in the Early Islamic World*.

16. Arib is the subject of Document 13.

17. See Document 6.

18. See Document 14.

CHAPTER 5

RELIGIOUS PRACTICE, LAW, AND SPIRITUALITY IN THE EARLY ABBASID ERA

Historians generally agree that Islam had assumed a distinct religious identity by the early Abbasid period. It might be helpful to make two preliminary points on Islam as a religious system. First, Islam should not be seen as "fully formed" at any point in its history. Key elements were in place by the early tenth century, but much else was to come as new generations of Muslims introduced their own ideas and practices. No religious system, in fact, is ever "complete": religious systems are as subject to change as any other facet of human society.

Second, it is more useful to speak of Islam in the plural—the *currents* of Islam—because of the variety of thought and practice shaped over the course of Islamic history. The different strands of Islam can all be identified as "religious." In one sense or another, they all wrestle with such topics as prophecy and scripture; divine will and sacred law; the nature of ritual practice; the responsibilities of leadership; and the ultimate meaning of human existence. The complexity and wealth of Islamic thought spring from the variety of ways in which such topics have been understood.

THE HADITH OF GABRIEL

Document 10 ("The Prophet's Wisdom") contains three texts. Each consists of a list of names (*isnad*) followed by an example of the Prophet's teaching (*matn*). The names are of the "transmitters" who are said to have passed on the *matn*, the text or report, from the time of the Prophet on. Each text is known as a *hadith* (pl., *ahadith*), which is also a collective noun (thus, "the books of Hadith"). Modern historians refer to the Hadith reports as "traditions," and to those who circulated the reports in the early Islamic period as "traditionists." By the ninth century, the Hadith probably numbered in the tens of thousands. Given the sheer bulk of material but, more important, the significance attached to it by the Muslim scholars, it is hardly surprising that the work of reading, debating, selecting, and even composing, new Hadith became their central activity. In very basic terms, it involved gathering the reports, carefully selecting those that were judged to be reliable (a controversial step), and organizing them, usually by topic, in written form. The Hadith collections, usually multivolume works, remain essential to Islamic practice, law, and education.

The third of the texts in Document 10 is known as the Hadith of Gabriel.[1] It probably first appeared in written form in a ninth-century Hadith collection titled *Sahih*, compiled by Muslim ibn al-Hajjaj (d. 875). The Gabriel Hadith is considered an authoritative statement of Islamic practice and faith, and therefore, serves as a useful start to a discussion of the early stages of Islamic religious history. It is composed of two sections. It begins with an exchange outside a mosque among three Muslim males. Early Arab-Islamic biographical dictionaries (which first appeared in late eighth-century Iraq) suggest that, of the three men, Abdallah ibn Umar (d. 693) was the most prominent. No surprise, really, since his father, Umar ibn al-Khattab, was the second of the Rashidun caliphs. Abdallah was widely respected for his piety, moral integrity, and learning, though he is best remembered as a reliable transmitter of Hadith. The Gabriel Hadith is among countless reports associated with his name.

It then turns to an encounter between the Prophet and Gabriel in which Muhammad identifies four essential elements, or dimensions, of Islam: *islam*, *iman*, *ihsan*, and the signs of the Last Day. This is the essential function assigned to Hadith from the ninth century on: to guide and instruct believers. The fourth element, concerning the Last Day (i.e., the end of time), will not be discussed here.[2]

The first element is *islam* (the term, lowercase, is used here to refer to an aspect of Islam, the formal religious tradition). Muhammad's response to the archangel's question is clear: *islam* entails five kinds of practice.

These would come to be known as the "pillars" (*rukn*; pl., *arkan*) of Islam. The first of the "Five Pillars" takes the form of a statement, the *Shahada* (bearing witness): "there is no god but God, and Muhammad is His messenger." It affirms the utter unity and distinctiveness that is the reality of the Qur'anic God and the essential role played by Muhammad as one who conveys divine guidance to humankind. (The Qur'an identifies Muhammad as the last and most perfect of the prophets, who include Moses and Jesus.) The statement itself is both an "act" and, it was generally presumed, an acceptance of these fundamental ideas. The second of the "pillars" is prayer (*salat*), to which Islamic tradition attaches enormous significance. The Qur'an refers frequently to (different kinds of) prayer though only *salat* emerged as one of the five "pillars." It not only refers, in fact, to the various forms of prayer, but also commands their performance. By the ninth century, and probably much earlier, Muslim scholars understood the major prayer to be that which Muslims were to carry out five times daily, following proper rites of ritual cleansing.

The third practice is *zakat* (purification), an alms or annual tithe usually paid to religious officials or representatives of the State, a practice often dated to the lifetime of the Prophet and the Rashidun period. Historians point out that the manner in which it was collected and its precise definition shifted over the course of early Islamic history. Its significance is clear: it was a means to contribute to the support of society at large. The fourth duty is to participate in the annual Ramadan fast (*sawm* or *siyam*). During the daylight hours of Ramadan, Muslims refrain from eating, drinking, sexual activity, and smoking. The monthlong fast, a remarkable display of communal worship, is marked throughout the Islamic world by a heightened religious sense and a greater emphasis upon social and family ties.

The fifth and final duty is the pilgrimage to Mecca (*Hajj*) which takes place in the final month of the Islamic calendar. It is required of every believer at least once in her/his lifetime and who is physically and financially capable of taking the journey and performing the specific rites of the *Hajj*. The nine prescribed rites include wearing the *ihram* (a two-part garment of plain white cloth), which symbolizes the pilgrim's state of purity; a circumambulation of the Ka'ba; and a "standing" at Mount Arafat, outside Mecca, which commemorates the Prophet's final pilgrimage and his Farewell Sermon. The physical demands of the pilgrimage have historically been very great, given the distances traveled and

the insecurity of roads and sea routes. In addition to its religious significance, the *Hajj* provides Muslims with the opportunity to gather with believers from every corner of Islamic society.

The term *islam*, to which the Prophet refers, is often translated as "submission" (i.e., to the will of God). In his statement to Gabriel, the
Prophet describes submission in terms of acts. The angel then asks about
faith (*iman*). The Prophet replies with a list of six items that the believer
is to understand and accept as necessary knowledge: God, the angels, the
revealed books, the messengers of God, the Day of Judgment, and "the
measuring out" (i.e., the idea that God determines all things). Much
more can be said about each of these items. The critical point is that if
islam consists of deeds or "outward" expressions of belief, then *iman* consists of the knowledge and understanding behind the deeds. The two elements, in other words, are to work hand in hand.

The angel then asks about righteous, or virtuous, conduct (*ihsan*). The
Prophet's reply is that every act should be performed in the full awareness of God's presence. This is probably best interpreted as intention: that
the believer is motivated fully by this awareness of God. A modern
scholar describes it this way:

> *Ihsan* connotes beauty, mastery, proficiency; it is achieved by main-
> taining a keen awareness of seeing and being seen by God. *Ihsan*
> means right virtue, which encompasses two states: a state of loving
> God with all your heart, and a state of being close to or intimate
> with God, of living in connection with God.[3]

The arrangement of the Gabriel Hadith makes very clear that an essential aspect of Islamic religious thought is the relationship between
practice and thought. From a very early point, Muslim thinkers understood the three elements of the Hadith (*islam, iman, ihsan*) as working
virtually as one, three parts of the same system. Faith and practice assume meaning only when both are in place and, equally, both are driven
by proper motivation. In addition, the ritual acts that make up the first
element (*islam*) constituted an important topic of Islamic law. In general
terms, the early Muslim legal scholars conceived of two broad sets of relationships: those between God and humankind, and those between one
human being and another. The first category, known as *ibadat*, refers to
the daily prayers, the month of fasting, *zakat*, and the pilgrimage to

Mecca. These are treated in the legal manuals as obligatory duties of the Muslim. The second broad category is known as *mu'amalat*.

The appearance of the Gabriel Hadith, in written form, indicates that by the ninth century essential features of the Islamic religious tradition were in place. A system of worship, informed by a set of principles, was available for Muslims at large and remained fundamental to Islamic practice from that point forward. If, however, the threefold system outlined above provided a certain unity to Islamic society across both regional and historical boundaries, other patterns of thought and practice became sources of division. To consider this point, it is necessary to turn to a discussion of the Muslim religious scholars and their role in early Islamic history.

THE RISE OF THE RELIGIOUS SCHOLARS

The Hadith of Gabriel can be read in a slightly different way. It records two instances in which knowledge, specifically religious knowledge, is transmitted. In the first instance, Abdallah ibn Umar relates to his companions what he was told by his father; in the second, the Prophet instructs the believers about the dimensions of Islam. The act of transmitting knowledge—from Muslim to Muslim, from one generation to the next—became an essential dynamic of Islamic religious and social history from a very early point. Religious knowledge is usually referred to in Islamic sources as *ilm*. The individuals associated with its collection and transmission, the religious scholars, are known by the related term *alim* (pl., *ulama*), literally "those in possession of *ilm*." Their commitment to knowledge is understood in part as a response to the Qur'an, in which references to knowledge, and specifically knowledge of God, occur with great frequency. Verses relate knowledge directly to faith: "And whenever you are told to go forth, then go forth, for God will elevate by many degrees those who act out of faith and to whom knowledge has been given, and God is Fully Aware of all that you do" (*Surat al-Mujadila*, 58:11).

But what did early Islamic society consider to be "religious knowledge," and how was that knowledge to be used? The formation of the major branches of Islam had everything to do with the varying responses of generations of *ulama*.

It might first be said that the *ulama* did not constitute an organized clergy. By the early Islamic period, the rabbinate had taken on a formal role in Judaism, as had the priesthood of the various Near Eastern Christian churches, including that of the Byzantine Empire. The Zoroastrian priesthood played a similar role in the late Sasanid period. Not so the *ulama*. Historians relate this, in part, to the claim by the caliphs to be the "deputies" of God. Their claim to religious authority left them with no obligation to create a religious hierarchy of this sort. When pressed to deal with legal or doctrinal questions, the caliphs provided responses, as did, in the provinces, their governors and *qadis*. How, then, does one explain the emergence of the religious scholars?

The history of scholarship in Islam begins with the Prophet's closest followers, those who had participated in the events of his career. The term *sahaba* (companions) is used for the first generation of these men and women; *tabiun* (successors), for the second. They are remembered, first and foremost, for the preservation of the Qur'an and the Prophet's teachings. A next stage was the formation of scholarly circles in Medina, Mecca, and the *amsar*. As the reputations of individual scholars grew, so did the demand by local communities for guidance in matters of the faith. The caliph may have exerted religious authority, but ordinary Muslims probably never thought to turn to the ruler or his entourage with everyday questions of this kind. It is unlikely, in any case, that access to the sovereign would have been granted. Rather, they turned to individuals whom they perceived to possess understanding and religiosity. Local scholars slowly acquired authority as teachers, spiritual guides, and moral exemplars.[4]

What motivated the early Muslim scholars? The answer is probably threefold. First, as believers, they sought to apply the teachings of the Qur'an and the Prophet to the creation of a just, equitable, and God-conscious society. They faced a difficult task: Islamic society was growing steadily as conversion accelerated, and each new generation of believers was posing new questions concerning the practice of the faith. The scholars formed their responses according to what seemed reasonable to them at the moment. Second, the early scholars had also to respond to the negative reactions of non-Muslims. The growth of Islamic urban society had set the stage for extended debate with Jews and Christians over the teachings of Islam. These were conducted in writing and face-to-face encounters. These experiences provided Muslim scholars with the opportunity to articulate the teachings of the Qur'an and the Prophet, a critical step in the development of Islamic thought.

The third part of the answer concerns the caliphs' claim to religious standing. By the mid-eighth century, the scholars increasingly saw the claim as hollow: the caliphs, in their view, were at best negligent of their religious duties and at worst, impious and unjust. The view that the caliphs were failing to uphold the norms of the Qur'an and the Prophet's own example took shape in the Umayyad period and carried forward into that of the early Abbasids. The scholars, it should be stressed, represented different groups: the Kharijis, the Shi'a and the proto-Sunnis. Each group will be considered below. The point of agreement was that the caliphate could no longer claim a primary religious role. Where disputes arose was over the proper source of religious guidance and on what terms it was to be exercised.

PROTO-SUFISM

It is worth stressing, however, that not all early Muslim scholars were caught up with questions of this kind. Early Muslim circles, particularly in Iraq, included those for whom a religious commitment entailed piety, asceticism, humility, and contemplation, matters that could be pursued only if one turned from a preoccupation with politics and wealth. A complex current of Islamic thought, centered on such attitudes, emerged formally by the tenth century. It is generally called Sufism (Arabic, *tasawwuf*), a term that may have originated with the word for wool (*suf*) and the rough garments worn by early Muslim ascetics.

Later Sufi thinkers—such as al-Sulami (d. 1021), al-Hujwiri (d. 1075), and al-Ghazali (d. 1111)—would stress the connection between Sufism, on the one hand, and the Qur'an and the example of the Prophet and his companions, on the other. Sufi texts, for example, make much of Muhammad as the exemplar of the inner, spiritual life. Just as the Qur'an descended, mankind—with Muhammad as the model—must "ascend" to meet it. Sufi texts would also make much of the Miraculous Journey (*Mi'raj*) taken by the Prophet from Mecca to Jerusalem (and then into God's presence). But all this is the explanation of later authors, at a time when Sufism was more clearly defined.

In its early stages, Sufism probably also had to do with two other matters. The first, indicated above, was a relative disinterest in material and political concerns. This did not necessarily involve a withdrawal from the world, however; Arab-Islamic sources indicate that early or proto-

Sufis participated in *jihad* against the Byzantine Empire. But it did entail a commitment to a life of spirituality and self-denial (*zuhd*) rather than one of indulgence and material comfort. A second aspect of early Sufism was the interaction of Arab-Muslim ideas of piety, as expressed in the Qur'an and teachings of the Prophet, with deeply rooted patterns of asceticism and piety among other religious groups of the Near East, notably the monastic movement in Egyptian and Syrian Christianity. Of particular interest, it seems, to the early Muslims was the phenomenon of the "saintly" person, an individual of heightened spiritual awareness and religious commitment who models the religious life. To the Muslims, there was no better example than Muhammad.

These early ideas are associated with such figures as Hasan al-Basri (d. 728), Rabi'a al-Adawiya (d. 801), al-Tustari (d. 896), and Junayd (d. 910), all of whom contributed to the first stages of Sufism. The ideas and reputations of the early ascetics attracted growing numbers of adherents and gave rise to informal circles of teachers and disciples by the ninth and tenth centuries. A prominent view was that the inner life was properly pursued along a progression of spiritual stages, to each of which the teacher leads his or her students. Just as the teacher, or master, derived knowledge and guidance through trust in God, so the student would do from the teacher. Also significant was the practice of *dhikr*, often translated as "remembering" God and His names, either in silent meditation or in quiet chanting. The idea derived from the Qur'an and Hadith, and is epitomized in the ritual prayer (*salat*) during which believers invoke the presence of God.

THE KHARIJI MOVEMENTS

Most Kharijis, by contrast, were deeply immersed in worldly matters. The Khariji movement was divided internally, with a number of splinter groups assembling and reassembling. Four groups are generally seen as historically significant. Basra was the earliest center of Khariji activity, though the movement quickly spread into other regions.

The first groups to emerge were the Azariqa and the Najdiya. Named after Nafi ibn al-Azraq (d. 685), an activist of *mawla* origins, the Azariqa are usually described as the most radical of the four groups. Umayyad forces, following a series of clashes, crushed the Azariqa by 698–699. The

Najdiya, relatively less radical but just as active militarily, were led by Najda ibn Amir (d. 692). Initially an ally of Ibn al-Azraq, Najda broke with him before proceeding to create a Khariji principality in eastern Arabia. An Umayyad force defeated the Najdiya in 693. The other two groups were the Sufriya and the Ibadiya. The Sufriya gained a following in areas of Arabia and North Africa into the tenth century. The Ibadiya, the longest surviving Khariji sect, established itself in Oman and areas of North Africa, where it still exists. The two groups are usually seen as representative of moderate Kharijism.

The Kharijis were divided, in part, over the problem of authority. Khariji scholars agreed in general that only men of merit (i.e., piety, faith, and knowledge) should lead; most refused to accept the leadership of the caliphs (except Abu Bakr and Umar), particularly those of the Umayyad house, who were denounced as tyrants. Disagreement arose over how to deal with illegitimate rulers: Should the true Muslim continue to live under such leadership? The Azariqa and Najdiya, each in its way, argued that Muslims, to remain untainted, must set themselves apart in separate communities and struggle against such leadership, even if outright war (*jihad*) resulted. The Sufriya and Ibadiya, in contrast, felt that life under corrupt leadership was unfortunate but usually unavoidable. True Muslims, then, should remain in place but follow only their own scholars and work tirelessly to "purify" society at large.

Closely related were debates over the problem of sin. A corrupt leader was viewed as a sinner because his conduct constituted a violation of God's rules as laid out in the Qur'an and Prophetic teachings. Khariji scholars widened the definition to take in any Muslim who violated these norms. Through adultery and stealing, for example, the Muslim became an "unbeliever" (*kafir*) or "idolater" (*mushrik*). Debate then centered on how that person was to be punished and whether repentance was permitted. These debates were among the very earliest attempts by Muslim scholars to define Islamic doctrine. Khariji ideas on these subjects, seen generally as too strict and divisive, were usually abandoned.

Kharijism as a formal movement lasted only through the early Abbasid period except in outlying regions, but the long-term contribution of Khariji thought was significant. The Khariji insistence on adhering closely to Qur'anic principles was adopted, in more moderate form, by most other currents of Islamic thought. Equally important to later generations was the Khariji emphasis on communal effort: Muslims were to work together, and only through joint commitment would salvation for all believers be achieved.

THE EARLY SHIʿA

Three events shaped early Shiʿi history. The first was the appointment of Abu Bakr as the Prophet's successor (632). The Shiʿi sources maintain that the appointment of Abu Bakr violated the Prophet's wishes since, in their view, the Prophet had designated Ali ibn Abi Talib to succeed him. Many Arab-Islamic sources relate an event that occurred during what is known as the Final Pilgrimage (to Mecca). At Ghadir Khumm, the Prophet delivered his last sermon, during which he instructed the believers to follow Ali much as they had followed him. Shiʿi scholars interpret this as a designation of succession (Sunni scholars disagree). From early on, therefore, Ali's supporters decried Abu Bakr's accession to office. It was only a short step for later Shiʿa to argue that Islamic society at large had gone astray in assigning authority to Abu Bakr and the caliphs who succeeded him (Umayyad and Abbasid). Little wonder that the Shiʿa would have such difficult relations with both dynasties.

The second event was the death of al-Husayn, Ali's son and the Prophet's grandson, at the hands of the Umayyads (680). Many historians argue that the killing of al-Husayn generated the first overt religious elements in the pro-Alid movement. Very early, the Shiʿa began to treat the death as martyrdom, a highly meaningful act of sacrifice. Al-Husayn's destination had been Kufa, an early garrison town and pro-Alid center. As seen earlier, anger at the treatment of al-Husayn had sparked the movement supporting Muhammad ibn al-Hanafiya, another of Ali's sons. Historians also point to the role of various groups of *ghulat* associated with the pro-Alid movement who were dubbed extremists because their ideas were rejected by later generations of Muslim scholars (Sunni and Shiʿi alike). Clearly, however, certain of these ideas influenced the early Shiʿa. Among the ideas of the "extremists" was that guidance was to be gained from divinely inspired figures; that such figures possessed secret knowledge; and that heroic individuals of this kind were capable of returning to life. This last notion was often described as a reemergence from hiding (occultation, "the state of being hidden from view").

The third event, the Abbasid revolution (749–750), was a key turn-ing point in early Shi'ism, marking a divide between the Shi'a and non-Shi'a. (The revolution was discussed earlier.) Just as significant was the divide among the Shi'i movements: three major branches of Shi'ism emerged from this contentious religious environment.

The Zaydiya took their name from Zayd ibn Ali (d. 740), a great-grandson of Ali ibn Abi Talib and leader of an anti-Umayyad revolt. The Zaydiya insisted that only Ali's descendants—through either al-Hasan or al-Husayn—could rightfully claim authority as the *imam*. Like most other Muslims, they stressed the need for the *imam* to play an active role: he should be prepared to teach but also to lead and fight when necessary. Two Zaydi states were established in the late ninth century. The first, in northern Iran along the Caspian Sea, survived to the twelfth century. Zaydi Shi'ism remained in the area until the sixteenth century. The sec-ond was founded (897) in Yemen by a Hasanid leader known as al-Hadi ila al-Haqq (d. 911), and survived, on and off, until 1962. Zaydi Shi'ism is still practiced in the Yemeni highlands.

The second group, known early on as the Imami Shi'a, later came to be called the *Ithna Ashariya* (Twelvers). Muhammad al-Baqir (d. 735) and his son, Ja'far al-Sadiq (d. 765), laid the foundation for a complex body of doctrine and law centered on the office of the *iman* (the imamate). Both were highly respected Medinan scholars, descendants of al-Husayn. Unlike the Zaydiya, they held that the *imam* could be only from the Husayni line; that, while in theory capable of ruling, he should avoid overt political activity; and, therefore, that he was principally a religious and spiritual figure. Imami scholarship, particularly in Kufa and Baghdad, built upon these early ideas.

Crisis occurred in 873 with the death, in Samarra, of Hasan al-Askari, a prominent scholar and leader of the Imami movement. His followers held that his infant son and successor, Muhammad, had gone into *ghayba* (hiding or occultation). Over time, the conviction formed that the ima-mate had been passed down a line of twelve individuals. The line began with Ali and included al-Husayn (third), Muhammad al-Baqir (fifth), Ja'far al-Sadiq (sixth), and Hasan al-Askari (eleventh). It ended with the infant Muhammad, now known as the (twelfth) hidden *imam*.

The effort devoted to developing the image of the hidden *imam* re-flected, in part, the influence of *ghulat* ideas once current in Iraqi circles.

The Twelfth Imam was now thought of as the Awaited One: he remained the living *imam* but would reappear in human form at a time decreed by God (usually held to be shortly before the Day of Judgment). He had become, in other words, the *Mahdi* (the rightly guided one). His role, in large part, was messianic: upon his return, he would lead the forces of righteousness against those of evil, restore the world to a state of justice, and assure the salvation of his true followers.

The *ghayba* of the Twelfth Imam meant that he could pose no challenge to the existing political order. In contrast with the Kharijis and the other Shi'i movements, the Twelver Shi'a would claim, not without justification, that they remained outside the political arena. Second, the idea of the Hidden Imam transformed the standing of the Twelver *ulama*. Their initial and limited role (as spiritual guides and legal experts) evolved over time as leading *ulama* defined themselves as the representatives of the Hidden Imam. Gradually, as a result, the leading scholars of each age were held to exercise the legal and religious authority of the *imam*. In part this meant control over the collection of alms, also referred to as religious taxes. Economic clout, combined with moral and religious standing, added up to significant influence.

The third movement, Isma'ili Shi'ism, probably originated around the debate over the succession of Ja'far al-Sadiq. One group of Shi'a backed the candidacy of Ja'far's son, Isma'il, and then *his* son, Muhammad ibn Isma'il; another group supported the imamate of another of Ja'far's sons, Musa ibn Ja'far (seventh of the Twelver *imams*). Isma'ili scholarship developed a rich and difficult body of doctrine in which ideas on the imamate contrasted sharply with those of the Twelvers. Isma'ili thought rested squarely on the idea of a living, active *imam*. Much of Isma'ili doctrine, however, developed in a later period following the success of one current of Isma'ili activism. Early Isma'ili Shi'a devoted themselves to the formation of a central organization, known as the *Da'wa*, that was dedicated to the spread of Isma'ili teachings. By the mid-ninth century, agents of the *Da'wa* had won adherents in various regions. One such region was eastern Algeria, in which the Kutama, a Berber people, formed a majority. Backed by Kutama forces, the Isma'ili movement seized control of the neighboring province of Ifriqiya (modern Tunisia), governed to that point on behalf of the Abbasids by the Aghlabid family. This was the foundation of the Fatimid state (909), a development discussed in Chapter 6.

EARLY SUNNISM

Since, as has been pointed out, Sunnism took longer to form than Kharijism or Shi'ism, the term "proto-Sunni" is used here for the period up to the mid-tenth century. The first proto-Sunni element to fall into place was acceptance of the legitimacy of the Rashidun caliphs. (The term "Rashidun" was coined, in fact, by later Sunni scholars.) This contrasted with the position of most Kharijis and meant a rejection of the Shi'i model of the imamate (as well as the Shi'i view that the Prophet had appointed Ali to succeed him). The essential idea is that in backing the first four caliphs, early Islamic society acted in harmony with God's will. The notion that the early believers were inherently correct in their actions and, as a result of "correctness," or consensus, unified in their views, is an essential Sunni idea.

Proto-Sunni scholars took a second, momentous step when they fixed the definition of *Sunna*. Originally meaning "path" or "beaten track," and probably used in pre-Islamic Arabia to refer to traditional practice, it came to mean, among early Muslim scholars, the general practice of the believers during the period of the Prophet and his companions. Proto-Sunni scholars then narrowed the definition even more to refer specifically to the practice of the Prophet. *Sunna*, in other words, came to mean "the path" of the Prophet. This sharpened the lines, of course, between the Shi'a and proto-Sunnis since, according to this view, no other model was acceptable, including that of the *imams*.

The shift contributed directly to the shaping of Hadith, the reports of the Prophet's words and deeds. The Hadith contain the *Sunna*. The Shi'a and proto-Sunnis created their respective collections of Hadith in the early period (other well-regarded Hadith works would be added in later centuries). Of six important Hadith collections, the Sunnis would assign particular status to two: the *Jami' al-Sahih* of al-Bukhari (d. 870) and the *Sahih* of Muslim (which contains the version of the Gabriel Hadith used here). The Shi'a would assign canonical status to four early Hadith collections of their own, including *al-Kafi fi Ilm al-Din* by Muhammad al-Kulayni (d. 939). A major difference between Sunni and Shi'i Hadith has to do with the *isnads*. The Sunni collections most frequently trace the Hadith to the Prophet and his companions. The Shi'a, however, usually cite the *imams* even when the Prophet is mentioned as well.

An important movement among the proto-Sunni scholars promoted Prophetic *Sunna* and, therefore, a central role for Hadith. Those who insisted on this point came to be known as the *ashab al-hadith* or, as one historian puts it, "The Hadith Party."[5] Another term for these circles of scholars was *ahl al-sunna wal-jama'a*, from which the term "Sunni" would spring. Modern historians call them "traditionist," which derives from "Prophetic traditions" (i.e., the Hadith). The activity of the Hadith movement was a critical step in the shaping of Sunnism. The traditionist scholars played an important part in the development of several further elements of proto-Sunnism.

Sunni Religious Law

The creation of religious law was the most significant accomplishment of the proto-Sunni scholars (with the traditionists playing a leading role). The seed that gave rise to the Sunni legal system was the conviction that God provided humankind with the means by which to create a righteous society. The term often used for Islamic law is *shari'a* which, in its ordinary meaning, refers to a "path" or "way." *Shari'a*, in the sense of law, might be thought of as a "blueprint," provided by God through revelation, by which to create such a society. By a very early date, the law was viewed as all-encompassing, as a full "way of life." One modern historian has described it as follows:

> The scope of the law is vast: the jurists [i.e., the religious scholars who specialized in law] expressed opinions on almost every conceivable arena of social life, from how to pray, to how to structure a business partnership, to how to trim one's beard. Islamic law, in other words, was not simply a matter for courts, judges (*qadis*), and the various institutional mechanisms of legal discipline. Rather, it was something which touched on believers' lives in intimate ways, and so all Muslims needed to have at least some rudimentary understanding of it.[6]

The challenge was to bring the vision of a true social order into being by creating the actual body of rules and principles.

The early history of Sunni law unfolded in stages. A first stage—in Medina, Mecca, Kufa, Basra, and elsewhere—was the effort to resolve questions posed by local believers. Local scholars expressed their views as personal opinions, but also in their capacity as judges (*qadis*) when reaching legal decisions. This led, however, to great diversity in the rules and opinions that emerged from one region to the next (and within each region). To bring about greater uniformity of belief and practice, the traditionists came to insist that only the Prophet Muhammad could be used as a normative model. This was a first step in the creation of the Hadith collections. The argument, to put it simply, was that rather than local rulemaking that depended largely on the opinions of individual scholars, Muslims should be guided by a more systematic model, that which was provided by the Prophet's *Sunna*.

A second stage occurred with the formation of the *madhhab* (pl., *madhahib*), often translated as "school of law." These were not institutions, but the bodies of opinion and teachings associated with specific early masters, such as Ahmad ibn Hanbal, a renowned Baghdadi scholar. Generations of his students—who formed the Hanbali "school"—wrote commentaries in which they elaborated upon the views of their legal tradition. In time, the *madhahib* came to rely as well upon manuals or digests of their legal teachings. To better identify themselves, each "school" produced biographical dictionaries that provided pertinent information on the early master and successive generations of his followers.

These efforts gave rise to a number of early Sunni *madhahib*. Only four, however, survived the early period (to the modern day). Each was named after a significant figure: the Hanafi *madhhab*, after Abu Hanifa (d. 767); the Maliki, after Malik ibn Anas (d. 795); the Shafi'i, after Muhammad al-Shafi'i (d. 820); and the Hanbali after Ibn Hanbal (d. 855). The Shi'a would create their own *madhahib*, the most prominent of which was the Ja'fari "school," named after Ja'far al-Sadiq, of the Twelver Shi'a. It should be noted, however, that the later, clear distinction between Sunni and Shi'i law was not so clear in the early period. Abu Hanifa, for example, was a student of Ja'far al-Sadiq and strong similarities between Ja'fari and Hanafi law remain to the present day.

Scholars of the early Abbasid period also fashioned what is known as the "sources" or "foundations" of the law (*usul al-fiqh*). As a result, by the tenth century Islamic law rested on two major disciplines or fields of study of Islamic religious education. *Fiqh* emerged first; it refers to the actual rules and regulations of the law. These were collected over time, organized by topic, and contained in a body of writing to which later genera-

tions of jurists would turn when deciding actual cases. It is useful to contrast *fiqh*, which was recognized as human knowledge, with *sharīa*, which
was knowledge contained in God's Word. *Usul al-fiqh* emerged at a later
stage in Islamic legal history. It was concerned with the theory of the law
or, in other words, the principles that guided the formulation of law. It
was only after extended, often very heated, debate that the early Sunni
ulama came to accept that the law was to be derived from a hierarchy of
four "sources" (*usul*). The Qur'an came first, followed by the *Sunna*, which
was followed in turn by two principles known as *qiyas* (analogical reasoning) and *ijma'* (consensus).

The latter two principles were controversial, particularly among the
more conservative traditionists. *Qiyas* came into play when a legal problem involved a subject that was not addressed explicitly in the Qur'an,
Sunna, or (later) the legal manuals. To reach their ruling, the scholars
used analogy ("Is situation x sufficiently like situation y that the same
rule should apply to both?"). The problem was that this required the exercise of reason or rational argumentation. Many traditionists were deeply
suspicious of a reliance on human reason, and made every effort to limit
the use of *qiyas*. *Ijma'*, the second principle, was defined ultimately as the
consensus of the jurists (the legal scholars). It held that an opinion or
ruling that was backed by such a consensus would be considered binding
from that point forward. This was a very powerful tool in asserting the
unity and authority of traditionist scholarly circles. It should be said,
however, that there were constant disputes among scholars over whether
consensus actually had been established around a given issue.

By the ninth century, the *sharīa* had become the basis upon which the
qadis reached their decisions. Modern scholars of Islamic law point out,
however, that *sharīa*, though all-encompassing in theory, was not so in
practice. From at least the early Abbasid period, it was customary for the
caliph, or a high official of his choosing, to hold public sessions (*mazalim*)
in which they received formal complaints of wrongdoing. These were
often petitions against abuses of power by local officials, but included
complaints against decisions by *qadis* as well. These sessions constituted,
in effect, a parallel system of law alongside the *sharīa* courts. In general,
the *sharīa* courts handled cases related to religious practice, marriage and
divorce, inheritance and other "domestic" areas, along with sales, con-
tracts, partnerships, and other areas of commercial and financial law. The

mazalim system dealt with all manner of disputes and, in particular, with most kinds of criminal cases.

A final question: How did the law affect the lives of ordinary Muslims? One might consider, by way of example, its impact on women. As seen earlier, in the view of many scholars the Qur'an treats women at two levels, the ethical and the practical. At the ethical level, it places women and men on equal footing, but in practical terms it creates a hierarchy of gender with women in a subordinate role, particularly in the public sphere (and when seen from a modern perspective).

Wide debate exists over the extent to which the early Muslim scholars used the law to enforce, even extend, that role. One view is that they simply adhered to Qur'anic teachings. They distinguished, in other words, the roles of women and men, maintaining that both roles were vital to the integrity of family and society even while affirming that men wielded ultimate authority within family and home. Even here, however, women at least in theory had the right to protest abuses of power on the part of men. A related view is that early Islamic law, when compared with standards of the wider, non-Muslim ninth- and tenth-century world, actually was quite progressive. An alternative view is that the early scholars discriminated on the basis of gender by inserting their own cultural views into the law, thereby assigning them normative value for all later generations of Muslims.[7] On this basis, the argument goes, Islamic law can be, and ought to be, reinterpreted on the basis of Qur'anic ethical principles. Such a step would reform the law insofar as women and gender are concerned.

The Muʿtazili-Traditionist Clash

Though the law was the central contribution of the early scholars, they devoted themselves to other areas of religious thought as well. The closely related disciplines of philosophy and theology, for example, preoccupied scholars throughout the early Islamic period. Both disciplines relied heavily upon rational argumentation. The debate over the appropriate use of human reason, strongly influenced by Greek philosophy, proved divisive. The proto-Sunni scholars held a spectrum of views on this problem. The general traditionist view—associated, for example, with the Hanbali *madhhab*—was that humankind should rely to the greatest extent possible upon divine guidance (Qur'an and *Sunna*); human reason was prone to error (and, therefore, sin), whereas divine guidance was infallible. Rationalist thought, in sum, was to be sharply limited.

A very different point of view is associated with the Mu'tazili movement, which emerged in Basra at an early stage and became prominent in Baghdad through the mid-ninth century. The movement was the foremost example in early Islamic history of a "rationalist school," heavily influenced by *kalam* (often translated as "rational theology") a major component of early Islamic thought. *Kalam* emerged from the interaction of early Muslims with proponents of other religious systems, principally Judaism and Christianity, and the influences of Greek philosophical thought. It provided Muslims with the techniques of argumentation long in use in the pre-Islamic Near East, and the early Muslims developed them as they engaged in polemics with non-Muslims (and each other).

Using the style and techniques of *kalam*, the Mu'tazilis developed controversial ideas concerning God and God's Word (i.e., the Qur'an). A key tenet concerned the Qur'anic insistence that God is utterly one and utterly different from all created things. This meant, to the Mu'tazilis, that any references to God's attributes (His hands, sight, and hearing, for example) must be considered in allegorical or symbolic terms. In other words, God cannot "see" or "act" as human beings do. On this basis, the Mu'tazilis concluded that the Qur'an itself ("God's speech") must also be separate from God. It followed, then, that since only God is eternal, the Qur'an, like all other things, was created. The Mu'tazilis placed emphasis upon reason and logic above all. If the Qur'an or *Sunna* held ideas that did not stand up to reason, they were to be rejected. In their view, the "createdness" of the Qur'an was the only logical way to solve the puzzle of "God's speech."

Their opponents were aghast: in their view, the Qur'an was a manifestation of God and could not be held apart. Any attempt to argue otherwise was to diminish the significance of the Book, an unimaginable step. Debate between the Mu'tazili and traditionist camps raged through the ninth century. Over the long term, Mu'tazili thought remained influential, particularly in Twelver Shi'i circles. But the debates with the traditionists took their toll among the proto-Sunnis, and by the tenth century, the Mu'tazili movement had largely faded from view.

The Mihna

The idea of the "createdness" of the Qur'an was not solely a Mu'tazili idea. It was shared by other groups, notably students of Abu Hanifa, a Baghdadi scholar and *qadi* under the caliph al-Mansur. (He is considered the founder of the Hanafi *madhhab*.) But it was closely associated with the Mu'tazilis. Controversy surrounding the doctrine mounted as leading Mu'tazilis came to exert influence over the early Abbasid court. One such figure, the *qadi* Ahmad ibn Abi Du'ad (d. 854), together with the caliph al-Ma'mun, used the "createdness" doctrine as the centerpiece of a campaign to assert authority over the religious scholars. The campaign, known as the *Mihna* (inquisition), was initiated very late in al-Ma'mun's reign (833). In letters sent to local officials in Baghdad, Egypt, and other locales, the caliph ordered leading scholars, most of them traditionists, to declare their support for the "createdness" doctrine.

Historians argue over the goal of the *Mihna*. All agree that al-Ma'mun was attempting to assert the full political and religious authority of the caliphate. One view is that he did so in order to reconcile with the Shi'a by representing the caliphate in terms similar to those of the Shi'i imamate. A more prominent view is that al-Ma'mun was seeking to renew the claim that the caliph, by virtue of his office and descent from the Prophet's clan, should wield full religious authority. If this was his goal, it failed. Most historians agree that the *Mihna* represented the final attempt to assert the right of the caliph to define Islamic law and doctrine. The *Mihna* continued through the reigns of al-Mu'tasim (833–842) and al-Wathiq (842–847), but was brought to an end by al-Mutawakkil (847–861). Although a number of scholars, under pressure, accepted the doctrine, the opposition of other leading figures, notably Ahmad ibn Hanbal, had made the campaign deeply unpopular, particularly in Baghdad. In this last confrontation, in sum, the scholars triumphed and authority over Sunni religious life remained in their hands from that point forward.

NOTES

1. For other discussions of the Hadith of Gabriel, see Sachiko Murata and William C. Chittick, *The Vision of Islam*, pp. xxv–xxxiv; and Vincent J. Cornell,

"Fruit of the Tree of Knowledge," in John Esposito, ed., *The Oxford History of Islam*, pp. 75–90.

2. See David Waines, *An Introduction to Islam*, pp. 129–132; and Farid Esack, *The Qur'an*, pp. 157–165.

3. Feisal Abdul Rauf, *What's Right with Islam*, p. 61.

4. See Patricia Crone, *Medieval Islamic Political Thought*, p. 43.

5. Patricia Crone, *Medieval Islamic Political Thought*, pp. 125–141.

6. Jonathan Berkey, *Formation of Islam*, p. 143.

7. Document 11 contains an extract of an early Hanbali legal text on marriage and divorce.

CHAPTER 6

THE ISLAMIC WORLD IN THE EARLY TENTH CENTURY

The Arab-Islamic conquests, the creation of a centralized empire, and the ongoing processes of Arabization and Islamization transformed the political, cultural, and religious landscape of the Near East, North Africa, and beyond. Muslims had become sizable minorities in many regions by the early tenth century. In Iran and the Near East, particularly in the large urban centers, they were poised to become a majority if they had not already done so. Through military expansion, conversion, trade, and education, Islam also was poised to make major inroads into Central Asia, Saharan Africa, and the Indian Ocean basin. Islam, in its variety of form and expression, had emerged as a major faith alongside Judaism, Christianity, and Buddhism. The present chapter considers features of the political and religious landscape of the tenth-century Islamic world.

THE POLITICAL MAP: THREE CALIPHATES

By the end of the ninth century, the Abbasid Empire had nearly collapsed, its military weakness particularly apparent. The civil war between al-Amin and al-Ma'mun early that century had divided the political and military elite of the empire. The defeat of the *Abna*, and the rise of new and unpopular Central Asian and Turkish regiments in Samarra, had further weakened the caliphate, in part by driving a wedge more deeply between the imperial state and the populace at large. Perhaps the most obvious sign of a faltering military capability was the length of time it took to contain an uprising in southern Iraq by the Zanj, a population of East African slaves employed to reclaim unproductive lands in the lower Tigris. The revolt persisted for roughly fifteen years (869–883), seriously draining the empire's military and fiscal resources. Added to these woes was the challenge of containing numerous Shi'i movements, particularly those of the Isma'ili Shi'a.

By the early tenth century, the imperial state faced internal crises as well, due to mismanagement, corruption, and the corrosive effect of rivalries among powerful civilian cliques. By this point most of the major provinces, including Egypt, Syria, and Khurasan, had become independent of the imperial center. Indeed, at times Abbasid authority barely extended beyond Iraq. Underlying the loss of political strength was a terrible economic situation brought on the permanent loss of provincial revenue. War, unrest, and poor administration brought a decline in agricultural production and further loss of revenue. The Abbasids had become poor and weak, and were hemmed in on all sides by political rivals. Al-Mustakfi (r. 944–946), the reigning caliph, had little choice but to welcome the newly arrived Buwayhids (945), a family from the northern region of Daylam who introduced a new style of government into the now fragmented Islamic political world: that of the military strongman. Amid this collapse of Abbasid authority, two rival powers announced their claim to the caliphate. In both cases, the challenge to the Abbasids was clear and deliberate.

The first of the two challenges came from the Fatimids in Ifriqiya. The Fatimid state had been established (909) by a branch of the Isma'ili Shi'i movement backed by Kutama Berber tribesmen. The Fatimids derived their name from that of Fatima (the Prophet's daughter and wife of Ali ibn Abi Talib). The Fatimids at first struggled to consolidate their new state. The effort required the suppression of Khariji and Sunni opposition in North Africa. A further step was to proclaim the first of the Fatimid rulers, Abdallah al-Mahdi (r. 909–934), as caliph, a gesture clearly aimed at the (Sunni) Abbasids in Baghdad. By this point, Abdallah had announced that he was a direct descendant of Muhammad ibn Isma'il (grandson of Ja'far al-Sadiq). Fatimid rulers, from this point on, would draw upon both sources of authority. For the majority of their subjects, they reigned as caliphs, the heads of an imperial state; in the eyes of their Isma'ili followers, they were the living and infallible representatives of God on earth, the *imams*.

Fatimid armies waged campaigns to the west as far as Morocco and seized control of Sicily. The Fatimids showed special interest in Egypt, however, control of which would provide substantial revenue and an important boost in the campaign to replace the Abbasid caliphate. Three initial campaigns against Egypt failed; a fourth attempt, under al-Mu'izz (r. 953–975), was successful. It followed extensive military and fiscal planning under Jawhar al-Siqilli, a former slave of Slavic origins and a longtime commander. Shortly after the conquest, the name of al-Mu'izz was proclaimed in the principal mosque of al-Fustat (969). Jawhar was also responsible for the creation of a new capital, known initially as al-Mansuriya, erected outside al-Fustat.

The stage was set for al-Mu'izz to take up residence in Egypt. Shortly after his arrival in 973, the new capital was renamed al-Qahira al-Mu'izziya or, simply, al-Qahira (the Victorious). (The English form of the name is Cairo.) This second phase of Fatimid history (969–1073) witnessed the transformation of Cairo from a small administrative center to one of the premier cities of the Mediterranean world. Control of Egypt provided the Fatimid caliphs with the human and financial resources to expand their realm. Territorial expansion, particularly into Syria and Iraq, allowed the Fatimids to make good on their challenge to the Abbasids. At its height, under the caliph al-Aziz (r. 975–996), Fatimid sovereignty was recognized across North Africa and the Near East.

The second claim to the caliphate was issued from across the Mediterranean. The Iberian Peninsula had fallen to Arab-Islamic forces in the first quarter of the eighth century and was known henceforth as al-Andalus. By roughly 750, the year of the Abbasid revolution, all but the northwestern corner of Spain was under Arab-Muslim control. Developments in the Near East, despite the distance of Spain from the eastern Mediterranean, had a direct effect upon the history of al-Andalus. The Abbasid rise to power, and the shift of the caliphate to Iraq, is a case in point. Among the very few Umayyads (in Syria) to survive the Abbasid takeover was a young prince, Abd al-Rahman. His dramatic flight across North Africa ended with his entry into Cordoba, the capital of Islamic Spain (756). His arrival marked the foundation of the Umayyad dynasty of al-Andalus.

The new Umayyad house at first paid homage to the Abbasids, though mostly in symbolic fashion since the Umayyads enjoyed nearly total fiscal and political autonomy. During his reign (756–788), Abd al-Rahman largely unified the peninsula through careful administration and a keen sensitivity to the ethnic complexity of his realm. Lavish construction in Cordoba, including the city's Great Mosque, marked the city's emergence as the premier urban center of the western Mediterranean. Historians cite the comment of a tenth-century Christian observer, Hroswitha of Gandersheim, that Cordoba was "the ornament of the world," a reference to the remarkable cultural life of the city. The energy of early Islamic Spain was rooted not simply in the wealth of the Umayyad state, in which agriculture, extensive Mediterranean trade, and technological advances all played their part. It was also related to the Umayyad commitment to intellectual and cultural pursuits by Muslim and non-Muslim alike.

Abd al-Rahman III (r. 912–961) asserted a claim to the caliphate some sixteen years into his reign. The evidence indicates that he did so in direct response to news of Abbasid frailty in Iraq and the rise of the Shi'i-Fatimid caliphate in Ifriqiya.[1] News of the announcement startled foes and supporters alike: rulers of three caliphates now reigned over distinct regions of the Islamic world (though by now the Abbasids were by far the weakest of the three). Each naturally viewed the others as rivals and usurpers. The significance of these developments is twofold. First, by the mid-tenth century, the Islamic world had taken on a striking cultural, political, and religious complexity. Second, the rival claims from Cairo and Cordoba signaled to the Abbasids—as if they needed a reminder—that the days of their preeminence were over.

THE RELIGIOUS LANDSCAPE

The major currents of Islamic thought and practice (Shi'i and Sunni) became more clearly defined in the tenth century. It was a significant period for all branches of Shi'ism. The Hamdanids, the dynasty that ruled northern Syria and areas of Iraq through the tenth century, were Shi'a. Their patronage led the Syrian city of Aleppo, for example, to flourish as a center of Twelver practice and scholarship. The Buwayhids were of Shi'i origin as well. The family, initially attached to the Zaydi sect, shifted its allegiance to the Twelver Shi'a following its rise to power in Iraq and Fars. Twelver scholars, with Buwayhid support, elaborated the system of doctrine concerning the Twelfth Imam and the theory of *ghayba*. Allowed to worship openly, the Twelvers also introduced new forms of practice, chiefly the public ceremonies marking al-Husayn's martyrdom at Karbala, a centerpiece of the Shi'i religious calendar to the present day.

No less significant were developments in Isma'ili Shi'ism. Fatimid patronage in Egypt led to a burst of Isma'ili scholarship. Al-Nu'man ibn Abi'Abdallah (d. 974), founder of a distinguished line of Fatimid *qadis*, contributed numerous works on law and doctrine during the North African phase of Fatimid history that became the basis for all later Isma'ili scholarship. The Fatimids also devoted considerable sums to architecture, including the construction of the congregational mosques of al-Azhar and al-Hakim. Al-Azhar acquired the reputation as a center of education and scholarship, in part due to the patronage of Ya'qub ibn Yusuf ibn Killis (d. 991), a convert from Judaism and the first *wazir* of the Fatimid state. It does not appear, however, that a majority of Muslims chose to adhere to Shi'ism, whether in Iraq or in Egypt. Most followed the example and leadership of the Sunni scholars.

Like their Shi'i counterparts, the Sunni scholars would be involved in a variety of forms of activity from this point on. Relations with the Buwayhids and, by extension, all successor states to the caliphate would consume much of their energy. The Abbasids, probably even more than the Umayyads before them, had claimed a mix of of religious and political authority. Though the Sunni scholars eventually negated that claim, the caliphs had played an active role in religious law and practice at an early stage. The Buwayhids could pretend to no such role: even a claim to religious authority would have seemed ludicrous. The Buwayhids were in power, however, so for the Sunni scholars the challenge was to create working relations with a new type of political regime, one dominated by military men and their civilian advisers. This delicate and often uneasy task quickly emerged as a major theme of Near Eastern/Islamic history.[2] The relationship was made all the more complex by virtue of the fact that the Buwayhids offered strong support to Twelver Shi'ism.

The law, the centerpiece of Sunni Islam, was a second area of activity. The legal scholars (*faqih*; pl., *fuqaha*) continued their work as educators, training new generations of jurists and judges. By this time the Shafi'i, Hanafi, and Hanbali "schools" (*madhahib*) dominated legal education in Baghdad and the surrounding provinces. The fourth Sunni school, the Maliki *madhhab*, predominated in North Africa (as it does to the present day). Alongside teaching, the *fuqaha* devoted much effort to

the writing of legal commentaries and manuals. Among the principal figures of the early Abbasid period was Muhammad ibn al-Hasan al-
Shaybani (d. 805), two of whose works are considered critical to the
emergence of the Hanafi school.[3] Abu al-Abbas ibn Surayj (d. 918) was
to play a similar role, at a somewhat later point, in relation to the Shafi'i
madhhab.

The careers of al-Shaybani and Ibn Surayj are a reminder that legal
scholars had professional options as well. Both men were employed by the
Abbasid administration as qadis. Al-Shaybani served as qadi of al-Raqqa
under Harun al-Rashid; Ibn Surayj held a similar post as a young scholar.
The office of qadi dated to the early Umayyad period and remained a vital
element of the judicial system of the Islamic world into the Abbasid period and beyond. The Abbasids established a new office, the qadi al-qudat
(chief qadi), a post generally held by a leading Baghdadi scholar. The religious scholars accepted such offices with discomfort, for it meant that
one was now an official of the state and therefore a participant in the
morally murky world of politics. It was a troubling choice and, from at
least the early Abbasid period, prominent scholars declined appointments
on these grounds. At a late point in his career, for example, Ibn Surayj
refused a second appointment as qadi (this time in Baghdad).

Scholars were also appointed to the post of market inspector
(muhtasib). The term means, literally, "one who practices hisba," an important Islamic concept generally translated as the duty of every Muslim
to "promote the good and forbid the wrong." The phrase appears numerous times in the Qur'an: "Let there arise from you one community,
inviting all to what is good, commanding what is right and forbidding
what is wrong" (Surat al-Imran, 3:104). The specific duties of the muhtasib
were rooted in this broad concept. First and foremost was the regulation
of weights and measures: shoppers were not to be cheated. He was also
to check the quality of merchandise, the preparation of cooked foods,
and the cleanliness of stalls, sidewalks, and streets. This was a government post: jurists, upon their appointment, were paid a regular salary and
were usually provided with scribes and troops to enable them to execute
their duties. The posts of qadi and muhtasib were closely related, and in
some cases were held by the same official. The history of both positions
underscores the complicated relationship between religious scholars and
the political establishment in early Islamic history.

NOTES

1. Document 15, which provides a rather glowing account of Abd al-Rahman's reign, refers to the decision.

2. See, for example, Jonathan Berkey, *Formation of Islam*, pp. 203–215.

3. Document 4 is an extract of one of his works.

1. The Ka'ba in Mecca. A pre-Islamic structure, it is referred to in the Islamic tradition as the House of God and is held to have been built by Adam, then reconstructed by Abraham. Before the Prophet Muhammad's lifetime, the site was devoted to idols. These the Prophet destroyed thereby "purifying" the Ka'ba. He is said to have then instituted the performance of pilgrimage rites at the site. *Library of Congress*.

2. Page from a ninth-century Qur'an. This fragment contains part of the second *Sura* (Surat al-Baqara) of the Qur'an and comes from a manuscript written either in Egypt or Iraq. Calligraphy, from very early on, became a dominant Arab-Islamic cultural form. This manuscript, written in an Arabic script known as Kufic, was produced on vellum. This was replaced by paper generally by the mid-ninth century though it remained in use for Qur'an manuscripts for several centuries thereafter. *Metropolitan Museum of Art, gift of Philip Hofer, 1937. (37.142)*

3. Three early Arab-Islamic coins. The coins, minted under Abd al-Malik (see Chapter 3), illustrate the creation of an Arab-Islamic coinage. The first, dated 693–694, retains the elements of pre-Islamic Sassanid coinage, such as the head of the Sassanid monarch, but adds an Arabic inscription. The middle coin, dated to 693–696, contains Arabic and an image of the standing caliph. The final coin, a gold dinar dated to 697–698, is totally Islamic. The left-hand image, for example, has the phrase "There is no god but God, the One [God], who shares [His divinity] with no one." *ANS/Michael Bates*.

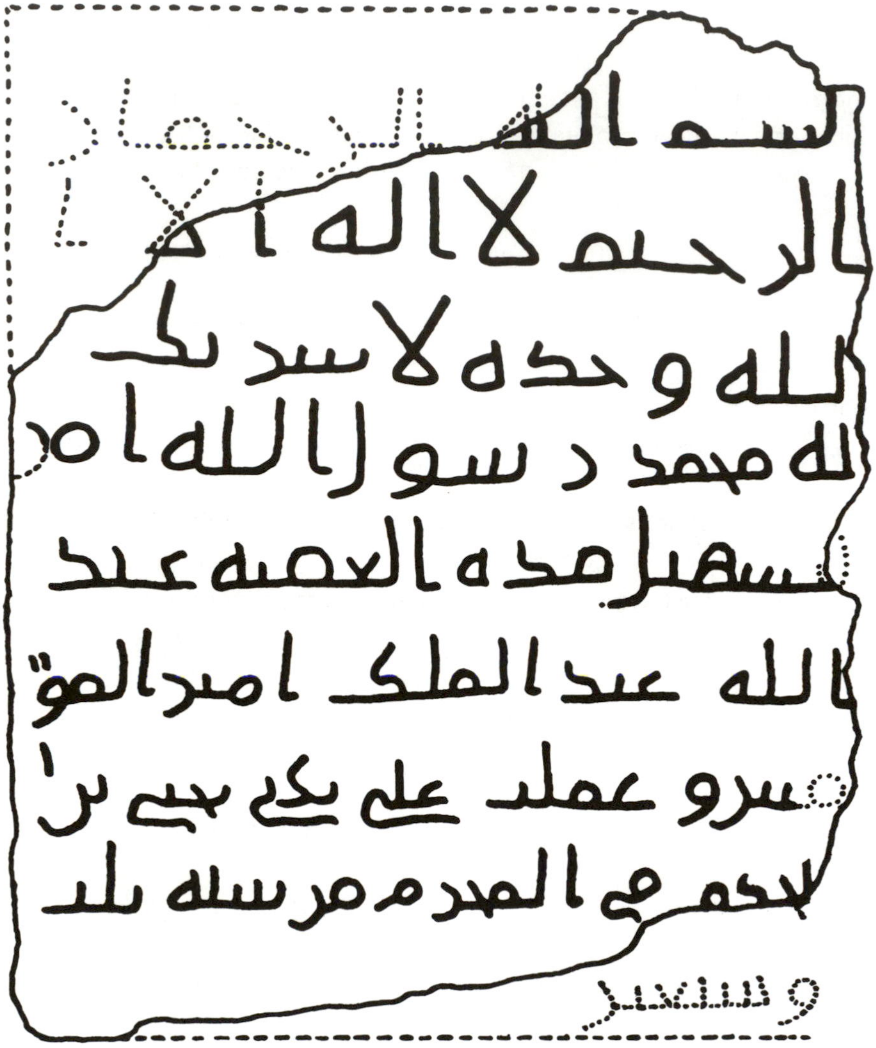

بسم الله الرحـ...

الرحمن لا اله الا

الله وحده لا شريك

الله محمد رسول الله

...ه صلى الله...

الله عبد الملك امير المؤ

...رو عمـل... علي يكي بر

...حم في المدد مر سله بل

وسـتين

4. An Umayyad-period milestone. Carved in the 690s, this milestone probably was meant to commemorate a new road connecting Damascus and Jerusalem. On it are the names of Yahya ibn al-Hakam, the official who likely carried out the project, and Abd al-Malik, the reigning caliph. Inscriptions of this kind served as a type of propaganda, to draw attention to the good works of the sovereign. *Miami University.*

5. The Great Mosque of Samarra. Samarra replaced Baghdad as the Abbasid capital from 836 to 892. It contained, as one would expect, much monumental architecture. The Great Mosque, completed around 852, was constructed by the caliph al-Mutawakkil. Its walls and distinctive minaret were restored by the Iraqi state in the late twentieth century. The unusual circular design of the minaret, found also at the Abu Dulaf mosque (Samarra) and the Ibn Tulun mosque (Cairo), was borrowed either from a Sassanid or possibly ancient Mesopotamian pattern. *Simmons Aerofilms Limited.*

6. Ceramic bowl from Nishapur or Samarqand. Measuring 18 inches in diameter, this is a fine example of ninth- and tenth-century Iranian/Central Asian ceramics. The development of new techniques of ceramic design points to a busy commerce in manufactured goods readily consumed by elite urban populations in this period. The stylized Arabic inscription around the top interior of the bowl reads: "Planning before work protects you from regret. Prosperity and peace." *Metropolitan Museum of Art, Rogers Fund, 1965. (65. 106.2)*

7. Seljuq incense burner. Made of bronze, this wonderful piece dates to around 1182. By that date, much of the Islamic Near East was controlled by the Seljuqs, a Central Asian Turkish clan. The Seljuqs had swept into the region in the mid-eleventh century, taking Baghdad from the Buwayhid Dynasty (see Chapter 6) in 1055. The inscriptions and design of this piece reflect a mix of Near Eastern and Central Asian motifs. Its elegance clearly suggests the lively commerce in luxury goods characteristic of the Near East throughout the early and middle Islamic periods. *Metropolitan Museum of Art, Rogers Fund, 1951. (51.56)*

BIOGRAPHIES

Abdallah al-Ma'mun (d. 833)

The eldest son of Harun al-Rashid (d. 809), al-Ma'mun seized the caliphate from his brother Muhammad al-Amin (r. 809–813) in the course of a bitter civil war. His years in power (813–833) were marred by regional unrest and conflict on the Byzantine frontier, a combination of factors that nearly led to the collapse of the Islamic Empire despite concerted efforts by al-Ma'mun to reverse their effect.

The conflict with al-Amin arose, in part, from sibling rivalry and other short-term causes and, in part, from more deeply rooted issues including a debate over relations between Baghdad (the imperial center) and the provinces. Provocative gestures on both sides led to civil conflict. Early in the war (811), outside the city of Rayy, Tahir ibn al-Husayn (d. 822), a Persian *mawla* from Khurasan, routed al-Amin's forces, commanded by Ali ibn Isa ibn Mahan (d. 811), a prominent member of the *Abna* of Baghdad. Al-Ma'mun was declared caliph following a yearlong siege of Baghdad and the killing of al-Amin (813). He soon faced empirewide opposition, first, to the policies of al-Fadl ibn Sahl (d. 817), al-Ma'mun's chief adviser, and, second, to al-Ma'mun's nomination of Ali al-Rida (d. 817), a Shi'i notable (and, later, Twelver Shi'i *imam*), as his successor (a decision soon reversed). Al-Ma'mun's arrival in Baghdad (819) brought relative calm to Iraq. To restore central control over Syria and Egypt, the caliph turned to Tahir's son Abdallah (d. 828), who waged several successful campaigns of reunification. The Tahirids, and new military forces recruited by al-Ma'mun and his influential brother, Abu Ishaq, replaced the *Abna* and other forces that had brought the dynasty to power. Abu Ishaq succeeded to the caliphate as al-Mu'tasim (r. 833–842).

As a younger man, al-Ma'mun received a classical education in Arabic, literature, the arts, and religious sciences. A devoted patron of culture and intellectual life throughout his long reign, he is associated with two broad initiatives. The first was the translation into Arabic of Greek, Persian, Syriac, and Sanskrit texts, works of pre-Islamic civilizations. The effort, probably initiated by Abu Ja'far al-Mansur, took a strong step forward under al-Ma'mun. The remarkable contributions of Arabic mathematics, medicine, astronomy, and philosophy were, in part, the fruit of Hellenistic, Iranian, and Indian influences upon Arab-Islamic thought. The second initiative was the *Mihna* (see Chapter 5), a campaign targeted at leading religious circles and probably rooted in al-Ma'mun's desire to assert the religious authority of the caliphate.

Abd al-Malik ibn Marwan (d. 705)

Abd al-Malik is widely viewed as the most significant member of the Umayyad dynasty after Mu'awiya I. He assumed office following the death of his father, Marwan I (r. 684–685). Recognition of his caliphate extended, however, only to Syria and Egypt, then governed by his brother, Abd al-Aziz ibn Marwan. The remaining provinces acknowledged the caliphate of Abdallah ibn al-Zubayr, a member of the Quraysh based in the Hijaz. Zubayrid forces, under Mus'ab ibn al-Zubayr, would control Iraq, and the garrison centers of Kufa and Basra, for an extended period. Following the conclusion of a truce with Byzantium, Abd al-Malik pursued the war with the Zubayrids, emerging triumphant following the death of Abdallah ibn al-Zubayr in Mecca (692).

The subsequent period of his reign brought campaigns against internal opposition (Khariji revolts and a military uprising led by one Ibn al-Ash'ath, partly in Iraq) and, on the northern frontier, the Byzantines. In these efforts, Abd al-Malik drew significant support from al-Hajjaj ibn Yusuf (d. 714), governor of Iraq after 694, and al-Muhallab ibn Abi Sufra (d. 702), an influential figure who led the campaign against the Azariqa Kharijis, then became governor of Khurasan (698–702). Al-Hajjaj worked closely with Abd al-Malik in fashioning a series of administrative reforms for which the latter's caliphate is perhaps best known. Historians associate the reforms with the related processes of Arabization and Islamization that are a hallmark of the Umayyad period. The principal aim of the reforms, however, was the centralization of the empire under Abd al-Malik's control.

The first, and perhaps most important, measures involved the substitution of Arabic as the language of administration in place of Greek and Persian, the languages of the Byzantine and Sasanid empires. Abd al-Malik also reformed the imperial coinage by introducing a new Islamic gold *dinar*. He is credited as well with the building of the Dome of the Rock, the well-known monument atop the Temple Mount in Jerusalem. As the first major structure of the Islamic era, it is variously understood as a powerful symbol of Islamic triumph over Judaism and Christianity and a clear assertion of Islam's distinctiveness as a religious tradition. In all, Abd al-Malik's reforms, in conjunction with the military successes of his reign, ushered in a period of stable rule that lasted through the reigns of his immediate successors. The first of these, his eldest son, al-Walid ibn Abd al-Malik (r. 705–715), was responsible for construction of the Great Mosque in Damascus.

Abu Ja'far al-Mansur (d. 775)

Abu Ja'far, the second ruler of the Abbasid dynasty, played only a secondary role in the early part of the Abbasid revolution. Following the accession to the caliphate of his brother, Abu al-Abbas al-Saffah (r. 750–754), Abu Ja'far oversaw the siege of Wasit in the final campaigns against Umayyad forces. Appointed as governor of the northern provinces of al-Jazira and Armenia, he used family ties and connections to the revolutionary forces to build a political base. Designated as heir apparent by his brother, Abu Ja'far took the title al-Mansur (the Victorious) upon his assumption of office (754).

His initial years in office were devoted to quelling opposition. His uncle, Abdallah ibn Ali (d. 764), having organized a force against Byzantium, chose instead to bid for the caliphate, an act that Abu Ja'far countered with the support of Abu Muslim's Khurasani army. His ability to mend fences thereafter with the Syrian and Khurasani commanders of his uncle's army was an early demonstration of his political acumen. Abu Muslim, a formidable figure, was dealt with in turn; his arrest and execution (755) allowed al-Mansur to appoint his own officials in Khurasan. The province remained largely autonomous, however, and was the site of occasional uprisings through the early Abbasid period. Following the suppression of a major proto-Shiʻi revolt (762), al-Mansur turned his attention to a consolidation of authority over the imperial state, widely seen as a hallmark of his reign.

Among his achievements in this regard were the integration of the Khurasani military elite into the imperial administration; the expansion of the central bureaucracy, with a notable rise in the numbers of officials of Iranian descent; and, above all, the foundation of a new capital at Baghdad. Intended initially to house the bureaucracy and the imperial regiments (specifically the Khurasani forces of the revolution), the city grew to include large commercial areas and civilian neighborhoods. It retained its role as a cultural and intellectual hub for centuries. Al-Mansur's style of government is noted for its severity in later Arab-Islamic sources; modern historians credit him with having firmly established Abbasid control over the empire. His son, and successor, Muhammad al-Mahdi (r. 775–785), continued many of his father's policies. A notable exception was his overture to the Shiʻa, with which al-Mansur had had poor relations.

Abu Musa Bugha the Elder (d. 862)

Bugha the Elder, a prominent member of the ninth-century Samarran Turkish military, served the Abbasid caliphate for roughly thirty years, primarily as a field commander. It is difficult to know to which of several Central Asian peoples Bugha belonged, though he is generally called a Turk. According to a tenth-century Arabic source, Bugha and his sons were enslaved by Ghassan ibn Abbad, governor of Khurasan (818–821) during the reign of al-Maʾmun. He and presumably his sons were then acquired, at great cost, by Abu Ishaq al-Muʻtasim, an Abbasid prince. The purchase took place in Baghdad around 820. Abu Ishaq offered hefty sums to elite Baghdadi households for their Turkish slaves, evidence of a lively market in slavery in the Abbasid capital. Abu Ishaq, perhaps on behalf of al-Maʾmun, formed the slave recruits into an elite guard.

Following his rise to power, al-Muʻtasim transferred his administration and military to Samarra (located north of Baghdad). Upon his foundation of Samarra, he distributed land grants to a number of civilian and military notables, Bugha among them. Over subsequent decades, Bugha led armies into various regions of the empire. His first command, under al-Mu'tasim, was against Babak al-Khurrami, head of a dangerous uprising in Azerbaijan. Under al-Wathiq (r. 842–847), Bugha led an army into southern Syria and the northern Hijaz to secure stretches of the pilgrimage route against Arab tribal raiders. Under al-Mutawakkil (r. 847–861), he waged his longest campaign, against an uprising of local nobles in Armenia (852–856). His next and final campaign (858–861) was along the Byzantine frontier. His death the following year (862) ended a long and impressive career.

Bugha was widely viewed as a loyal and reliable member of the military command—quite in contrast with other Turkish officers, whose involvement in palace intrigues led them, during a particularly unsettled period of Samarran history, to assassinate three, if not four, sitting caliphs. The evidence indicates that Bugha played little part in the events in Samarra. He was survived by three sons, one of whom, Musa ibn Bugha (d. 877), played a prominent role in both politics and the military in the late ninth century. A second son, Abu Nasr Muhammad, fell victim to one of many outbreaks of violence in Samarra (870).

Abu Ubayda al-Buhturi (d. 897)

Al-Buhturi, a leading ninth-century poet and anthologist, was born in Manbij (northern Syria), into the Buhtur clan of the Arab Tayyi tribe. As a young poet, he produced love poetry and panegyric odes known as *qasidas* (see below) in praise of his tribe. His verse caught the attention of a Tayyi military chief, at whose house he met Abu Tammam (d. 845). The older poet had earned a place at the court of al-Mu'tasim, largely for his panegyric verse in honor of the caliph. Abu Tammam took the younger man under his wing, providing him with instruction in versemaking and introductions to elite society, initially in provincial Mesopotamia and later in Baghdad. Al-Buhturi's failure to express much grief at the death of Abu Tammam is seen as the first instance of the selfabsorption for which he would become famous.

His break came in 848 when al-Fath ibn Khaqan (d. 861), a leading member of al-Mutawakkil's court, introduced him to the caliph. Al-Buhturi established close ties to both men and remained a fixture of the Abbasid court for years. Al-Mutawakkil is the subject of a significant portion of his extant verse. His poems contain many references to political developments in the Samarra period, among them the construction of al-Mutawakkiliya, a new area of the city. Upon the caliph's assassination (861), al-Buhturi retired briefly to Manbij, then re-emerged as a favorite of al-Mu'tazz (r. 846–869), for whom he wrote panegyrics. His last Abbasid patron was al-Mu'tadid (r. 892–902). Al-Buhturi subsequently moved to Egypt, where he established himself at the court of Khumarawayh ibn Tulun (r. 884–896), the second member of the Tulunid dynasty. He retired to Manbij, where he died after a long illness.

Al-Buhturi devoted most of his writing to the panegyric form. He relied, for the most part, on the classical form of the *qasida*, which was a traditional three-part poem, usually of uniform rhyme and meter. He remained a favorite of literary critics through the centuries for his clear, musical style and fine descriptions. He is usually listed, along with Abu Tammam and al-Mutanabbi (d. 955), as one of the great Abbasid poets. Many of his peers apparently thought little of him. He had many rivals, which was natural enough, given his standing in palace society—although his obnoxious behavior probably was also to blame. One biographer refers to al-Buhturi's habit of roundly criticizing audiences for insufficient appreciation of his genius.

Ahmad ibn Hanbal (d. 855)

A preeminent figure of early Islamic scholarship, Ibn Hanbal is probably best known for the Sunni legal tradition (*madhhab*) that bears his name. (The Hanbali "school" predominates today in Saudi Arabia.) Of Arab descent, Ibn Hanbal was born into the Banu Shayban of the Rabi'a tribe that had played an important role in the Arab conquest of Iraq and Khurasan. His father and grandfather having played a part in the Abbasid revolution, Ibn Hanbal was raised and educated in Baghdad. As a young man, he traveled through Iraq and the Hijaz, carrying out the *Hajj* on several occasions and studying. Listed among his teachers are several prominent eighth-century scholars.

He gained public attention during the *Mihna* (see Chapter 5) for his vigorous opposition to the doctrine of the "createdness" of the Qur'an. For their stance, he and a like-minded colleague, Muhammad ibn Nuh (d. 833), were ordered arrested and brought before al-Ma'mun. Upon the caliph's sudden death, he was returned to prison in Baghdad. The new caliph, al-Mu'tasim, an unenthusiastic supporter of the *Mihna*, was pushed by his adviser, Ahmad ibn Abi Du'ad (d. 854), to harshly interrogate Ibn Hanbal. Some Arabic sources report that Ibn Hanbal, after a particularly humiliating session, finally gave in, though other sources, particularly those by later Hanbali scholars, insist that he stood firm. He is said to have remained in seclusion for some years thereafter. Following the decision by the caliph al-Mutawakkil (r. 847–861) to reverse the *Mihna*, Ibn Hanbal regained favorable standing at court, at one point invited to a meeting with the caliph al-Mu'tazz (r. 866–869).

Ibn Hanbal's best-known work, a collection of Hadith of the Prophet and his companions, is known as the *Musnad*. Following Ibn Hanbal's death, his tomb became the site of Sunni pilgrimage until the fourteenth century, when it is reported to have been swept away in a flood. Two of his sons, Salih ibn Ahmad (d. 880) and Abdallah ibn Ahmad (d. 828), were among his closest followers and, as such, contributed to the formation of the Hanbali *madhhab*.

A'isha bint Abi Bakr (d. 678)

The Prophet is said to have entered into additional marriages only after the death of his first wife, Khadija, in most cases in order to strengthen ties either to his own following or to prominent Hijazi tribes. A'isha, the daughter of Abu Bakr, an influential Meccan and the Prophet's close adviser, probably was chosen for this reason. Born in Mecca, she became the Prophet's third wife in 623, at the age of nine, according to the early biographies. The sources report that the Prophet took part in her childhood games early in their marriage and that she was his preferred wife at the time of his death. One line of argument sees in her eventful life evidence that women enjoyed wide access to public life prior to the introduction of Islamic law. The point is controversial since it is widely maintained, in the Islamic tradition, that Islamic law in fact improved the standing of women by initiating social and legal reforms.

The first of several noteworthy episodes in her life occurred outside Medina (627). On the return from one of the Prophet's campaigns, A'isha was accidentally left behind when the caravan moved on. She was rescued by a young man, Safwan ibn al-Muʿattal, who accompanied her to Medina. When opponents accused her of having committed adultery with Safwan, Muhammad hurried to her defense, citing revelation (*Surat al-Nur*, 24:11–20) that spoke of her innocence and roundly condemning her accusers. Other defenders noted the lack of evidence against her. Despite her vindication, the accusation remained and, over the centuries, was repeated by detractors, Shiʿi scholars most notably (see below).

Following the Prophet's death (632), Aʾisha, now a childless widow, apparently took no part in politics until Uthman's caliphate. She joined the opposition to Uthman ostensibly on religious grounds, arguing, like others in the community, that his policies violated Qurʾanic teachings and the Prophet's example. Her political activity continued following Uthman's assassination when she joined Talha and al-Zubayr in opposing Ali's caliphate. The respective armies clashed at the Battle of the Camel, so called because much of the fighting is said to have taken place around the camel bearing her litter. Upon Ali's victory, Aʾisha was placed under house arrest in Medina and apparently took no further part in politics.

The biographical dictionaries indicate that she devoted the remaining years of her life to scholarship and religious instruction. As a result of her role in transmitting information about the Prophet's life and teachings, she is regularly named as an authority in Sunni Hadith collections. Aʾisha remains a controversial figure in Islamic society. Alongside Khadija and the Prophet's daughter Fatima, she is among the best-known women of the early Islamic period. Various strands of modern Islamic feminism see her as an exemplary Muslim, both for her relationship to the Prophet and for her piety and scholarship. In Shiʿi writings, however, she is still sharply criticized, both for her alleged adultery and for her opposition to Ali ibn Abi Talib.

Ali ibn Abi Talib (d. 661)

Ali, a member of the Prophet's clan, the Banu Hashim, was the fourth of the Rashidun caliphs. Abu Talib (d. 619), his father, protected the Prophet against the Quraysh early in Muhammad's career. One of the first converts to Islam, Ali became the Prophet's son-in-law upon his marriage to Fatima. Their sons, al-Hasan and al-Husayn, played a significant role in early Islamic politics and are revered as *imams* by the various Shi'i traditions. Following Fatima's death, Ali married again. A third son, Muhammad ibn al-Hanafiyya, born to a concubine, achieved prominence as well among the early Iraqi Shi'a.

Following the Prophet's death, Ali gained wide respect for his knowledge of the Qur'an and the events of the Prophet's life. He went on to counsel Abu Bakr and Umar, the first two Rashidun caliphs. The Shi'i tradition insists that the Prophet had appointed Ali to succeed him as leader of the nascent Islamic community, a position rejected by Sunni commentators. The sources are hazy, however, on the question of whether Ali felt he was the legitimate heir to the Prophet's mantle. His relations with the third of the Rashidun caliphs, Uthman, were badly strained. Ali is said to have accused Uthman of having violated Qur'anic principles and the teachings of the Prophet.

Ali assumed the caliphate following Uthman's assassination (656). His claim to the office was rejected by the Umayyads, Uthman's clan, who accused Ali of complicity in the murder. Leading the Umayyads was Mu'awiya, the powerful governor of Syria. Ali also faced opposition from A'isha (the Prophet's controversial wife) and two influential companions of the Prophet, Talha ibn Ubayd Allah and al-Zubayr ibn al-Awwam. The Battle of the Camel, near Kufa (656), led to the deaths of Talha and al-Zubayr, and A'isha's house arrest in Medina.

The conflict with Mu'awiya unfolded in stages. A period of open warfare ended at Siffin, along the Euphrates River, with the decision to open negotiations. Ali was condemned by a group of his followers, known as the Kharijis, for agreeing to hold the talks. Though Ali's forces went on to decimate the Kharijis, the conflict worsened Ali's position by indirectly strengthening Mu'awiya's hand in Syria and Egypt. Ali's assassination, at the hands of a Khariji extremist, occurred in the principal mosque of Kufa (661). Rule over the Arab-Islamic Empire fell to Mu'awiya and, in time, the Umayyad dynasty.

Ali's significance to Islamic history is twofold. He was instrumental in the formation of the early Islamic community. The Shi'i sects regard him, however, as also the founder of a line of divinely inspired figures, the *imams*. The Shi'i *imams*, a line of male descendants of the Prophet's house through Ali and Fatima, are viewed as the sole legitimate leaders of the Islamic *umma*. Ali's tomb in Najaf (southern Iraq) remains a principal site of Shi'i pilgrimage.

Amr ibn Bahr al-Jahiz (d. 868)

Born in Basra (776) to a *mawla* family of the Banu Kinana tribe, al-Jahiz was probably of mixed East African and Arab descent. His nickname, *jahiz* (goggle-eyed), suggests an unusual physical appearance. A prolific and often acerbic essayist, he earned a place in Arab-Islamic letters for his prose writings and, to a lesser extent, his embrace of the Mu'tazili movement, to which he contributed minor writings.

The Arabic biographical sources provide a generous amount of information on his life. As a young man, he is said to have displayed a keen intelligence in endless hours of conversation in the mosques of Basra—a hub of early Arab-Islamic culture—in which he debated religion, law, and politics with local scholars. Though he never took up permanent residence in Baghdad, as did other Basran intellectuals, he spent extended periods in the Abbasid capital (and, later, Samarra). He appears never to have held permanent employment (in a court-appointed post or in teaching), though the biographers refer to the patronage of leading figures of the Abbasid court, notably the vizier Muhammad ibn al-Zayyat (d. 847) and the chief *qadi* and leading light of the Mu'tazili movement, Ahmad ibn Abi Du'ad (d. 854). Al-Jahiz is also said to have impressed al-Ma'mun with several early essays on the caliphate.

A prolific writer, al-Jahiz produced essays on topics including Mu'tazili doctrine; the animal kingdom; the caliphate; thieves and bandits; slave girls and singers; slave owners; the characteristics of God; secretaries and bureaucrats; the jokes and slang of the common folk of Baghdad; and books. His essays fill several long volumes in their modern editions. His best-known work, a staple of upper-level university courses in Arabic and Arabic literature, is a multivolume work titled *Kitab al-Hayawan* (*Book of Animals*). Like most of his other work, it is written in a rambling style in which al-Jahiz turns frequently from his main subjects to digress on related and unrelated topics. Like other writers, al-Jahiz was drawn to the translation movement then under way in the Abbasid capital, and appears to have read many of the works of Greek, Persian, and Indian origin. Running as a thread through the *Book of Animals* is a deeply learned defense of the wisdom and poetry of the Arabs, a response to those who promoted Persian, Greek, and other non-Arab cultural traditions. Legend holds that al-Jahiz, an avid bibliophile, died beneath a cascade of volumes falling from an overburdened bookshelf.

Arib al-Ma'muniya (d. 890)

Nearly everything that is known of Arib's life is contained in a long biographical entry in the *Kitab al-Aghani* (*Book of Songs*), a remarkable, multivolume work by the tenth-century Iraqi historian Abu al-Faraj al-Isfahani (d. 967). Though it is not easy material to use because of its combination of historical information and literary anecdote, it recounts a remarkable life and sheds valuable light upon the patterns of ninth-century elite Abbasid culture.

Arib was renowned as a singer, composer, and music instructor. Her reputation as a courtesan rested on both her artistic excellence and her witty, outspoken, and compelling companionship. As was true of most entertainers of the Abbasid court, Arib was of slave origins. Born in 797, she is reported to have been the daughter of Ja'far ibn Yahya—a member of the Barmakid family—and his concubine Fatima, a young hand-maiden employed by his mother. Ja'far turned the girl over to a Christian nursemaid who, upon the fall of the Barmakids, sold her to a slave merchant who, in turn, sold her to a leading official of the Abbasid court. As was the pattern, the official moved with her to Basra, where he oversaw her training as musician and singer. She arrived in Baghdad at some point thereafter, and it appears that she spent most of her career there and in Samarra, where she was acquired by several members of the Abbasid house. She was finally manumitted, according to one report, by al-Mu'tasim.

As might be expected, her public life—next to nothing is known of her private affairs—centered on the musical and literary salons (*majlis*; pl., *majalis*) that were a regular feature of Abbasid-era culture. The musical *majalis* were often long sessions in which songs were not only performed but analyzed and debated as well. More formal and lavish sessions, often those in which the caliphs took part, were governed by strict rules of etiquette and conduct. The information in the *Book of Songs* makes clear that Arib was very much in demand in the elite homes of Baghdad and Samarra in which sessions of this kind were held. She is said to have excelled in besting her professional rivals. At a later stage in her life, she trained younger singers, a group of whom accompanied her to parties and salons.

Over the course of her career, Arib established a network of contacts throughout elite Abbasid society. Among her strongest supporters was

Ishaq al-Mawsili (d. 850), perhaps the greatest singer of the age. Her love affair with Ibrahim ibn al-Mudabbir (d. 893), a high-ranking official, was one of several such relationships with members of the Abbasid military and administration. An anecdote preserved in an early source suggests that by the close of her life, Arib had acquired considerable material wealth and high social rank. She died, according to al-Isfahani's sources, at the considerable age of ninety-three.

Harun al-Rashid (d. 809)

Al-Rashid is familiar to English-language readers from translations of the *The Thousand and One Nights*. His reign (786–809)—despite the wealth and authority of the Abbasid state at that point—witnessed the first stages in the disintegration of the Islamic Empire.

Appointed by his father, Muhammad al-Mahdi, as second in line to the caliphate after his brother Musa al-Hadi (r. 785–786), al-Rashid received the support of his mother, al-Khayzuran (d. 789)—a former slave from Yemen and a significant player in early Abbasid politics—and Yahya ibn Khalid al-Barmaki (d. 805), his tutor and secretary. Due mostly to the efforts of his two patrons, Harun gained valuable experience first as titular head of expeditions against Byzantium, then as governor of Egypt and other central provinces. His accession to the caliphate followed the abrupt death, perhaps by assassination, of his brother, which occurred amid intense infighting between influential military and palace cliques, his own included.

For a decade, the Barmakids—Yahya ibn Khalid, his brother Muhammad, and his sons, al-Fadl and Ja'far—exerted a virtual monopoly of authority over the central administration. Harun's decision to remove the family from power (803) may have been related to the caliph's political maturation as well as long-term palace politics. The family had led a renewed effort to centralize the imperial administration through tighter regulation of local governors and a relative easing of Abbasid relations with the Alid family and its Shi'i supporters. The immediate cause of the Barmakids' downfall, however, was probably the tensions born of the caliph's succession arrangement, formalized in an elaborate ceremony in Mecca (802). It designated Muhammad al-Amin (d. 813) and Abdallah al-Ma'mun (d. 833), the oldest of al-Rashid's sons, as his heirs.

Harun al-Rashid's reign witnessed considerable unrest, particularly in outlying regions including Yemen. Two local dynasties in North Africa—the Idrisids in Morocco and the Aghlabids in Ifriqiya—asserted autonomy from the Abbasid center (though the Aghlabids continued to send tribute to Iraq). Military factionalism in Syria and tax revolts in Egypt added to the woes of the central administration, as did Shi'i and Khariji uprisings in northern Mesopotamia and western Iran. On campaign against Rafi ibn al-Layth, head of a particularly difficult revolt in Khurasan, al-Rashid fell ill and died. The succession arrangement, which brought al-Amin to power, quickly ran aground with the onset of civil war between the two brothers.

Khadija bint Khuwaylid (d. 619)

Khadija, the first of Muhammad's wives, was the first convert to Islam, according to the Arab-Islamic sources. Her father, Khuwaylid, belonged to the Asad branch of the Quraysh. She is reported to have been married twice as a young woman. The death of her second husband, a successful trader, left Khadija a wealthy widow and heir to her husband's caravan trade. She hired the young Muhammad—attracted, it is said, by his reputation for honesty and piety—to oversee her business. He is said to have conducted trade on her behalf between the Hijaz and Syria. While some sources state that she was fifteen years his senior, other sources suggest they were close in age. Her marriage proposal to Muhammad, possibly presented through a male guardian, followed. The marriage produced four girls (Zaynab, Umm Kalthum, Fatima, and Rukayya) and at least one son (Abdallah). Abdallah is reported to have died as a child. Of the four girls, Fatima gained the greatest significance through her marriage to Ali ibn Abi Talib. Rukayya married Uthman, the third of the Rashidun caliphs.

Many details of Khadija's life are uncertain. Her significance to early Islamic history is at least twofold. Modern historians are interested in her status as a merchant and property owner and her seeming independence. One line of argument is that these show the greater autonomy enjoyed by women prior to the introduction of Islamic regulations that limited their rights and social mobility. Arab-Islamic sources generally laud her role in Muhammad's life following the start of his prophetic mission. She is reported to have provided the encouragement he required to proceed with his public preaching, at an early point when the hostile response of the Quraysh grew particularly fierce. She is also associated with her cousin, Waraqa ibn Nawfal, a Christian convert revered by the Islamic tradition for having acknowledged Muhammad's prophetic standing.

Khadija's relationship with Muhammad and her standing as a woman of conviction and piety are reflected in the honorific phrase often attached to her name. She is counted among the "mothers of the believers" (*ummahat al-mu'minin*). Her death (619) occurred some three years before the *Hijra*, and just after the death of Abu Talib, the Prophet's uncle and protector. Faced with a mounting campaign of abuse and violence by the Quraysh, Muhammad found his situation made all the more precarious by the loss of his two cherished supporters.

Mu'awiya ibn Abi Sufyan (d. 680)

Mu'awiya, a member of the Banu Umayya clan of the Quraysh, is generally described as the founder of the Umayyad caliphate. His second cousin, Uthman ibn Affan (d. 656), the third of the Rashidun caliphs, was the first member of the clan to control the caliphate, though it fell to Mu'awiya to establish the dynasty in Damascus. The reconstruction of the history of his caliphate is made difficult by the generally hostile treatment of the Umayyads in later Arab-Islamic sources. Generally the sources are respectful of Mu'awiya himself.

His rise to office followed an extended conflict with Ali ibn Abi Talib, who was accused of at least indirect complicity in Uthman's murder. Following Mu'awiya's refusal to recognize Ali's caliphate, armed struggle ensued. Negotiations between the two sides at Siffin (657) were inconclusive but resulted in a weakening of Ali's authority, to Mu'awiya's advantage. Strengthened by the seizure of Egypt (658), then Ali's assassination (661), Mu'awiya's bid for the caliphate was settled with the decision by al-Hasan, Ali's son, to forgo a bid for the caliphate (661). In that year—known in the Arabic sources as the "year of unity"—Mu'awiya was proclaimed head of the Arab-Islamic Empire.

His years in office were marked by advances in Anatolia against the Byzantine Empire as well as campaigns in the eastern Mediterranean and North Africa, with Egypt serving as the springboard into the latter territory. Mu'awiya also largely overcame the challenges posed by unruly elements within the conquest armies, notably nomadic forces from Arabia. He did so, in good part, through a policy of cooperation with tribal chiefs (*ashraf*) in Syria and Iraq. The result was the establishment of relative order in the garrison cities of Iraq (Kufa and Basra). This was consistent with his generally conservative approach: a reliance on traditional patterns of political leadership. His use of the title *Khalifat Allah* (deputy of God), appears to have been limited, as does his use of central government; he seems to have preferred to rely on the muscle of his Syrian troops and the loyalty of his provincial governors.

Muʿawiya's death (680) followed his controversial decision to appoint his son, Yazid I (r. 680–683), as his successor. The Arab-Islamic sources, associating it with the traditions of the Byzantine and Sasanid monarchies, roundly condemn the decision as un-Islamic. It apparently was opposed by contemporary elite circles as well, and served to spark a new period of conflict within the Arab-Islamic Empire. The events of the civil war turned largely on the bid for the caliphate by Ibn al-Zubayr and the abortive attempt by Husayn ibn Ali to unite with his family's followers in Iraq.

Muhammad ibn Jarir al-Tabari (d. 923)

Al-Tabari, historian and Qur'an commentator, ranks among the greatest scholars of early Islamic history. Born in Tabaristan (hence his name) in 839, he inherited a modest estate from his landowning father, from which he received an annual income that enabled him to pursue a life of scholarship (and freed him, for the most part, from having to seek patronage and employment). A gifted student, he was educated in Rayy, a northern Iranian city, then in Baghdad, which was home for most of his adult life. As an older student (856–870), he traveled extensively through the Near East, studying with prominent scholars and, it appears, keeping copious notes. Upon returning from Egypt, he settled in Baghdad, where, for roughly a half-century, he devoted himself to teaching and writing (only two later journeys to Tabaristan are recorded). His early biographers indicate that he led a modest, celibate life, and there is no evidence that he ever married. He was buried in the same house, located on the city's east side, in which he lived and wrote.

In contrast with prominent contemporaries, al-Tabari stayed clear of politics and is reported to have declined several official appointments. His writings are associated with early Sunni thought (Sunnism was taking on distinct form by the early tenth century), and though detractors accused him of Shiʿi sympathies, there is little evidence to support the claim. His interest in, and commitment to, legal scholarship drew a following that, for a brief period, constituted itself as a distinct law "school" (*madhhab*). The Jaririya, as it was known, lasted through the tenth century, then disappeared. The controversies of al-Tabari's life were related to his difficult relations with the large and vocal following of Ahmad ibn Hanbal. They are said to have harassed al-Tabari and his students; some reports speak of disturbances on their part during al-Tabari's funeral.

Although, as a prolific author, al-Tabari produced works on a number of subjects, there is much debate over the number and titles of his works. Best known are the *Taʾrikh al-Rusul wa al-Muluk* (The History of the Prophets and Kings) and his commentary (*tafsir*) on the Qurʾan. Both works, modern editions of which run to many volumes, stand among the essential texts of classical Islamic thought. The first is a universal history, dealing with the Creation, the Old Testament and ancient Israel, the pre-Muhammadan prophets, and the Sasanid dynasty, followed by a detailed account of Islamic history. The commentary, a close analysis of the language and meaning of the Qurʾan and the basis of a number of later supplementary commentaries, immediately gained a large readership and remains essential to Islamic religious education.

Umar ibn al-Khattab (d. 644)

Umar, the second of the Rashidun caliphs and one of the Prophet's earliest companions, is said to have converted to Islam in 617. As a member of the Adi ibn Kaʿb clan of the Quraysh, he vigorously opposed the Prophet's teachings up to the moment of his conversion. Only following the *Hijra* did Umar assume a prominent role among the Prophet's followers. The marriage of his daughter, Hafsa bint Umar, to the Prophet bolstered his standing as a leader of the *Muhajirun* (the Meccans who accompanied the Prophet to Medina). Umar later assumed a leading role in the debate over succession to the Prophet by throwing his support to Abu Bakr. The two men remained close, despite disagreement over key policy matters, and upon Abu Bakr's death (634), Umar assumed the office of caliph.

The evidence suggests that Umar was a prickly and demanding leader, deeply devoted to the nascent Islamic cause. The Arab-Islamic sources speak, in particular, of Umar's efforts to broaden the authority of the caliphate. Many reports indicate strained relations with top field commanders as a result of his insistence on directing the course of the early conquests. He is also reported to have ventured to Syria in the 630s and, according to some accounts, to Jerusalem, where he is said to have drawn up a document, known as the Pact of Umar, in which he set out the rules governing relations between the Muslims and the "People of the Book" (*ahl al-dhimma*), Christians and Jews. In all likelihood, however, the document was written at a much later date and simply associated with Umar. Over his ten years as caliph, the conquests entended into Egypt and the Fertile Crescent and to the western edges of Iran.

Umar also is credited with the development of several early Arab-Islamic institutions. He is said to have adopted the title of *Amir al-Mu'minin* (Commander of the Faithful), for example, perhaps in an effort to define the authority of his office. He is also credited with the development of the military payroll register (*diwan*) and the system of military stipends (*ata*; pl., *ata'at*). Historians tend to interpret these measures as an effort by Umar to prevent Arab-Muslim tribesmen from settling in the conquered territories, which were assigned the status of the collective property of the Islamic *umma*. Other developments, such as use of the office of *qadi* (judge), are also associated with Umar. On his deathbed, it is said, he called for the creation of a *shura* (consultative council) to select his successor.

Widely revered in Sunni Islamic sources, Umar is maligned by Shi'i authors for having denied the office of caliph to Ali ibn Abi Talib and his descendants. Umar was assassinated (644) by a Persian slave in Medina.

PRIMARY
DOCUMENTS

DOCUMENT 1
Selections from the Qur'an

The Qur'an consists of 114 suras, or "chapters," each of which contains a given number of individual verses (aya; pl., ayat). Surat al-Fatiha, the opening chapter of the Qur'an, plays a role not unlike that of the Lord's Prayer in Christian practice. The Qur'anic passages provided here reflect key themes of the Qur'an: the majesty of God; the genius of Divine creation; the certainty of Divine judgment; and mankind's responsibility, assigned by God, to create a just, equitable society. In Surat al-Nisa, for example, the Qur'an treats marriage, inheritance, parent-child relations, and the relationship between God and mankind. All are essential aspects of the kind of society envisioned by the Qur'an. The verses concerning Iblis (Satan) illustrate the Qur'anic cosmology, the organization of the universe into different realms. Iblis, following his banishment by God, will reign eternally over Hell (Gehenna) while leading astray those who choose to respond to his invitation.

Surat Al-Fatiha (The Opening, 1:1–7)

(The Koran Interpreted, vol. 1, p. 1)

*In the Name of God, the Merciful, the Compassionate
Praise belongs to God, the Lord of all Being,
the All-Merciful, the All-Compassionate,
the Master of the Day of Doom.
Thee only we serve; to Thee alone we pray for succour,*

Guide us in the straight path,
the path of those whom Thou hast blessed,
not of those against whom Thou art wrathful,
nor of those who are astray.

Surat Al-Nisa (The Women, 4:1–33)

(The Koran Interpreted, vol. 1, pp. 100–101)

In the Name of God, the Merciful, the Compassionate
Mankind, fear your Lord, who created you
of a single soul, and from it created
its mate, and from the pair of them scattered
abroad many men and women; and fear God
by whom you demand one of another,
and the wombs; surely God ever
watches over you.

Give the orphans their property, and do not
exchange the corrupt for the good; and devour
not their property with your property; surely
that is a great crime.
If you fear that you will not act justly
towards the orphans, marry such women
as seem good to you, two, three, four;
but if you fear you will not be equitable,
then only one, or what your right hands own;
so it is likelier you will not be partial.
And give the women their dowries as a gift
spontaneous; but if they are pleased
to offer you any of it, consume it
with wholesome appetite.
But do not give to fools their property
that God has assigned to you to manage;
provide for them and clothe them out of it,
and speak to them honourable words.
Test well the orphans, until they reach
the age of marrying; then, if you perceive
in them right judgment, deliver to them
their property; consume it not wastefully
and hastily

ere they are grown. If any man is rich,
let him be abstinent; if poor, let him
consume in reason.
And when you deliver to them their property,
Take witnesses over them; God suffices
For a reckoner.

To the men a share of what parents and kinsmen
leave, and to the women a share of what
parents and kinsmen leave, whether it be
little or much, a share apportioned;
and when the division is attended by
kinsmen and orphans and the poor,
make provision for them out of it,
and speak to them honourable words.
And let those fear who, if they left
behind them weak seed, would be afraid
on their account, and let them fear
God, and speak words hitting the mark.
Those who devour the property of orphans
unjustly, devour Fire in their bellies,
and shall assuredly roast in a Blaze.

God charges you, concerning your children:
to the male the like of the portion
of two females, and if they be women
above two, then for them two-thirds
of what he leaves, but if she be one
then to her a half; and to his parents
to each one of the two the sixth
of what he leaves, if he has children;
but if he has no children, and his
heirs are his parents, a third to his
mother, or, if he has brother, to his
mother a sixth, after any bequest
he may bequeath, or any debt.
Your fathers and your sons—you know not
which out of them is nearer in profit
to you. So God apportions; surely God is
All-knowing, All-wise.

Surat Al-Hijr (The Rock, 15:17–51)

(The Koran Interpreted, vol. 1, pp. 282–284)

We have set in heaven constellations
and decked them out fair to the beholders,
and guarded them from every accursed Satan
excepting such as listens by stealth—
and he is pursued by a manifest flame.
And the earth—We stretched it forth, and cast
on it firm mountains,
and We caused to grow therein of every thing
justly weighed, and
there appointed for you livelihood, and for those
you provide not for.
Naught is there, but its treasuries are with Us,
and We send it not down
but in a known measure.
And We loose the winds fertilising,
and We send down out of heaven water,
then We give it to you to drink, and
you are not its treasures. It is
We who give life, and make to die,
and it is We who are the inheritors.
We know the ones of you who press forward, and
We know the laggards;
and it is thy Lord shall muster them, and He is
All-wise, All-knowing.

Surely We created man of a clay
of mud moulded,
and the jinn created We before
of fire flaming.
And when thy Lord said to the angels,
"See, I am creating a mortal of a clay
of mud moulded.
When I have shaped him, and breathed My spirit in
him, fall you down, bowing before him!"

Then the angels bowed themselves
all together,
save Iblis; he refused to be among

those bowing.
Said He, "What ails thee, Iblis, that
thou art not among those bowing?"
Said he, "I would never bow myself
before a mortal
whom Thou hast created a clay
of mud moulded."
Said He, "Then go thou forth hence;
thou art accursed.
Upon thee shall rest the curse, till
the Day of Doom."
Said He, "My Lord, respite me till the day
they shall be raised."
Said He, "Thou art among the ones
that are respited unto the day
of a known time."
Said he, "My Lord, for Thy perverting me
I shall deck all fair
to them in the earth,
and I shall pervert them, all together,
excepting those Thy servants among them
that are devoted."
Said He, "This is for Me a straight path:
over My servants
thou shalt have no authority, except those
that follow thee;
being perverse;
Gehenna shall be their promised land
all together.
Seven gates it has, and unto each gate
a set portion
of them belongs."
But the godfearing shall be amidst gardens
and fountains:
"Enter you them, in peace and security!"
We shall strip away all rancour that is
in their breasts;
as brothers they shall be upon couches
set face to face;
no fatigue there shall smite them, neither
shall they ever be driven forth from there.

Tell My servants
I am the All-forgiving, the All-compassionate,
and that My chastisement
is the painful chastisement.

Source: The Koran Interpreted, 2 vols., translated by A. J. Arberry (London, 1955).

DOCUMENT 2
Muhammad and the Quraysh

SELECTION FROM THE SIRAH OF MUHAMMAD IBN ISHAQ

> *The passage, from one of the earliest biographies of the Prophet Muhammad, the Sirat Rasul Allah of Muhammad ibn Ishaq (d. 767), identifies Muhammad as the "apostle [of God]." Ibn Ishaq, a Medinan scholar, spent much of his adult life in Baghdad as an official of the Abbasid administration under the caliph al-Mansur (r. 754–775). His biography survives, however, only in a version produced by Abd al-Malik ibn Hisham (d. 834), a later Iraqi scholar who lived and worked in Egypt. Ibn Hisham, in editing the biography, omitted significant sections, so we cannot claim to have Ibn Ishaq's book in its original form. Described here is the angry response of the Quraysh, the leading clan of Mecca, to the content and spread of Muhammad's teachings. The Quraysh seek to persuade the Prophet's influential uncle, Abu Talib (d. 619), to withdraw his support and protection so that they can deal with Muhammad as they wish. The role played by kinship in contemporary society is clear.*

When the [companions of the apostle, i.e, Muhammad] prayed they went to the glens so that their people could not see them praying, and while Sa'd b. Abu Waqqas was with a number of the prophet's companions in one of the glens of Mecca, a band of polytheists came upon them while they were praying and rudely interrupted them. They blamed them for what they were doing until they came to blows, and it was on that occasion that Sa'd smote a polytheist with the jawbone of a camel and wounded him. This was the first blood to be shed in Islam.

When the apostle openly displayed Islam as God ordered him his people [i.e., the Quraysh] did not withdraw or turn against him, so far as I have heard, until he spoke disparagingly of their gods. When he did that they took great offence and resolved unanimously to treat him as an enemy, except those whom God had protected by Islam from such evil, but they were a despised minority. Abu Talib his uncle treated the apostle kindly and protected him, the latter continuing to obey God's commands, nothing turning him back. When the Quraysh saw that he would not yield to them and withdrew from them and insulted their gods and that his uncle treated him kindly and stood up in his defence and would not give him up to them, some of their leading men went to Abu Talib, namely 'Utba and Shayba, both sons of Rabi'a b. 'Abdu Shams . . . and Abu Sufyan b. Harb . . . and Abu'l-Bakhtari whose name was al-'As b. Hisham b. al-Harith b. Asad . . . and al-Aswad b. al-Muttalib b. Asad . . . and Abu Jahl (whose name was 'Amr, his title being Abu'l-Hakam) b. Hisham b. al-Mughira . . . and al-Walid b. al-Mughira . . . and Nubayh and Munabbih two sons of al-Hajjaj b. 'Amir b. Hudhayfa . . . and al-'As b. Wa'il. They said, "O Abu Talib, your nephew has cursed our gods, insulted our religion, mocked our way of life and accused our forefathers of error; either you must stop him or you must let us get at him, for you yourself are in the same position as we are in opposition to him and we will rid you of him." He gave them a conciliatory reply and a soft answer and they went away.

The apostle continued on his way, publishing God's religion and calling men thereto. In consequence his relations with Quraysh deteriorated and men withdrew from him in enmity. They were always talking about him and inciting one another against him. Then they went to Abu Talib a second time and said, "You have a high and lofty position among us, and we have asked you to put a stop to your nephew's activities but you have not done so. By God, we cannot endure that our fathers should be reviled, our customs mocked and our gods insulted. Until you rid us of him we will fight the pair of you until one side perishes," or words to that effect. Thus saying, they went off. Abu Talib was deeply distressed at the breach with his people and their enmity but he could not desert the apostle and give him up to them.

Ya'qub b. 'Utba b. al-Mughira b. al-Akhnas told me that he was told that after hearing these words from the Quraysh, Abu Talib sent for his nephew and told him what his people had said. "Spare me and yourself," he said. "Do not put on me a burden greater than I can bear." The apostle thought that his uncle had the idea of abandoning and betraying him, and that he was going to lose his help and support. He answered, "O my uncle, by God, if they put the sun in my right hand and the moon in my left on condition that I abandoned this course, until god has made it victorious, or I perish therein, I would not abandon it." Then the apostle broke into tears, and got up. As he turned away his uncle called him and said, "Come back, my nephew," and when he came back, he said, "Go and say what you please, for by God I will never give you up on any account."

When the Quraysh perceived that Abu Talib had refused to give up the apostle, and that he was resolved to part company with them, they went to him with ʿUmara b. al-Walid b. al-Mughira and said, according to my information, "O Abu Talib, this is ʿUmara, the strongest and most handsome young man among Quraysh, so take him and you will have the benefit of his intelligence and support; adopt him as a son and give up to us this nephew of yours, who has opposed your religion and the religion of your fathers, severed the unity of your people, and mocked our way of life, so that we may kill him. This will be man for man." He answered, "By God, this is an evil thing that you would put upon me, would you give me your son that I should feed him for you, and should I give you my son that you should kill him? By God, this shall never be." Al-Mutʿim b. ʿAdiy said, "Your people have treated you fairly and have taken pains to avoid what you dislike. I do not think that you are willing to accept anything from them." Abu Talib replied, "They have not treated me fairly, by God, but you have agreed to betray me and help the people against me, so do what you like," or words to that effect. So the situation worsened, the quarrel became heated and people were sharply divided, and openly showed their animosity to their opponents.

Source: The Life of Muhammad, edited and translated by Alfred Guillaume (London, 1955).

DOCUMENT 3
The Conquest of Syria

SELECTIONS FROM *FUTUH AL-BULDAN* OF AHMAD B. YAHYA AL-BALADHURI

Al-Baladhuri's history of the Arab-Islamic conquests, the Futuh al-buldan, *is an invaluable source for the early Islamic period. Little is known about the author. Of Iranian descent, he was probably raised in Baghdad, and is reported to have been a close companion of the Abbasid caliph al-Mutawakkil (r. 847–861). Al-Baladhuri describes the Arab campaigns and provides very useful details on political and economic developments that arose in the aftermath of the conquests. Here, for example, he comments on the arrangements made between the Arab forces and the defenders of Fihl following the city's surrender. The battle of Ajnadayn (fought between 634 and 637) was among the first significant encounters between the Arab-Islamic forces and those of the Byzantine Empire, led overall by the Byzantine emperor Heraclius (r. 610–641). Note that the document uses Islamic dates in reference to the battles and other events.*

The Battle of Ajnadin (or Ajnadain)

The battle of Ajnadin ensued. In this battle about 100,000 Greeks [i.e., Byzantine troops] took part, the majority of whom were massed one band after the other by Heraclius [Hirakl], the rest having come from the neighboring districts. On that day, Heraclius was in Hims [Emesa]. Against this army, the Moslems fought a violent battle, and Khalid ibn-al-Walid particularly distinguished himself. At last, by Allah's help, the enemies of Allah were routed and shattered into pieces, a great many being slaughtered.

Those who suffered martyrdom on that day were 'Abdallah ibn-az-Zubair ibn-'Abd-al-Muttalib ibn-Hashim, 'Amr ibn-Sa'id ibn-al-'Asi ibn-Umaiyah, his brother Aban ibn-Sa'id (according to the most authentic report. Others, however, claim that Aban died in the year 29), Tulaib ibn-'Umair ibn-Wahb ibn-'Abd ibn-Kusai (who fought a duel with an "unbeliever" who gave him a blow that severed his right hand making his sword fall down with the palm. In this condition he was surrounded and killed by the Greeks. His mother Arwa, daughter of 'Abd-al-Muttalib, was the

Prophet's aunt. His surname was abu-'Adi), and Salamah ibn-Hisham ibn-al Mughirah. According to others, Salamah was killed at Marj as-Suffar. Other martyrs were: 'Ikrimah ibn-abi-Jahl ibn-Hisham al-Makhzumi, Habbar ibn-Sufyan ibn-'Abd-al-Asad al-Makhzumi (who, according to others, was killed in the battle of Mu'tah), Nu'aim ibn-'Abdallah an-Nahham al-'Adawi (who, according to others, was killed in the battle of al-Yarmuk), Hisham ibn-al-'Asi ibn-Wail as-Sahmi (who is also supposed by others to have been slain in the battle of al-Yarmuk), Jundub ibn-'Amr ad-Dausi, Sa'id ibn-al-Harith, al-Harith ibn-al-Harith, and al-Hajjaj ibn-al-Harith ibn-Kais ibn-'Adi as-Sahmi. According to Hisham ibn-Muhammad al-Kalbi, an-Nahham was killed in the battle of Mu'tah.

Said ibn-al-Harith ibn-Kais was slain in the battle of al-Yarmuk; Tamim ibn-al-Harith, in the battle of Ajnadin; his brother, 'Ubaidallah ibn 'Abd-al-Asad, in al-Yarmuk; and al-Harith ibn-Hisham ibn-al-Mughirah, in Ajnadin.

When the news of this battle came to Heraclius, his heart was filled with cowardice and he was confounded. Consequently, he took to flight to Antioch [Antakiyah] from Hims [Emesa]. It was mentioned by some-one that his flight from Hims to Antioch coincided with the advance of the Moslems to Syria. This battle of Ajnadin took place on Monday twelve days before the end of Jumada I, year 13. Some, however, say two days after the beginning of Jumada II, and others two days before its end.

After that, the Greeks massed an army at Yakusah which was a valley with al-Fauwarah at its mouth. There the Moslems met them, dispelled them and put them to flight with a great slaughter. Their remnants fled to the cities of Syria. The death of abu-Bakr took place in Jumada II, year 13, and the Moslems received the news in al-Yakusah.

The Battle of Fihl in the Province of the Jordan

The battle of Fihl in the province of the Jordan was fought two days before the end of dhu-l-Ka'dah and five months after the proclamation of 'Umar ibn-al-Khattab as caliph. The commander-in-chief was abu-'Ubaidah ibn-al-Jarrah, to whom 'Umar had sent a letter with 'Amir ibn-abi-Wakkas, a brother of Sa'd ibn-abi-Wakkas, conferring on him the governorship of Syria and the chief command.

Some say that the appointment of Abu-'Ubaidah to the governorship of Syria was received when Damascus was under siege. Khalid being the chief commander in time of war, abu-'Ubaidah concealed the appointment from him for many days. When asked by Khalid for the reason, abu-'Ubaidah said, "I hated to dishearten thee and weaken thy position as thou stoodst facing an enemy."

The way this battle came about was that when Heraclius came to Antioch he summoned the Greeks and the inhabitants of Mesopotamia to go forth to war, putting them under the command of one of his men in whom he trusted. These met the Moslems at Fihl in the province of the Jordan and a most fierce and bloody battle ensued, which ended, by Allah's help, in the victory of the Moslems. The Greek patrician with about 10,000 men was slaughtered, and the rest of the army distributed themselves in the cities of Syria, some of them joining Heraclius. The inhabitants of Fihl took to the fortifications where they were besieged by the Moslems until they sought to surrender, agreeing to pay tax on their heads and *kharaj* [the land tax] on their lands. The Moslems promised them the security of life and property, agreeing not to demolish their walls. The contract was made by abu-'Ubaidah ibn-al-Jarrah, but according to others, by Shurahbil ibn-Hasanah.

Source: The Origins of the Islamic State, vol. 1, translated by Philip Khuri Hitti (New York, 1916).

DOCUMENT 4
The Spoils of War

Selection from al-Siyar al-Saghir of Muhammad ibn al-Hasan al-Shaybani

Al-Shaybani (d. 805), the author of this passage, is the Muhammad ibn al-Hasan mentioned in the text. Educated in the southern Iraq town of Kufa, al-Shaybani studied with two leading Muslim scholars, Abu Hanifa (d. 768) and Abu Yusuf (d. 798), before emerging as a prominent legal scholar. He was appointed late in his career as qadi (judge) of al-Raqqa and, later, of the Iranian city of Rayy. Here he deals with touchy political and legal matters that arose during the period of the conquests. How were the Arab-Islamic forces to treat conquered regions and their inhabitants? How were conquest spoils to be distributed? These problems were hotly debated in the early Islamic community. The practice of di-

*viding conquered lands and their revenue into fifths may have originated
in pre-Islamic Arabia. One important distinction that emerged in Islamic
law was that between lands seized by force and those taken peacefully, as
a result of negotiation.*

In the Name of God, the Merciful, the Compassionate. Praise Be to
God, the One, the Just. [This was transmitted to] Abu Sulayman al-
Juzjani from Muhammad b. al-Hasan al-Shayban from Abu Hanifa from
Alqama b. Marthad from ʿAbd-Allah b. Burayda from his father, Burayda
b. al-Husayb al-Aslami, who said:

Whenever the Apostle of God [i.e., Muhammad] sent forth an army
or a detachment, he charged its commander personally to fear God, the
Most High, and he enjoined the Muslims who were with him to do good
[i.e., to conduct themselves properly].

And [the Apostle] said:

Fight in the name of God and in the "path of God" [i.e., truth]. Com-
bat [only] those who disbelieve in God. Do not cheat or commit treach-
ery, nor should you mutilate anyone or kill children. Whenever you meet
your polytheist enemies, invite them [first] to adopt Islam. If they do so,
accept it, and let them alone. You should then invite them to move from
their territory to the territory of the "emigrants" [Medina]. If they do so,
accept it and let them alone. Otherwise, they should be informed that
they would be treated like the Muslim nomads (Bedouins) [who take no
part in the war] in that they are subject to God's orders as [other] Muslims, but that they will receive no share in either the ghanima (spoils of
war) or in the fayʾ [spoils of war taken peacefully]. If they refuse [to accept Islam], then call upon them to pay the jizya (poll tax); if they do,
accept it and leave them alone. If you besiege the inhabitants of a fortress
or a town and they try to get you to let them surrender on the basis of
God's judgment, do not do so, since you do not know what God's judgment is, but make them surrender to your judgment and then decide their
case according to your own views. But if the besieged inhabitants of a
fortress or a town asked you to give them a pledge [of security] in God's
name or in the name of His Apostle, you should not do so, but give the
pledge in your names or in the names of your fathers; for, if you should
ever break it, it would be an easier matter if it were in the names of you
or your fathers.

[This was transmitted to] Muhammad b. al-Hasan from Abu Yusuf from Muhammad b. al-Sa'ib] al-Kalbi from Abu Salih [al-Samman] from ['Abd-Allah] b. 'Abbas [who said]:

The one-fifth [share of the spoil] was divided in the time of the Apostle of God into five parts: one for God and the Apostle, one for the near of kin, one for the poor, one for the orphans, and one for the wayfarer.

He [Ibn 'Abbas] said that [the caliphs] Abu Bakr, 'Umar, 'Uthman, and 'Ali divided [the one-fifth share] into three parts; one for the orphans, one for the poor, and one for the wayfarer.

[This was transmitted to] Muhammad [b. al-Hasan] from Abu Yusuf and Muhammad b. Ishaq, from Abu Ja'far [Muhammad b. 'Ali b. al-Husayn] [from Yazid b. Hurmuz], who said:

I asked [Ibn 'Abbas]: "What was [the caliph] 'Ali b. Abi Talib's opinion concerning the one-fifth [share]?" He [Ibn 'Abbas] replied: "His ['Ali's] opinion was like the opinion of his House [the house of the Prophet Muhammad], but he disliked to disagree with Abu Bakr and 'Umar [on the subject]."

[This was transmitted to] Muhammad [b. al-Hasan] from Abu Yusuf from Abu Ishaq from Ismail b. Abi Umayya from 'Ata b. Abi Rabah from ['Abd-Allah] b. 'Abbas, who said:

[The caliph] 'Umar offered to defray the expenses of marriage for [the unmarried members of] our House and to pay our debts [from the one-fifth share]. When we insisted that [the share] instead should be handed over to us, he refused.

[This was transmitted to] Muhammad [b. al-Hasan] from Abu Yusuf from Muhammad b. Ishaq from [Muhammad b. Shihab] al-Zhuri from Sa'id b. al-Musayyib, who said:

The Apostle of God, in dividing up the one-fifth [share] of the spoil after the campaign of Khaybar, divided between the Banu Hashim and the Banu al-Muttalib the part assigned to the near kin. Thereupon, 'Uthman b. 'Affan and Jubayr b. Mut'im asked the Apostle to treat them on equal footing on the ground that they were as closely related to him as Banu al-Muttalib. The Apostle replied: "We and the Banu al-Muttalib have stood together in [the days of] both al-Jahiliya [i.e., the pre-Islamic period] and of Islam."

[This was transmitted to] Muhammad [b. al-Hasan] from Abu Yusuf from al-Ash'ath b. Sawwar from Abu al-Zubayr [Muhammad b. Muslim] from Jabir [b. 'Abd-Allah], who said:

The Prophet used to assign the one-fifth [share] to "the path of God" [i.e., pious purposes] and out of it he gave to some members of the community, but when the revenue increased, he included others.

Source: Majid Khadduri, trans. *The Islamic Law of Nations* Pp. 75–79. © 1966 [Johns Hopkins University Press]. Reprinted with permission of the Johns Hopkins University Press.

DOCUMENT 5
Harun al-Rashid and the Succession Arrangement

SELECTION FROM TA'RIKH AL-RUSUL WA'L-MULUK OF MUHAMMAD IBN JARIR AL-TABARI

> *Muhammad ibn Jarir al-Tabari (d. 923), the author of a multivolume* History, *spent much of his career in Baghdad. One of the foremost scholars of the early period, he also composed a deeply learned commentary on the Qur'an. In this passage from the* History, *he describes the succession scheme arranged by the Abbasid caliph Harun al-Rashid (r. 786–809) for his two sons. Following al-Rashid's death, however, the arrangement collapsed. Muhammad al-Amin (r. 809–813) succeeded his father; his brother Abdallah al-Ma'mun (r. 813–833) became governor of Khurasan. Abdallah's decision to challenge his brother's authority sparked civil war. The conflict (809–819) led to extended warfare in and around Baghdad during which al-Amin fell to his brother's troops (813). The conflict ended only with al-Ma'mun's return to Iraq from Khurasan. Both the document and al-Tabari's account shed useful light on the elaborate ceremony and language of Abbasid political culture.*

He related: [The caliph] Harun [al-Rashid] made the Pilgrimage, accompanied by [his two sons], Muhammad and 'Abdallah, and by his military commanders, ministers and judges, in the year 802. He left behind at al-Raqqah Ibrahim b. 'Uthman b. Nahik al-'Akki in charge of his womenfolk, the treasuries and material wealth, and the army, and he dispatched his son al-Qasim to Manbij and then installed him there with the military commanders and soldiers whom he had attached to al-Qasim's side.

When he had accomplished the rites of the Pilgrimage, he composed for his son 'Abdallah al-Ma'mun two letters, over the composition of which the religious lawyers and judges had expended intensively their intellectual efforts. One of them comprised stipulations laid upon Muhammad setting forth the conditions which Harun had imposed on him regarding Muhammad's faithful adherence to the arrangements in the document concerning the handing over of the administrative regions for which 'Abdallah was to assume responsibility, and he conveyed to him estates, sources of revenue, jewels, and wealth. The other was the documentary text of the oath of allegiance which the Caliph had extracted from the nobles and commoners alike, and that of the obligations due to 'Abdallah and incumbent upon both Muhammad himself and those nobles and commoners.

[Harun al-Rashid] placed the two documents in the Holy House [the Ka'bah in Mecca] after he had extracted the oath of allegiance to Muhammad and after he had called to witness in his favor regarding the terms of the oath, God, His angels and all those who were with him in the Ka'ba, comprising the rest of his children, his family, his [clients], his military commanders, his ministers, his secretaries, and so forth. The act of witness to the succession oath and the (other) document took place in the Holy House, and he ordered the doorkeepers to guard the two documents and to prevent anyone from taking them away and making off with them. 'Abdallah b. Muhammad, Muhammad b. Yazid al-Tamimi, and Ibn al-Hajabi have mentioned that al-Rashid was present and that he summoned the leading members of the Hashimite family, the military commanders and the religious lawyers. They were taken into the Holy House, and he ordered the document to be read out to 'Abdallah and Muhammad, and made the whole of those present bear witness to the attestation of the two of them to the document. Then he thought it fitting to hang up the document in the Ka'bah, but when it was lifted up in order to attach it for suspension, it fell down, and people commented that this arrangement would speedily be dissolved before it could be carried through completely.

The text of the document was as follows:

In the name of God, the Merciful, the Compassionate One. This is a document composed by the servant of God Harun the Commander of the Faithful, which Muhammad son of Harun the Commander of the Faithful has written out in a state of soundness of mind and full exercise of his powers, willingly and unconstrainedly. The Commander of the Faithful has appointed me as his successor after him and has imposed acknowledgement of allegiance to me on the whole of the Muslims. He has appointed ʿAbdallah the son of Harun the Commander of the Faithful as his successor and as caliph and as the one responsible for all the affairs of the Muslims after myself, with my full agreement and freely conceded by me, willingly and unconstrainedly. He has given responsibility for Khurasan, its frontier regions and its districts, for the conduct of warfare there and its army, its land tax, its official textile workshops, its postal relay system, its pubic treasuries, its poor-tax, its religious tithe, the sums collected as tribute, and all its administrative divisions, both during his own (i.e., Harun's) lifetime and afterwards. I have accepted the obligation laid on me by the servant of God Harun the Commander of the Faithful with my full agreement and a contented mind, that I will faithfully fulfill and hand over to my brother ʿAbdallah b. Harun the right of succession, the executive power, the caliphate and the affairs of the whole of the Muslims, which Harun the Commander of the Faithful has granted to him after me.

Source: Reprinted by permission from *The History of al-Tabari*, vol. 30, *The ʿAbbasis Caliphates of Musa al-Hadi and Harun al-Rashid A.D. 785–809/A. H. 169–193*, translated by C. E. Bosworth, the State University of New York Press © 1989, State University of New York. All rights reserved.

DOCUMENT 6
Housing the Turkish Units at Samarra

SELECTION FROM THE KITAB AL-BULDAN OF AHMAD B. ABI YAʿQUB AL-YAʿQUBI

The document treats the foundation of Samarra by the caliph al-Muʾtasim (r. 833–842). For roughly sixty years, Samarra replaced Baghdad—founded by al-Mansur roughly a half-century earlier—as the Abbasid capital. The history of Samarra was shaped in large part by the activity of a sizable Turkish military. Turkish commanders played, for a short and violent period, the role of kingmakers by selecting and assassinating a series of caliphs. The Turkish rank and file, toward the end of this period, engaged in riots and civil war. Little wonder that the Abbasids finally abandoned the city for their original capital, during the reign of al-Muʿtadid (892–902). The author of this selection, al-Yaʿqubi (d. 897), wrote not only the Geo-

graphy *from which this passage is taken but also a well-regarded* History. *Raised in Baghdad, al-Ya'qubi served in several provincial administrations in Armenia and Egypt, probably as a finance official.*

When the rough and ill-mannered Turks rode their horses, [they did so] at full gallop, knocking down people right and left. The urban toughs would seize hold of them, killing some, beating others. The [Turks'] blood was shed with impunity, while [the local authorities] did nothing to retaliate against those committing such deeds. This [state of affairs] weighed heavily on al-Mu'tasim, and he resolved [finally] to leave Baghdad. He went to al-Shammasiya, the place where al-Ma'mun use to go for days, sometimes months. [He] decided to build a city in al-Shammasiya, which was located [a distance] outside Baghdad. The area of the site grew too cramped for him, however, and he was uncomfortable with its proximity to Baghdad so he departed for al-Burdan on the advice of al-Fadl b. Marwan, who was then his chief minister. This was in the year 836.

[The text goes on to say that al-Mu'tasim visited to several other sites along the Tigris River, none of which he found suitable. He then came across a new site—which was to be known as Samarra—and ordered the start of construction. He distributed areas of the new settlement to his officials and commanders, and settled his military forces in their new quarters. For the Turkish units, he adopted specific measures, as the following passage indicates].

Al-Mu'tasim isolated all of the areas on which he settled the Turks from those on which he settled the civilians, setting the one entirely apart from the other, so that the Turks would not interact with any of the local population nor would any but the Faraghina live beside them. He allotted to Ashinas and his companions the area known as al-Karkh, and assigned to him a number of Turkish officers and soldiers. He ordered him to build the mosques and markets.

He allotted to Khaqan Urtuj and his companions the area adjoining al-Jawsaq al-Khaqani, and ordered him to settle in one place all those who were assigned to him, that is, by forbidding them to mix with the townspeople. He allotted to Wasif and his companions the area adjoining al-Hayr; he had built a long wall which he called Ha'ir al-Hayr. He ordered that all of the distributed areas on which the Turks and the "uncivilized" Faraghina were settled were to be built far from the markets and everyday hubbub, on wide avenues and long side streets. In their allotted areas and along their streets, no townspeople, whether merchants or others, would be allowed to mix with them.

Then al-Mu'tasim purchased (for the Turks) slave women and married them to these women. He forbade them or anyone related to them from marrying into the local populace so that their offspring would marry only among themselves. He ordered that the slave women assigned to the Turks be given fixed salaries and that their names be placed in the military registers. None of them would be allowed to divorce or abandon his wife.

When he assigned Ashinas al-Turki and his companions their area at the western edge of the settlement, calling the site al-Karkh, he ordered that he not allow any stranger, merchant or any other, to reside near them, nor any interaction on their part with the civilian populace. In an area north of al-Karkh, he assigned an area to another group and called it al-Dur. Throughout al-Dur and the other assigned areas, he had mosques and bathhouses built for them, and in each area a small market which included a number of shops belonging to grain merchants, butchers, and others who provided basic goods and necessities.

Source: Author's translation.

DOCUMENT 7
The Cities of Egypt: Alexandria and al-Fustat

Selection from Ahsan al-Taqasim fi Ma'rifat al-Aqalim of al-Muqaddasi

Little is known of al-Muqaddasi's life. Probably raised in Jerusalem, he died sometime after 990. He is considered one of the foremost Arab geographers of the early Islamic period on the strength of his Ahsan al-Taqasim, from which this description of two Egyptian cities is drawn. Note that he makes no mention of al-Qahira (Cairo), the capital founded by the Fatimid dynasty (970) outside al-Fustat. Cairo was to become Egypt's principal urban center, and one of the great cities of the premodern Mediterranean world. At the time of al-Muqaddasi's visit, however, it is clear that al-Fustat, not Cairo, was the locus of commerce and public life in Egypt. Al-Muqaddasi was a fine writer, capturing in extraordinary detail many aspects of medieval Egyptian society.

Al-Iskandariyya (Alexandria) is a delightful town on the shore of the Romaen Sea [i.e., the Mediterranean]. Commanded by an impregnable fortress, it is a distinguished city with a goodly [populace] of upright and devout people. The drinking water of the inhabitants is derived from the Nile, which reaches them in the season of its flood via an aqueduct and fills their cisterns. It resembles Syria in climate and customs; rainfall is abundant; and every conceivable type of product is brought together there. The countryside round about is splendid, producing excellent fruits, and fine grapes. It is a clean town, and their buildings are of the kind of stone suited for maritime construction; it is also a source of marble. It has two mosques. On their cisterns are doors which are secured at night so that thieves may not make their way up through them. The remaining towns here are very well developed; and in the surrounding area grow locust, olives, and almonds, and their cultivated lands are watered by the rain. It is near here that the Nile [lets out] into the Romaen Sea. It is the city founded by Dhu al-Qarnayn (Alexander the Great), and has, indeed, a remarkable citadel.

Al-Fustat is a metropolis in every sense of the word; here are together all the departments of government administration, and moreover, it is the seat of the Commander of the Faithful. It sets apart the Occident [i.e., Egypt and North Africa] from the domain of the Arabs, is of wide extent, its inhabitants many. The region around it is well cultivated. Its name is renowned, its glory increased; for truly it is the capital city of Egypt. It has superseded Baghdad, and is the glory of Islam, and is the marketplace for all mankind. It is more sublime than the City of Peace [Baghdad]. It is the storehouse of the Occident, the entrepôt of the Orient, and is crowded with people at the time of the Pilgrimage festival. Among the capitals there is none more populous than it, and it abounds in noble and learned men. Its goods of commerce and specialities are remarkable, its markets excellent as is its mode of life. Its baths are the peak of perfection, its bazaars splendid and handsome. Nowhere in the realm of Islam is there a mosque more crowded than here, nor people more handsomely adorned, no shore with a greater number of boats. It is more populous than Nishapur, more splendid than al-Basra, larger than Damascus. Victuals here are most appetizing, their savories superb. Confectioneries are cheap, bananas plentiful, as are fresh dates; vegetables and firewood are abundant. The water is palatable, the air salubrious. It is a treasury of learned men; and the winter here is agreeable. The people are well-disposed, and well-to-do, marked by kindness and charity. Their intonation in reciting the *Qur'an* is pleasant, and their delight in good deeds is evident; the devoutness of their worship is well-known throughout the world. They have rested secure from injurious rains, and safe from the tumult of evildoers. They are most discriminating in the selection of the preacher and of the leader in prayer; nor will they appoint anyone to lead them but the most worthy, regardless of expense to themselves. Their judge is always dignified, their *muhtasib* [market inspector] deferred to like a prince. They are never free from the supervision of the ruler and the minister. Indeed were it not that it has faults aplenty, this city would be without compare in the world.

The town stretches for about two-thirds of a *farsakh*, in tiers one above the other. It used to consist of two quarters, al-Fustat and al-Jiza, but later on, one of the [Abbasid caliphs] had a canal cut around a portion of the town, and this portion became known as al-Jazira (the island), because of its lying between the main course of the river and the canal. The canal itself was named the "Canal of the Commander of the Faithful," and from it the people draw their drinking water. Their buildings are of four storeys or five, just as are lighthouses; the light enters them from a central area. I have heard it said that about two hundred people live in one building. In fact, when al-Hasan bin Ahmad al-Qarmati arrived there, the people came out to meet him; seeing them, as he considered, like a cloud of locusts, he was alarmed, and asked what this meant. The reply was: "These are the sightseers of Misr [the city]; those who did not come out are more numerous still."

I was one day walking on the bank of the river, and marveling at the great number of ships, both those riding at anchor, and those coming and going, when a man from the locality accosted me, saying: "Where do you hail from?" Said I, "From the Holy City [i.e., Jerusalem]." Said he, "It is a large city. But I tell you, good sir—may God hold you dear to Him—that of the vessels along this shore, and of those that set sail from here to the towns and the villages—if all these ships were to go to your native city they could carry away its people, with everything that appertains to it, and the stones thereof and the timber thereof, so that it would be said: 'At one time here stood a city.' "

Source: *The Best Divisions for Knowledge of the Regions*, translated by Basil Collins (Reading, UK, 2001).

DOCUMENT 8
The Wealth of the Abbasid Court

SELECTION FROM *KITAB AL-HADAYA* BY AN ANONYMOUS AUTHOR

The author of the Kitab al-Hadaya *(Book of Gifts) is unknown, though there is evidence (contained in the book itself) that he lived in Egypt in the late eleventh century, possibly as an official of the Fatimid dynasty. The reader should not assume that the information provided here is accurate: the estimates of costs and revenue are suspiciously large, and cannot, in any case, be confirmed. The value of the two passages lies in the evidence they provide regarding the level and complexity of material wealth at the highest levels of Near Eastern/Islamic society. Exotic animals, fine fabrics, precious stones and metals, superb instruments, weapons, and furnishings: this was the stuff of commerce and elite consumption. So, too, were human beings: slaves were employed in the military, administration, and elite homes in a variety of capacities. In a number of cases, slaves and freedmen assumed a significant role in early Islamic social and political life.*

When [the Abbasid Caliph] al-Mutawakkil ʿala-Allah was assassinated, the total sum in coin in his private treasury was a million [gold] dinars in cash and fifty million [silver] dirhams. He left eleven thousand eunuchs and slave girls, six thousand of these being eunuchs. He also left eight thousand military slave boys. As for his private expenditures, [they amounted] to two million one hundred thousand [gold] dinars and twenty-six million five hundred thousand [silver] dirhams every year, and for his mother Shuja' six hundred thousand dinars. The [other] expenses were two hundred thousand dinars for the kitchens; three hundred thousand dinars for construction and restoration; ten million dirhams in wages for the entourage; five million dirhams for expenditure on his private attendants; three hundred thousand dinars for clothing; a hundred thousand dinars for scents; a hundred thousand dinars for refurbishing the equipment in the treasuries, and for fabricating gold and silver articles; one million two hundred thousand dirhams for canvas and candles; two million dirhams for ice; a hundred thousand dinars for furnishings; two million dirhams for beverage storage vaults; five hundred thousand dirhams for the allowances of his boon companions; five hundred thousand dirhams for the wages of dog trainers, falconers, and cheetah attendants; five million dirhams for expenditure on light boats and the like; a hundred thousand dinars for the purchase of slaves; three hundred thousand dinars for the purchase of precious stones; eight hundred thousand dinars for the wages of the house servants; five hundred thousand dirhams for the wages of [entertainers such as] slapstick comedians, jesters, trainers of fighting rams, trainers of fighting [roosters], [and] those in charge of fighting dogs.

[The Abbasid caliph] al-Mu'tazz bi-Allah had once requested from his mother, Qabihah, fifty thousand dinars to spend on the soldiers. She told him that she could not lay her hands on a single coin. But after she was assassinated in the year 869, her wealth was revealed, as there was found in one of her treasuries a million dinars and three caskets, one of which contained one measure of emeralds, more precious than anyone had ever seen. In another casket there was a half measure of pearls; no one had ever seen anything more beautiful and regular than these. The third contained a measure of rubies, the like of which had never been seen. They were estimated at a value of two million dinars. This was in addition to the savings found for her in the above-mentioned year. The revenue from her agricultural land amounted to ten million dinars per year. There were also found quilts for her [personal] use; the value of each was estimated at more than a thousand dinars. For each quilt, sable pelts would be taken, their fur shaved off [for the stuffing], and the skins thrown away. When enough fur had been collected for [the stuffing of] one quilt, musk and amber crumbs would be sprinkled among the fur, which was then placed between the lining and the outside cover, instead of cotton, and then quilted. The covers were of Khurasani cloth [with silk warp and a weft of another fabric], which was the lightest and warmest [of all fabrics].

Source: Book of Gifts and Rarities, translated by Ghada al-Hijjawi al-Qaddumi (Cambridge, MA: Harvard University, Center for Middle Eastern Studies, 1996).

DOCUMENT 9
The Markets of Baghdad

Selection from Ta'rikh al-Rusul wa'l-Muluk of Muhammad ibn Jarir al-Tabari

The Near East, in the early Abbasid period, underwent rapid urban-
ization. Of the types of urban centers in early Islamic history, Baghdad,
along with Samarra and Cairo, is often considered a "planned" city—es-
tablished for specific purposes, as the selection suggests. Also suggested
here, however, is that over the course of his caliphate, al-Mansur was
obliged to introduce significant changes to the structure of his new capi-
tal, changes having to do with security as well as population growth. The
story of the Byzantine ambassador, impossible to verify, may be nothing
more than a story rather than the account of an actual event.

According to Yahya b. al-Hasan b. 'Abd al-Khaliq, the maternal uncle
of al-Fadl b. al-Rabi': 'Isa b. 'Ali complained to [the Abbasid caliph] Abu
Ja'far [i.e., al-Mansur], "O Commander of the Faithful, it is tiring for me
to walk from the gate of the courtyard to the palace, for I have become
weak," and he replied, "Have yourself carried in a litter," but he responded, "I am embarrassed because of the people." Al-Mansur said, "Is
there anyone who continues to be embarrassed because of them?" but 'Isa
continued, "Allow me, O Commander of the Faithful, what is allowed,
one of the water-carrying camels." He said, "Does any water-carrying or
riding animal enter the city?" Thus he ordered that everyone move their
doors to the intervalla of the arcades and that no one should enter the
courtyard except on foot. When al-Mansur ordered that the doors that
led into the courtyard should be blocked and opened to the intervals of
the arcades, the markets were established in the four arcades of the city,
each one having a market. This continued until one of the [officials] of
Byzantium came as an ambassador, and he ordered al-Rabi' to take him
on a tour of the city and its surroundings to see the development and the
building. Al-Rabi' took him on a tour, and when it was finished [al-
Mansur] asked, "What do you think of my city?" [The ambassador] had
gone up on the walls of the city and in the domes of the gates, and he
said, "I saw a beautiful building, but I saw your enemies with you in the

city." The caliph asked him who they were, and he replied, "The market people." Abu Ja'far [al-Mansur] was silent about it and, when the [Byzantine official] had gone, he ordered that the market be sent out of the city. He appointed Ibrahim b. Hubaysh al-Kufi and attached Jawwas b. al-Musayyab al-Yamani, his freedman, and ordered the two of them to build the markets in the Karkh area and ordered them to make booths and houses for every trade and to hand them over to the people. When they had done this, he moved the market there from the city and imposed rents on them according to size [of structure].

When the number of people grew, they built markets on sites that Ibrahim b. Hubaysh and Jawwas had not sought to build on because they were unable to construct the booths from their sources. They were charged less in rents than was collected from those who settled in the buildings of the authorities.

One of them said: The reason Abu Ja'far [al-Mansur] moved the merchants from the city to al-Karkh and the nearby areas outside the city was that it was said to Abu Ja'far that foreigners and others stayed the night in it and that it was not safe because there might be spies and intelligence agents among them or they might open the gates of the city by night because of the position of the markets. So he ordered that the market be removed from the city and he established the [security force] and [palace guard] in it and for the merchants, built at the Gate of the Harrani Arch, the Syrian Gate, and in al-Karkh.

According to al-Fadl b. Sulayman al-Hashimi from his father: The reason for the removal of the markets from the City of Peace and the City of al-Sharqiyyah to the Karkh Gate, the Barley Gate and the Muhawwal Gate, was that al-Mansur had appointed a man called Abu Zakkariyya' Yahya b. 'Abdallah in charge of the [accounts] of Baghdad and the markets in the year 773–774, when the market was in the city. Al-Mansur was pursuing those who had rebelled with Muhammad and Ibrahim sons of 'Abdallah b. Hasan. This [market inspector] had some connection with them, and he gathered a group against al-Mansur and led the lower classes of them astray, and they caused a commotion and gathered together. Al-Mansur sent Abu al-'Abbas al-Tusi to them, and he calmed them down and took Abu Zakariyya' and put him in his custody. Abu Ja'far ordered him to kill him, so a chamberlain of Abu al-'Abbas al-Tusi, called Musa, killed him with his own hands at the Golden Gate in the courtyard on the order of al-Mansur. Abu Ja'far ordered that those houses that extended into the street of the city be destroyed and that the street be forty cubits wide. He demolished whatever had been extended into that width and ordered that the markets be removed to al-Karkh.

Source: Reprinted by permission from *The History of al-Tabari*, vol. 29, *Al-Mansur and al-Mahdi A.D. 763–786/A. H. 146–169*, translated by Hugh Kennedy, the State University of New York Press © 1990, State University of New York. All rights reserved.

DOCUMENT 10
The Prophet's Wisdom

SELECTIONS FROM TWO HADITH COLLECTIONS: *SAHIH AL-BUKHARI* OF MUHAMMAD AL-BUKHARI AND *SAHIH MUSLIM* OF MUSLIM IBN AL-HAJJAJ

The three selections are examples of Hadith, a term that originally meant "report" of an event or utterance; the term Sunna originally meant "practice, custom." Following the Prophet's death, as Muslims collected accounts of his teachings and activities, the two related terms took on a more technical meaning. Prophetic Sunna came to refer to Muhammad's words and deeds; Hadith, to the reports that contained these accounts. The early Islamic scholars, Sunni and Shi'i alike, devoted considerable effort to the analysis and organization of Hadith. The three selections derive from the two best-known collections of Sunni Hadith, those produced, respectively, by Muhammad al-Bukhari (d. 870) and Muslim ibn al-Hajjaj (d. 875). Both men hailed from Khurasan in eastern Iran. Shown here are the two parts from which nearly all Hadith were formed: the list of transmitters ("the chain of authorities," the isnad) and the text of the report (matn).

From *Sahih al-Bukhari* (Book of Faith, no. 6/13)

Musaddad related to us, saying that Yahya reported to him, from Shu'bah, from Qatadah, from Anas, may God be pleased with him, who said: The Prophet, may God bless him and give him peace, said: "None of you has faith unless he desires for his brother what he desires for himself."

From *Sahih al-Bukhari* (Book of Faith, no. 8/16)

Muhammad ibn al-Muthanna related to us, saying that Abd al-Wahhab al-Thaqafi reported to him, saying that Ayyub reported to him, from Abu Qilabah, from Anas, who said: The Prophet, may God bless him and give him peace, said: "There are three matters in which he who has them revealed to him will discover the sweetness of faith: that he cherishes God and His messenger [the Prophet Muhammad] over everything other than them; that he loves a person, loving him only for the sake of God; that a return to [a state] of unbelief [in God] is as hateful to him as being cast into the fire [of Hell]."

From *Sahih Muslim* (Book of Faith, no. 1/1)

Kahmas related to us, from Abu Buraydah, from Yahya ibn Ya'mar, who said: "Humayd ibn Abd al-Rahman and I were on pilgrimage or on Umra [the minor pilgrimage] . . . when we happened upon Abd Allah ibn Umar ibn al-Khattab as he was entering the mosque. My companion and I went up to him, one standing on his right, the other on his left . . . [Abd Allah ibn Umar] said: my father, [the caliph] Umar ibn al-Khattab, related to me: "One day we were sitting in the company of the Prophet of God, may God bless him and give him peace, when suddenly there stood before us a man, clothed in brilliant white and with the darkest hair, who bore no signs of having traveled. None of us recognized him.

He sat before the Prophet, may God bless him and give him peace, and, leaning his knees against his, and placing his palms on his thighs, he said, "Tell me, Muhammad, about *islam*." The Prophet of God, may God bless him and give him peace, replied: "*islam* means that you bear witness that there is no god but God and that Muhammad is God's messenger; that you carry out the ritual prayer; pay the obligatory alms; fast during [the month of] Ramadan; and perform the pilgrimage [*Hajj*] to the House [of God; i.e., the Ka'ba in Mecca] if you have the means to do so." [The man] said: "You have spoken truly." We were astonished that he would [even] ask the question and that he would [then] declare it true.

[The man] said: "Then tell me about faith [*iman*]." [The Prophet] said: "Faith means that you have faith in God, His angels, His books, His messengers, and the Day of Judgment, and that you have faith in the measuring out [by God] of both good and evil." [The man] said: "You have spoken truly."

He said: Then tell me about the performance of righteous deeds [*ihsan*]." [The Prophet] said: "That you worship God as if you see Him, for though you do not see Him, He sees you."

[The man] said, "Tell me about the [Final] Hour." [The Prophet] replied, "On this [matter], he who is questioned knows no more than he who asks the question." [The man] said: "Then tell me about its signs." [The Prophet] replied: "The slave girl will give birth to her mistress, and you will see the barefoot, unclothed, destitute shepherds vying with each other in the construction [of buildings]."

[Umar] said: "Then the man was taken off. I waited a long while then [the Prophet] said: 'O Umar, do you know who the questioner was?' " I replied, "God and His messenger know best." He said, "Why, that was Gabriel. He came to teach you your religion.' "

Source: Author's translation.

DOCUMENT 11
The Rules of Marriage

SELECTION FROM A TENTH-CENTURY COMPILATION BY ABD ALLAH IBN AHMAD IBN HANBAL

Muslim scholars, from the very earliest period of Islamic history, have devoted enormous energy to developing the rules that govern Islamic social and religious life. The result is the vast and complex body of Islamic law. The passage presented here comes from a collection of legal opinions issued by Ahmad ibn Hanbal (d. 855) and collected by his son, Abdallah (d. 903). Ibn Hanbal, an early giant of Islamic legal history, is known for both his scholarship and his opposition to the Abbasid caliphate during the episode known as the Mihna *(see Chapter 5). Marriage is viewed by the Islamic tradition, much as it is in most other religious communities, as an essential social institution. As shown here, the early Muslim scholars examined marriage in the most intricate detail.*

[What Happens When] a Man Marries a Woman without a *Wali* [legal guardian] and Who Gives a Woman in Marriage When She Has No *Wali*

Abd Allah said, "I heard my father [i.e., Ahmad ibn Hanbal] say, about a man who marries a woman without a *wali*, in the presence only of witnesses, 'That is not valid.' "

Someone said to my father while I was listening, "Does the governor or the judge have the most right to give [a woman] in marriage?" He said, "The judge, because he is in charge of sexual relations and legal judgement."

I asked my father about a woman who entrusts her matter to a Muslim man who thereby gives her in marriage. But she has brothers and agnates. He said, "The marriage contract is concluded over again by her brothers or agnates."

I asked my father about a man who is one of the witnesses to a woman's marriage. Then later [after a certain period of time] the woman comes to him and says, "My husband has divorced me and my *'idda* [the cycle of menstrual periods] is over." Can the witness accept what she says and marry her [himself]? My father said, "If he acted as a witness to her marriage with a *wali* and [other] witnesses present, then she comes and says, 'My husband divorced me,' he should inquire about her husband's divorcing her. Then if he can be certain that her husband has divorced her and that with regard to what she has claimed about the end of her *'idda* she is telling the truth, [he can marry her]. If, however, he turns out to be her nearest *wali*, in order to marry her he must arrange to have another man act as her *wali* and give her in marriage to him in the presence of witnesses. Further, he must award her a fair dower."

I asked my father about a secret marriage. "Do you think it is a [valid] marriage contract? If there are two witnesses and a *wali*, is it secret?" He said, "It is preferable that a marriage be made public and not be secret, that it be with a *wali*, and that musical instruments be played at it, so that it becomes well known and acknowledged."

I asked my father about a man who is a woman's *wali*, and puts her matter into the hands of a second man, and the second man uses that authority to marry her himself with the woman's consent. Then the marriage takes place. "Do you consider this marriage valid?" My father said,

"As long as he really was her nearest *wali* and there was no one nearer than he, and he gave his authority as her guardian to a second man who married her with her consent, the marriage is valid." I said, "What if there was a *wali* nearer than he?" He said, "Then the nearest *wali* has the right to give her in marriage with her consent."

[My father said,] "There is no disagreement about the [woman who has been married before]: she is given in marriage only with her permission."

I said to my father, "What about the [virgin, i.e., a woman who has not been married]?" He said, "There are those who disagree concerning the matter [of the virgin]." I said, "What do you prefer?" He said, "Her *wali* should consult her. Then if she grants permission, he can giver her in marriage." I said, "But if she does not grant it?" He said, "If her father is [her *wali*], and she has not reached seven years of age, then her father's giving her in marriage is valid, and she has no option. But if she has reached her ninth year, neither her father nor anyone else should give her in marriage without her permission. [As for] the orphan who has not reached nine years of age, if someone other than her father is giving her in marriage, I do not like him to do so until she reaches nine years of age. When she reaches nine, she should be consulted. Then if she grants her permission, she has no option thereafter."

I asked my father about a woman who gives herself in marriage to a man, in the presence of two witnesses, during a period in which her *wali* is absent. Then her *wali* writes that what she has done for herself is valid. "Is that permissible?" He said, "The marriage contract should be concluded again."

I asked him about a woman who orders a certain man to give her daughter in marriage, and he does so. He said, "The marriage contract should be concluded again." I said, "[What if] the girl is five years old?" He said, "I do not approve of such a marriage. Only her father gives an underage girl in marriage; when he does so, the marriage is valid. Only her father should give a girl in marriage, until she reaches nine years of age and can be consulted about herself. Then, if she gives her permission, her agnates may give her in marriage: her brother, her paternal uncle, his son. But if she has no agnates, then the judge [gives her in marriage]." I said to my father, "But if her agnates refuse to give her in marriage?" He said, "They should not do that. [But if they do,] she brings her situation to the [attention] of the judge."

DOCUMENT 12
The Death of al-Husayn ibn Ali

Selection from Ta'rikh al-Rusul wa'l-Muluk of Muhammad ibn Jarir al-Tabari

The death of the Prophet's grandson, al-Husayn ibn Ali, was a key event in early Shi'i history. The passage provided here is a short section of al-Tabari's lengthy description of the attack on al-Husayn and his followers at Karbala (680). Their opponents were Syrian forces sent by the Umayyad caliph, al-Yazid ibn Mu'awiya (r. 680–683). The text underscores the significance that early Muslim scholars attached to the event: it was not simply a political episode, but a moment of profound religious meaning as well. Since al-Husayn was the Prophet's grandson, how could it have been otherwise? Over subsequent centuries of Islamic history, the events at Karbala would become the centerpiece of elaborate rituals of lamentation in which the deaths of al-Husayn and the other Shi'i imams are remembered.

According to Abu Mikhnaf: A young lad came out against us. His face was young like the first splinter of the moon, and there was a sword in his hand. He was wearing a shirt and a waistcloth, and a pair of sandals, one of whose straps was broken—as I remember, it was the left. Amr b. Sa'd b. Nufayl al-Azdi said to me, "By God! Let me attack him." I said, "Praise be to God! What do you want to do that for? Is it not enough for you that these people who, you see, have surrounded them should do the killing?" But he insisted, "By God! Let me attack him." So he rushed against him and did not turn back until he had struck his head with his sword. The young lad fell face downward as he called out, "O uncle!" Al-Husayn [his uncle] showed himself just like the hawk shows itself. He launched into attack like a raging lion and struck Amr [b. Sa'd b. Nufayl] with his sword. That man tried to fend off the blow with his arm, but his arm was cut off from the elbow; he gave a great shriek. As al-Husayn turned away from him, the cavalry of the Kufans attacked in order to save Amr [b. Sa'd b. Nufayl] from Husayn. Their horses collided against Amr with their chests, their hooves kicked out and they galloped with their riders over him so that they trampled him to death. The dust fell; there was al-Husayn standing by the head of the young lad; the lad had his feet stretched out on the ground. Husayn was saying, "May the people who killed you perish, for the one who will oppose them on the Day of Resurrection on your behalf will be your grandfather. By God! It is hard on your uncle that you called him and he did not answer you, or rather he answered but your cry did not help you, for, by God, those who kill his relatives are many but those who help him are few." Then he carried him.

It is just as if I can see the two feet of the boy leaving tracks in the ground while Husayn held his breast close to his own. I asked myself what he would do with him. He brought him and put him with his son Ali b. al-Husayn and the other members of his family who had been slain. I asked about the boy and was told that he was al-Qasim b. al-Hasan b. Ali b. Abi Talib.

Al-Husayn remained there for a long time during that day. Whenever one of the people came against him, he would turn aside from him and was unwilling to be responsible for his death and such a dreadful sin. A man from the Banu Badda' of Kindah called Malik b. al-Nusayr came against him and struck him on the head with his sword. Al-Husayn was wearing a hooded cloak. The sword cut through [the hood of] the cloak and wounded his head. The cloak became covered with blood. Al-Husayn declared, "Because of that may you never eat and drink with your hand. May God gather you on the [Day of Judgment] with those people who are wrongdoers." He threw down the cloak and called for a cap. He put on the cap and wound a turban around it. He was tired and had become less active.

The man from Kindah had managed to take the cloak, which was made of silk. Later, when he brought it to his wife, Umm 'Abdallah bt. al-Hurr—she was the sister of Husayn b. al-Hurr al-Baddi—he began to wash the blood from the cloak. His wife said to him, "Have you brought plunder from the son of the daughter of the Apostle of God into my house? Take it away from me." His colleagues mentioned that he remained poor as a result of the wicked action until he died.

According to Abu Mikhnaf: Abu Ja'far Muhammad b. Ali b. al-Husayn told me that the blood of his family was on the hands of us from

Banu Asad. I said: "Is it my fault? May God have mercy on you." Then I asked him what our guilt was. He answered, "Al-Husayn was brought his young child; he was on his knee. Then one of you, Banu Asad, shot an arrow that slaughtered the child. Al-Husayn caught the blood [in his hand]. When the palm of his hand was full, he poured the blood onto the ground and said, "O Lord, if it be that You have kept the help of heaven from us, then let it be because Your purpose is better than [immediate] help. Take vengeance for us on these oppressors."

Source: Reprinted by permission from *The History of al-Tabari*, vol. 19, *The Caliphate of Yazid b. Mu'awiyah A.D. 680–683/A. H. 60–64*, translated by I.K.A. Howard, the State University of New York Press © 1991, State University of New York. All rights reserved.

DOCUMENT 13
Arib's Visit to Her Former Lover

SELECTION FROM NISHWAR AL-MUHADARAH OF AL-MUHASSIN IBN 'ALI AL-TANUKHI

Al-Tanukhi (d. 994), an official in the Buwayhid administration (see Chapter 6), contributed several collections of adab (belles-lettres) literature. Anecdotes of the kind contained in this selection were popular in medieval Islamic/Near Eastern society. They were intended not only to entertain but also, in many cases, to convey instruction and wisdom, often through well-known historical figures. Arib (d. 890) and Ibn al-Mudabbir (d. 893), the former lovers featured here, were influential participants in ninth-century Abbasid palace society. Arib is described by one biographer as well-versed in poetry, backgammon, chess, and calligraphy, though it was her singing and composition that stood out. (Her chosen instrument was the oud, a stringed instrument akin to the lute, a preference she would pass on to her students.) Ibrahim ibn al-Mudabbir, a high-ranking finance official during the Samarra period, is reported to have been a boon companion of al-Mutawakkil (r. 847–861) and a competent poet.

I was informed by Abu Mohammed after Abu Ahmad al-Fadl b. 'Abd al-Rahman of Shiraz, state-secretary, as follows: I was told, he said, by a trustworthy person that Ibrahim b. al-Mudabbir narrated how he was for a long time in love with [the musician and singer] 'Arib, and spent large sums upon her. When, he said, I was hit by fortune, abandoned office and stayed at home, she too had aged, repented of her singing, and become paralysed. One day when I was sitting, my porter came and announced that 'Arib's boat was at the door, and that she was in it and solicited an interview. I was surprised, but my heart warmed towards her, and rising went down to the river-bank, where I found her sitting in her boat. Madam, I said, how comes this?—I longed for you, she replied, and wished to renew old times, and drink with you today.—I bade her come up, but she told me she must wait for her litter to come; and then I saw an elegant boat approach containing a litter, wherein she was placed, which her servants then brought up. We conversed for a time, then food was brought which we ate, then wine. I drank, and when I filled her cup, she drank and ordered her slave-girls to sing. Of these there were with her a number of highly accomplished performers, who sang with sweetness and in excellent style, which I greatly enjoyed. Some days before I had composed some verses, for indeed I was always devoted to the repetition and recitation of poetry; they were

> *If thy night be sleep unbroken,*
> *Wakeful eyelids close not I.*
> *In the dark my sides seem rent by*
> *Scissors' edges as I lie.*
> *In God's care I place her for whom*
> *Openly I may not sigh.*

Madam, I said to her, I have composed some verses which I wish you to set to music.—What, she exclaimed, Abu Ishaq, when I have repented!—Find, I said, some expedient for that.—Then she told me to recite the lines to two of her singing girls, pointing to Bid'ah and Tuhfah, whom I accordingly got to learn them by heart. She then thought for a little, striking her fan on the ground and humming to herself, and then told these girls to arrange a certain string in a particular style, to strike with a particular finger and to do various things until she had got the tune right, when she bade them sing the verses in a particular key, and put so and so in such and such a place. Then they proceeded to sing the lines as though they had heard them many times before. Ere the notes had issued from their lips I thought to myself: Here is 'Arib visiting me and setting my verses to music, and acting as a professional singer; is she to go away without a present? Never, not though I were to die of want, hunger, and poverty!—So I went to my slave-girls, and explained the situation, asking them to help me with anything which they had handy. One gave me an anklet, another a bracelet, another a bead necklace, and another an ornament of some kind, until I had got together a collection in value of about a thousand dinars. I then called for a [heavy] basket of gold filigree in which I placed the ornaments, and then bringing it to her, told her it contained a few presents which I wished to bestow on the two maidens, and hoped she would order them to accept them. She declined, but not resolutely, saying: Abu Ishaq, [could there be no finer moment than this we are sharing now?]. I told her it must be, and thereupon she bade her maids accept [the presents], which they did. She sat with me until sunset, when she rose to depart, and I accompanied her as far as the Tigris, and when about to take her place in her boat, she told me she had a request to make. I bade her command me. She then stated that a certain lady, mother of my children, had purchased a particular estate adjoining hers; that she was anxious to add it to her property, and wanted me to ask my wife to take the purchase money and let her have it. Seeing that this was the reason for her visit, I asked her to stop where she was, and while she remained in the boat, I went to speak to my wife, promised her the price, and obtained her sanction for the sale of the property. This I brought to 'Arib, saying: Hereby I present you with the property of which I have guaranteed the price to the owner, and tomorrow I will see that witnesses' names are signed on the back of the document, which you may take with you at once.—She thanked me and departed. Now the price of the property was a thousand dinars, so that her day's society and her setting my verses to music cost me two thousand, one hundred dinars.

Source: The Table-talk of a Mesopotamian Judge, translated by D.S. Margoliouth (London: Journal of the Royal Asiatic Society, 1922).

DOCUMENT 14
A New Capital in Egypt

SELECTION FROM *SIRAT AHMAD IBN TULUN* OF ABD ALLAH IBN MUHAMMAD AL-BALAWI

The Tulunid dynasty (868–905) ruled Egypt virtually independent of the Abbasid caliphate in Iraq. The dynasty's founder, Ahmad ibn Tulun (d. 884), was born into a Turkish military family in Samarra, his father having been among the Turkish slave soldiers incorporated into the Abbasid military in the early-to-mid-ninth century. Ahmad, with the backing of his father's supporters, rose quickly through the ranks and, as a well-regarded member of the officer corps, was appointed governor of Egypt (868). Faced with unrest in Samarra and the Zanj revolt in southern Iraq, the late ninth-century caliphs could do little to prevent Ibn Tulun from assuming wide authority over Egypt's affairs. The selection comes from the detailed account of the Tulunid period by al-Balawi, a tenth-century Egyptian historian about whom, unfortunately, there is little information.

Ahmad ibn Tulun returned to Egypt [from Syria], having gathered large numbers of slaves and troops and [stores] of equipment. The result was that space in his palace grew constricted. He and the governors [of Egypt] before him had resided in the palace known to the present day [i.e, mid-tenth century] as Balad al-Imarah. [The palace] had two gates, one facing the area called Hawd Abi Qudayra; to the present day, the gate has been known as Bab al-Khassa. The other [gate] was adjacent to [the headquarters] of the police force assigned to Upper Egypt, the gate of the headquarters being another of the [palace's] gates.

This all composed a single palace with [an additional] gate leading to the mosque located beside the police headquarters and in which the Friday prayer service was held. It still contains [Ibn Tulun's] own pulpit and *maqsurah* [the special enclosure for the ruler]. The palace, however, was demolished brick by brick following Muhammad ibn Sulayman's entry into the province. During the reign of Harun ibn Khumarawayh, [the palace] had been used to house the Bureau of Land Taxes.

[Space in the old palace being at a premium,] Ahmad ibn Tulun rode to the foot of the mountain and, there, mapped out a [new] palace complex. He ordered his closest companions, elite guardsmen, and attendants to map out [areas] for themselves surrounding or in proximity to the [new palace]. They did so and began construction. Eventually the [newly] constructed zone came up against the existing town along a stretch from the Badr marketplace to the livestock market. On the opposite side, the [new] building and construction [zone] reached a point that extended beyond the limits of the old town.

[Areas of the new settlement] were then distributed [to the military] as land grants. Each of these concessions was named after its inhabitants. The Nubian [units] were assigned a separate concession which was named after them; the Byzantines [Byzantine mercenaries] another concession; the auxiliary troops a separate concession; and [similarly] for each category of [Ibn Tulun's] military forces. The military commanders built [their residences] in a number of areas.

A fine city resulted. It was divided by streets and lanes, and within it were constructed elegant mosques, flour mills, baths and public ovens. Its markets were designated. They included the Ayyarin Market, in which were placed the cloth and perfume merchants; the Famiyyin Market, in which were gathered the butchers, greengrocers, and meat grillers—in the shops of the Famiyyin [Market] was everything one would find in similar shops in the old town but in greater quantity and of finer quality—and the Tabbakhin Market, in which were gathered the money changers, bakers and sellers of sweets. [Ibn Tulun similarly] assigned to each of the trades and crafts a separate market, each splendid, well-constructed, elegant and secure.

The [new] city was as well appointed as any of the large cities of Syria, indeed, larger and a great deal more handsome.

[Ibn Tulun] constructed his [own] residence, making it spacious and grand. In it he built a handsome plaza in which polo was played. The entire residence was known as al-Maydan [the plaza] on account of the plaza. Everyone, young and old, [upon being] asked, when going out, about their destination, would reply "to al-Maydan."

Source: Author's translation.

DOCUMENT 15
Abd al-Rahman III of al-Andalus

SELECTION FROM *NAFH AL-TIB* OF
AHMAD IBN MUHAMMAD AL-MAQQARI

Abd al-Rahman III (r. 912–961), a member of the Umayyad dynasty of Islamic Spain, brought about significant achievements, including a new level of sophistication in the ceremonial life of the dynasty. The document probably exaggerates the extent of his accomplishments, however; it should be read with a dose of skepticism. It does refer to his decision to adopt the titles caliph and Commander of the Faithful and, in this way, declare himself the equal of the Abbasid caliph in Baghdad. The announcement was meant to counter the claims of the Fatimid rulers in Egypt to the same title. Al-Maqqari (d. 1632), the source of this text, was a North African scholar; his large book on Islamic Spain is an invaluable source on the history of Islamic society in the western Mediterranean.

'Abd al-Rahman [III] died at [his palace] al-Zahra on the second or third day of the month of Ramadhan of the year 961, of a paralytic fit, at the age of seventy-three. He was born in the year 890, and was only twenty years old when his father Muhammed was put to death. His mother's name was Muznah. In addition to the honourable appellation of al-Nasir li-din-illah (the defender of the true faith), 'Abd al-Rahman received from his subjects the surname of *Abu al-Mutarrif* (the victorious). Never was the [Islamic realm] more prosperous, or the true religion more triumphant, than under his reign. The infidels of Andalus [Islamic Spain] were driven back to the mountainous districts of the north, where they insured their safety only by paying tribute to the Commander of the Faithful. Commerce and agriculture flourished; the sciences and arts received a new impulse, and the revenue was increased ten-fold. Notwithstanding the costly magnificence with which 'Abd al-Rahman surrounded his person—the unusual number of troops which he constantly kept in his pay, the multitude of eunuchs, Slavs, and other servants employed about his palace, the bounteous gifts which he distributed to the learned, and the splendid buildings which he caused to be erected in various parts of his extensive dominions, in Africa as well as in Andalus—it is said that when he died he left in the coffers of the treasury the enormous sum of five millions of dinars.

The amount of the revenue under this reign has been estimated by several contemporary writers at six million, two hundred and forty-five thousand dinars; namely, five million, four hundred and eighty thousand arising from the land-tax levied in the towns and districts, and seven hundred and sixty-five thousand being the amount of indirect taxation, and duties imposed upon goods. As to the sums which entered the royal coffers, being the fifth of the spoil taken from the infidels, they were beyond calculation, and cannot be estimated, as no precise account of them was kept in the treasury books.

Of this immense sum one-third went to pay the troops and the public officers; another third was destined for ['Abd al-Rahman's] own use; and the remainder was spent in public buildings. Many, indeed, were the works of public utility which this just and enlightened monarch caused to be erected in various parts of his extensive dominions. As to his capital, Cordova, he is well known to have embellished it and widened its precincts, so that it equaled, if it did not surpass, in size and splendour the proud metropolis of the ['Abbasids][i.e., Baghdad]. His addition to the great mosque of Cordova, and the construction of the palace of al-Zahra in the vicinity of that capital, are two splendid erections, which will transmit the name of 'Abd al-Rahman to posterity. Of both those buildings we have elsewhere given as accurate a description as it was in our power; and therefore we need not now return to the subject.

It is said that after the death of 'Abd al-Rahman a paper was found in his own hand-writing in which those days which he had spent in happiness and without any cause of sorrow were carefully noted down, and on numbering them they were found to amount only to fourteen. O man of understanding! Wonder and observe the small portion of real happiness the world affords, even in the most enviable position! The Caliph al-Nasir, whose prosperity in mundane affairs and whose widely-spread empire became proverbial, had only fourteen days of undisturbed enjoyment during a reign of fifty years, seven months, and three days. Praise be given to him, the Lord of eternal glory and everlasting empire! There is no God but He! The Almighty, the giver of empire to whomsoever he pleases!

As above stated, 'Abd al-Rahman was the first sovereign of the Umayyad house in Andalus who assumed the title of *Amir al-Mu'minin* (Commander of the Faithful). The authors of the time say that when 'Abd al-Rahman saw the state of weakness and abjectness to which the

['Abbasid] Califate had been reduced, and perceived that the Turkish freedmen in the service of the ['Abbasids] had usurped all authority and power in the state—when he heard that the Caliph al-Muktadir had been put to death, in the year 929, by one of his freedmen, called Munis al-Muzaffar—he no longer hesitated to assume the insignia of the Caliphate, and call himself *Amir al-Mu'minin*.

Source: *The History of the Mohammedan Dynasties in Spain*, translated by Pascual de Gayangos (London, 1840).

GLOSSARY

Abna: Literally, "sons"; the descendants of the Khurasani troops who settled in Baghdad upon the conclusion of the Abbasid revolution.

Ahl al-dhimma: Non-Muslim populations under Muslim rule subject to the stipulations of *dhimma*.

Alim: See *Ulama*.

Amir (pl., umara): Commander; military chief; governor.

Amir al-Mu'minin: "Commander of the Faithful"; standard title of the caliph.

Ansar: Literally, "helpers"; the Medinans who joined Muhammad in creating the first Islamic polity.

Ashraf (sing., sharif): Nobles, tribal leaders; descendants of the Prophet.

Aya (pl., ayat): Symbol or sign of God; line or verse of the Qur'an.

Barid: Intelligence and postal system.

Bay'a: Oath of allegiance given to a new caliph by the military and political elite.

Da'wa: Call, summoning; used for the missionary activity of the Isma'ili and other early religiopolitical movements.

Dhikr: Remembrance, mention; usually associated with Sufi practice of "remembering" the name of God.

Dhimma: "Guarantee of security"; legal protection extended to the non-Muslims (*dhimmi*) living under Arab-Islamic rule in exchange for loyalty and payment of the *jizya*.

Dinar: Standard gold coin in early Islamic period.

Dirham: Standard silver coin in early Islamic period.

Diwan (pl., dawawin): List or register of names; pay register of participants in Arab-Islamic conquests; government bureau.

Faqih (pl., fuqaha): Jurist, jurisprudent, scholar of Islamic law.

Fiqh: "Understanding"; the science of Islamic jurisprudence; Islamic religious law.

Fitna: Literally, "trial, temptation," or any source of socioreligious division.

Ghayba: Occultation (especially of the Twelfth Imam).

Ghazw: Military expedition, raid.

Ghulat: Extremists; term used for proto-Shi'i groups of early period that espoused heretical doctrines.

Hadith: Reports of the words and deeds of the Prophet and his companions (*Sunna*); usually accompanied by a list of transmitters (*isnad*).

Hajj: Pilgrimage to Mecca; one of the "Five Pillars," or ritual duties, required of the Muslim.

Haram: Sacred enclave or sanctuary, such as area around the Ka'ba.

Hijra: The "emigration" of Muhammad and his followers from Mecca to Yathrib (Medina), traditionally dated to 622; marks year 1 of the Islamic calendar and foundation of Islamic society.

Hilm: The blend of qualities (wisdom, experience, forbearance and generosity) characteristic of sound leadership in Arab tribal society.

Hisba: Qur'anic principle "to promote the good and forbid the wrong"; office of the *muhtasib*.

Ibadat (sing., ibada): Act of worship (e.g., prayer, fasting); one of the two major categories of acts in Islamic law.

Ibn: Son (e.g., Ahmad ibn Hanbal = Ahmad the son of Hanbal).

Ihsan: Righteous or virtuous deed; beauty, perfection of faith.

Ijma: Consensus of the religious scholars; one of the "sources" of Islamic law.

Ilm: Knowledge, particularly religious knowledge, contained in the fields of Islamic law and other "religious sciences."

Imam: Supreme leader over the Muslims; legitimate successor to the Prophet as used by the Shi'a; prayer leader.

Iman: Faith, belief.

Islam: As a religious term, "acknowledgment of, and submission to, the Will of God."

Isnad: Chain of transmitters or authorities. See *Hadith*.

Isra: The Prophet's "Night Journey" from Mecca to Jerusalem.

Jihad: Struggle or effort, on "the path of God"; key Qur'anic concept, often translated as "holy war," which places undue stress upon military rather than religious or spiritual effort.

Jinn: Category of spirits believed to inhabit heaven and earth.

Jizya: Head or poll tax levied upon non-Muslims living under Muslim rule.

Jund (pl., ajnad): Military district of early Arab-Islamic Empire; army.

Ka'ba: Shrine, of pre-Islamic origin, located in Mecca; Islamic teachings associate its origins with Abraham.

Kafir: "Unbeliever," "infidel"; one who is "ungrateful" for God's mercy and gifts.

Kalam: Rationalist theology; broad current in Islamic thought that stressed the use of human reason in religious argumentation.

Khalifa: Representative or deputy; the caliph, or leader, of the early Islamic Empire. Used both in *khalifat Allah*, "the deputy of God," and *khalifat rasul Allah*, "the agent (or successor) of the Prophet of God."

Kharaj: Land tax levied initially on non-Muslims, then on all landowners in Arab-Islamic Empire.

Khutba: Sermon delivered at the Friday congregational prayer.

Madhhab (pl., madhahib): "School" of Islamic religious law, especially in Sunni Islam.

Madrasa: College for the study and teaching of Islamic law.

Mahdi: "One rightly guided by God"; in Shi'i usage, the Twelfth Imam, who, as the Awaited One, will return to bring the Last Day and restore the community to the right path.

Majlis (pl., majalis): Sitting area, audience hall; literary or musical session.

Malik (pl., muluk): King; tyrant (in early Islamic usage).

Maqsura: Enclosure in a mosque, usually near the *mihrab*, generally set aside for use by the ruler or other prominent persons.

Matn: The substance or body of a report. See *Hadith*.

Mawali (sing., mawla): Clients or freedmen in early Islamic society; takes on other meanings later in Islamic history.

Mazalim: Court of complaints, often led by the caliph or top official of the court.

Mihrab: Niche in the wall of a mosque indicating the direction of prayer (*qibla*).

Minbar: "Platform"; raised structure in a mosque from which the Friday sermon (*khutba*) is delivered.

Mi'raj: "Ascension"; specifically, the ascent of the Prophet from Jerusalem into the presence of God.

Misr (pl., amsar): Arab-Islamic garrison towns (e.g., Kufa, Basra, Fustat).

Muhajirun: The believers from Mecca who joined Muhammad in the "emigration" to Yathrib (Medina).

Muhtasib: Market inspector, "one who implements *hisba*."

Mushrik: Idolater; polytheist; one who "associates" anything with God.

Qadi (pl., quda): Judge, magistrate.

Qibla: Direction of prayer (toward the Ka'ba in Mecca).

Qital: Fight, struggle, armed conflict; used in the Qur'an, often in relation to "the struggle in God's path."

Qiyas: Analogical reasoning; one of the "sources" of Islamic law.

Rashidun: "Rightly-guided"; term coined by later generations of Sunni scholars for the first four, Medina-based successors to the Prophet (Abu Bakr, Umar, Uthman, Ali).

Ridda: Literally, "return"; used in Islamic history in sense of "rejection, repudiation," to refer to the Arab tribes that renounced their ties to Medina (and Islam) following the Prophet's death.

Rukn (pl., arkan): "Support"; the religious duties of Islam, often referred to as the "Five Pillars" of Islam.

Sahaba (sing., sahib): Companions (of the Prophet).

Salat: Canonical prayer, obligatory for believers, conducted five times daily; one of the "Five Pillars" of Islam.

Sawm (or siyam): Obligatory fast during the month of Ramadan; one of the "Five Pillars" of Islam.

Shahada: "Bearing witness"; Muslim profession of faith ("there is no god but God and Muhammad is His messenger"); one of the "Five Pillars."

Shariʿa: The "path of God" as laid out in the Qurʾan and *Sunna*; Islamic law.

Shura: Consultation, counsel, elective process.

Shurta: Police force; military escort.

Sira: Biographical account of the life of the Prophet.

Suf: Wool.

Sunna: "Beaten path," term used for tribal custom of pre-Islamic Arabs; normative practice of the Prophet as described in the Hadith reports.

Sura: Section or chapter of the Qur'an.

Tabi'un (sing., *tabi'*): "Successors"; the second generation of the Prophet's followers.

Tafsir: "Explanation"; Qur'anic commentary; exegesis.

Tasawwuf: Arabic term for Sufism.

Ulama (sing., *alim*): Literally, "those in possession of religious knowledge"; the scholars of the Islamic "religious sciences."

Umma: Qur'anic term for "religious community"; usually refers to the worldwide community of Muslims.

Usul al-Fiqh: The theoretical "sources" of religious law; theoretical jurisprudence.

Wafd (pl., *wufud*): Delegation.

Wazir (pl., *wuzara*): Vizier, minister, high-ranking state official.

Zakat: Obligatory alms or "religious tax"; one of the "Five Pillars" of Islam.

Zuhd: Asceticism, renunciation (of worldly temptations).

ANNOTATED BIBLIOGRAPHY

Books

Abdul Rauf, Feisal. *What's Right with Islam*. San Francisco: HarperCollins, 2004. Discussion of relations between the Islamic world and the West. Contains useful comments on the Hadith of Gabriel.

Ahsan, M. M. *Social Life under the Abbasids*. London: Longman, 1979. Provides much useful information on ordinary patterns of early Islamic society.

Ali, Abdallah Yusuf. *The Holy Qur'an: Text, Translation, Commentary*. Washington, DC: The Islamic Center, 1978. Widely used translation of the Qur'an. The commentary reflects contemporary, moderate interpretation.

Ali, Maulana Muhammad. *A Manual of Hadith*. London: Curzon Press, 1977. Straightforward, accessible introduction to Hadith.

al-Baladhuri, Ahmad ibn Yahya. *The Origins of the Islamic State [Futuh al-Buldan]*. Translated by Philip Hitti and Francis Murgotten. 2 volumes. New York: Columbia University Press, 1916–1924. A readable translation of a critically important work of early Arab-Islamic historiography.

Berkey, Jonathan. *The Formation of Islam: Religion and Society in the Near East, 600–1800*. Cambridge: Cambridge University Press, 2003. A fine discussion of early Islamic society and religious trends. Very up-to-date comments on debates of modern scholarship on the formation of Islam.

Black, Antony. *The History of Islamic Political Thought: From the Prophet to the Present*. Edinburgh: Edinburgh University Press, 2001. Initial chapters introduce readers to the major debates over religion and politics in early Islamic society.

Blankinship, Khalid Yahya. *The End of the Jihad State: The Reign of Hisham Ibn Abd al-Malik and the Collapse of the Umayyads*. Albany: State University of New York Press, 1994. Detailed account of the final decades of the Umayyad dynasty.

Bloom, Jonathan M. *Paper Before Print: The History and Impact of Paper in the Islamic World*. New Haven, CT: Yale University Press, 2001. Detailed and wonderfully illustrated history of the production of paper and its impact on the premodern Islamic world.

Bloom, Jonathan, and Sheila Blair. *Islamic Arts*. London: Phaidon Press, 1997. Accessible and copiously illustrated introduction to the variety of Islamic arts.

Book of Gifts and Rarities [Kitab al-Hadaya wal al-Tuhaf]. Translated by Ghada al-Hijjawi al-Qaddumi. Cambridge, MA: Harvard University Press, 1996. Fine translation of an Arab-Islamic text of the eleventh century.

Bulliet, Richard. *Conversion to Islam in the Medieval Period: An Essay in Quantitative History*. Cambridge, MA: Harvard University Press, 1979. Intriguing attempt to deal with the complex topic of conversion to Islam in the early period.

————. *Islam: The View from the Edge*. New York: Columbia University Press, 1994. Discussion of the development of early Islam that steps outside the history of empire and elite Near Eastern society.

The Cambridge History of Iran. Volume 3: *The Seleucid, Parthian, and Sasanian Periods*. Edited by Ehsan Yarshater. Cambridge: Cambridge University Press, 1983. Useful introduction to pre-Islamic Iranian history.

Crone, Patricia. *Medieval Islamic Political Thought*. Edinburgh: Edinburgh University Press, 2004. A detailed discussion of the debates and ideas of Arab-Islamic politics and religion into the premodern period. For very advanced students.

Crone, Patricia, and Martin Hinds. *God's Caliph: Religious Authority in the First Centuries of Islam*. Cambridge: Cambridge University Press, 1986. An influential work on the early history of the caliphate.

Donner, Fred McGraw. *The Early Islamic Conquests*. Princeton, NJ: Princeton University Press, 1981. A detailed history of the Arab-Islamic conquests, full of very useful information on early Islamic society.

Egger, Vernon O. *A History of the Muslim World to 1405: The Making of a Civilization*. Upper Saddle River, NJ: Pearson Prentice-Hall, 2004. A survey of Islamic history with helpful reading lists and original documents.

Esack, Farid. *The Qur'an: A Short Introduction*. Oxford: Oneworld Publications, 2002. Lively and wide-ranging discussion of the Qur'an, Qur'anic exegesis, and Islamic scholarship, past and present.

Esposito, John L., ed. *The Oxford History of Islam*. New York: Oxford University Press, 1999. A fine collection of essays on many aspects of Islamic history, society, and culture. The essays by Fred Donner, Vincent Cornell, and Ahmad Dallal are cited in the notes.

The Essential Koran: The Heart of Islam. Translated and presented by Thomas Cleary. San Francisco: HarperSanFrancisco, 1993. A useful introduction to the major themes of the Qur'an, although readers should also look at translations of the full text.

Ettinghausen, Richard, Oleg Grabar, and Marilyn Jenkins-Madina. *Islamic Art and Architecture 650–1250*. Second edition. New Haven, CT: Yale University Press, 2001. A superb overview, with excellent maps and diagrams, of Islamic art and architecture from the seventh to the thirteenth centuries.

Gayangos, Pascual de, trans. *The History of the Mohammedan Dynasties in Spain*. London: W. H. Allen and Co., 1940. Readable translation of a significant Arab-Islamic source on the history of al-Andalus.

Haldon, J. F. *Byzantium in the Seventh Century: The Transformation of a Culture*. Cambridge: Cambridge University Press, 1990. An advanced introduction to one of two dominant states of the pre-Islamic period.

Hawting, G. R. *The First Dynasty of Islam: The Umayyad Caliphate AD 661–750*. Second edition. London: Routledge, 2000. Detailed survey of the political history of the Umayyad dynasty. An excellent introduction to the subject.

Hillenbrand, Robert. *Islamic Architecture: Form, Function and Meaning*. New York: Columbia University Press, 1994. A wide-ranging, detailed, and wonderfully illustrated discussion written for the lay audience.

Hodgson, Marshall G. S. *The Venture of Islam: Conscience and History in a World Civilization*, vol. 1. Chicago: University of Chicago Press, 1974. Contains a superb discussion of the emergence of Islamic society set against the backdrop of the religious and sociopolitical history of the Near East. For advanced students.

Hourani, Albert. *A History of the Arab Peoples*. Cambridge, MA: Belknap Press of Harvard University Press, 1991. A nicely written and accessible history of Arab society from the dawn of Islam to the present day.

Hoyland, Robert G. *Arabia and the Arabs: From the Bronze Age to the Coming of Islam*. London: Routledge, 2001. An up-to-date survey of the economic, cultural, and religious history of pre-Islamic Arab society.

Humphreys, R. Stephen. *Islamic History: A Framework for Inquiry*. Revised edition. Princeton, NJ: Princeton University Press, 1991. Extremely useful survey of the literature (modern and medieval) on Arab-Islamic history and major areas of debate in modern scholarship.

Ibn Ishaq, Muhammad. *The Life of Muhammad [Sirat Rasul Allah]*. Translated by Alfred Guillaume. London: Oxford University Press, 1955. A challenging but extremely valuable starting point for the study of the Prophet's life and the first stage of Islamic history.

Irwin, Robert, ed. *Night and Horses and the Desert: An Anthology of Classical Arabic Literature*. London: Allen Lane, 1999. Broad selection of Arabic-Islamic texts dating from the pre-Islamic period into the sixteenth century. Includes selections from the Qur'an and most forms of medieval Arabic literature.

Kennedy, Hugh. *The Armies of the Caliphs: Military and Society in the Early Islamic State*. London: Routledge, 2001. A helpful introduction to the military history of the early Islamic period.

————. *An Historical Atlas of Islam*. Second edition. Leiden: Brill, 2002.

————. *The Prophet and the Age of the Caliphates*: Second edition. New York: Pearson Longman, 2004. A detailed survey of the political history of the Islamic world into the middle Abbasid period. A good complement to the Lapidus volume.

Khadduri, Majid, trans. *The Islamic Law of Nations: Shaybani's Siyar*. Baltimore: Johns Hopkins University Press, 1966. Useful translation of chapters on warfare and taxation from an important early Arab-Islamic work.

Knysh, Alexander. *Islamic Mysticism: A Short History*. Leiden: Brill, 2000. Clearly written introduction to the subject. The early chapters offer a balanced view of early "proto-Sufism" and major early historical figures.

The Koran Interpreted. Translated by A. J. Arberry. 2 volumes. London: Allen & Unwin, 1955. A careful and readable translation, still widely used by modern scholars.

Lapidus, Ira. *A History of Islamic Societies*. Second edition. Cambridge: Cambridge University Press, 2002. A lengthy account of Islamic social history from the pre-Islamic period to the modern day. For the political history surrounding sociocultural developments, see Kennedy, *Prophet.*

Lassner, Jacob. *The Topography of Baghdad in the Early Middle Ages.* Detroit, MI: Wayne State University Press, 1970. Translation and study of the introduction of *The History of Baghdad* by al-Khatib al-Baghdadi (d. 1071).

Lings, Martin. *Muhammad: His Life Based on the Earliest Sources.* London: Allen & Unwin, 1983. A detailed biography that uses the early Arab-Islamic sources, such as Ibn Ishaq and al-Tabari, to good effect.

Margoliouth, D. S., trans. *The Table-talk of a Mesopotamian Judge.* London: Royal Asiatic Society, 1922. Translation of selections from a work by al-Tanukhi, a tenth-century Iraqi author.

Momen, Moojan. *An Introduction to Shi'i Islam: The History and Doctrines of Twelver Shi'ism.* New Haven, CT: Yale University Press, 1985. A thorough and well-organized presentation of mainly Twelver Shi'i history and thought.

al-Muqaddasi, Abu Abdallah Muhammad. *The Best Divisions for Knowledge of the Regions [Ahsan al-Taqasim fi Ma'rifat al-Aqalim].* Translated by Basil Collins. Reading, UK: Garnet Publishing, 2001. Reliable translation of a highly significant work of Arab-Islamic geography.

Murata, Sachiko, and William C. Chittick. *The Vision of Islam.* New York: Paragon House, 1994. A detailed introduction to the guiding principles of the Islamic religious system.

Petry, Carl F., ed. *The Cambridge History of Egypt.* Volume 1: *Islamic Egypt, 640–1517.* Cambridge: Cambridge University Press, 1998. A set of chapters on many facets of Egypt's history to the sixteenth century.

Robinson, Chase F. *Islamic Historiography.* Cambridge: Cambridge University Press, 2003. An up-to-date introduction to the principal genres and problems of Arab-Islamic historical writing.

———. *Abd al-Malik.* Oxford: OneWorld Publications, 2005. A revisionist history of Abd al-Malik's caliphate. Challenges standard interpretations of the reign itself and the course of Umayyad history.

Robinson, Francis, ed. *The Cambridge Illustrated History of the Islamic World.* London: Cambridge University Press, 1996. A collection of fine essays on Islamic history, economics, and society to the present day. The topical essays by K. N. Chaudhuri and Basim Musallam are cited in the notes.

Rodinson, Maxime. *Mohammed*. New York: Pantheon Books, 1971. English translation of an influential Western biography of the Prophet. Like the work by W. M. Watt (see below), it is widely considered out of date, but nevertheless relies on a close analysis of the Prophet's career.

Sells, Michael, trans. *Desert Tracings: Six Classic Arabian Odes*. Middletown, CT: Wesleyan University Press, 1989. Translation of major pre-Islamic Arabian poems.

Spectorsky, Susan A., trans. *Chapters on Marriage and Divorce: Responses of Ibn Hanbal and Ibn Rahwayh*. Austin: University of Texas Press, 1993. Clear translation of difficult early legal texts with a very useful introduction and notes by the translator.

al-Tabari, Muhammad ibn Jarir. *The History of al-Tabari*, 39 volumes. Albany: State University of New York Press, 1985–1999. Translated by a number of modern scholars, the work is an invaluable source for early Arab-Islamic history and is a good introduction to Islamic historiography.

Waines, David. *An Introduction to Islam*. Cambridge: Cambridge University Press, 1995. A excellent introduction to the origins, doctrines, and practices of the Islamic tradition to the present day. Very useful discussion of the rise of the religious scholars.

Watson, Andrew. *Agricultural Innovation in the Early Islamic World: The Diffusion of Crops and Farming Techniques, 700–1100*. Cambridge: Cambridge University Press, 1983. A detailed study of the spread of new crops and farming technology into the Near East through the early Islamic period.

Watt, W. Montgomery. *Muhammad: Prophet and Statesman*. London: Oxford University Press, 1961. A shorter version of the author's well-known two-volume work on the Prophet. Though considered out of date by many historians, it is still a very useful source for the course of the Prophet's career.

Wheatley, Paul. *The Places Where Men Pray Together: Cities in Islamic Lands, Seventh through the Tenth Centuries*. Chicago: University of Chicago Press, 2001. Detailed and challenging discussion of urbanization in early Islamic history, based on the work of al-Muqaddasi.

Audio and Video

Gardner, Robert A., director. *Islam: Empire of Faith*. Available from Public Broadcasting Service (www.pbs.org/empires/islam/shop.html). VHS and DVD.

Excellent introduction to many aspects of early Islamic society and culture, with commentary by a team of scholars in various disciplines of Islamic and Middle East studies.

An excellent collection of Middle Eastern and Islamic world films can be found at www.lib.unc.edu/house/mrc/bodman/.

Web Sites

The Internet Islamic History Sourcebook, Paul Halsall, editor, Fordham University Center for Medieval Studies. Link to Islamic and Middle East section: www.fordham.edu/halsall/islam/islamsbook.html. The first set of pages contains documents from pre-modern Arabic, Persian, and Turkish sources, as well as articles and book chapters by modern scholars. Other sections contain links to maps and to a range of further resources.

Islam, Islamic Studies, Arabic and Religion by Alan Godlas, Department of Religion, University of Georgia. Contains remarkable array of links to all things Islamic at www.uga.edu/islam.

INDEX

About the Author

MATTHEW S. GORDON studies the sociopolitical history of the early Islamic Near East. His book, *The Breaking of a Thousand Swords: A History of the Turkish Military of Samarra*, appeared in 2001. A primer, entitled *Understanding Islam*, was published in 2002.